METROPOLITAN MUTATIONS

Canadian Cataloguing in Publication Data

Main entry under title:

Metropolitan mutations : the architecture of
emerging public spaces

Published on the occasion of a travelling exhibition
organized by the Royal Architectural Institute of
Canada.
ISBN 0-316-56783-3

1. Architecture – Canada. 2. Public architecture –
Canada. 3. Architecture, Modern – Canada. I. Mer-
tins, Detlef. II. Royal Architectural Institute of
Canada.

NA745.M48 1989   720'.971   C89-093532-7

Printed and bound in Canada

METROPOLITAN MUTATIONS

The Architecture

of Emerging

Public Spaces

RAIC Annual 1

Little, Brown and Company (Canada) Limited

Boston London Toronto

Royal Architectural Institute of Canada

CONTENTS

FOREWORD

by Esmail Baniassad, Vice-President, Commission on Research and Education

This first volume of the RAIC ANNUAL concerns the architecture of the public place — the theme of the 1988 conference of the Royal Architectural Institute of Canada. In bringing together the proceedings of the conference and the catalogue of the exhibition that was prepared for it, it presents a searching examination of the roots, the developments and the permutations of the public place as an **essential** dimension of architecture. This stands in welcome contrast to the view that sees architecture solely in terms of individual buildings and that regards "urban design" as separate from architecture. The public place is an indispensable part of everyday concerns of architecture and is not replaceable by private and individual interests and actions however grand they may be.

The "public place" may appear at first to address desirable but optional, or at any rate not critical, concerns in architecture. But, in fact, the majority of the papers reveal the depth and urgency with which the authors have regarded the question. At the same time, these papers cannot be regarded as merely the resurgence of a picturesque or city beautiful movement. The demise of public places, which we witness on an ongoing basis, is as fundamental in our society as is the problem of homelessness, which was the theme of the 1987 conference. Both are indications of a single mode of poverty; both arise from the lack of sufficient generosity toward the public realm and from the seriously narrow limitation of the scope of design to the individual building in a potentially derelict urban fabric.

The high quality of the conference and exhibition obviously draws from the serious work of the many contributors, but as a whole it owes much to the hard and focused work of their curator, architect Detlef Mertins.

This record of the exhibition and conference serves not only to disemminate valuable new thought and research about public places, but also to promote a more informed practice in which the architecture of the public place and the design of any individual building are inexorably interwoven. It reminds us that public places are perhaps the most valuable legacy of the past and that, as architects, we have a professional responsibility to advocate the importance of this legacy in the shaping of our world. By our actions we may, hopefully, enhance this legacy and add to it in response to the ever-permutating nature of social gathering.

INTRODUCTION

by Detlef Mertins, Curator and Editor

Time makes inexorable changes in community life, and these changes alter the original significance of architectural forms. Important events of today are published in the newspapers, rather than by public criers, and we cannot change that. Retail trade has made a steady progression from the market square into dull buildings and the pedlar's satchel, and we cannot change that. Fountains have been reduced to mere decorative function by the piping of water directly into houses, and that is not a thing we would change. Popular festivals, parades, religious processions and open-air theatrical events will soon be but memories.

As the slow succession of the centuries has removed feature after feature of civic activity from public open places, it has shorn the plaza of its principal purpose. Artistic city development got more encouragement from the quality of ancient life than it does from our severely regulated modern existence, for modern ideas of urban beauty differ from the old in basic character as well as in detail.

Great population increases in our modern capitals, more than anything else, have shattered the old forms. With the growth of a city its streets widen and its buildings grow taller and bulkier. Appreciation of style has become so blunted by the incessant dreariness of modern architecture, that only an exceptionally striking effect can now arouse interest. But we cannot turn the clock back, and consequently the modern planner, like the modern architect, must draw his plans for a metropolis to the scale of several million inhabitants.

Is it really possible to plan on paper the kind of effect that was produced by the passage of centuries? Could we actually derive any satisfaction from feigned naiveté and sheer artificiality? Certainly not. The vitality of the glorious old models should inspire us to something other than fruitless imitation. If we seek out the essential quality of this heritage and adapt it to modern conditions we shall be able to plant the seeds of new vitality in seemingly barren soil.

Camillo Sitte, *The Art of Building Cities*, Vienna: 1889

Written in Vienna one hundred years ago, these passages from Camillo Sitte's important study of European urban spaces are surprisingly applicable today. And more surprising still, in his acceptance of changes that he understood to be problematic, Sitte appears to be much more modern than has been portrayed in recent years.

Throughout the 1970s the young, radical architects Leon and Rob Krier of Luxembourg conducted a highly influential critique of the erosion of urban space in 20th-century architecture and town planning, in Sitte's name. As some of the principal voices of the Rationalist movement, they attacked the excessive emptiness of

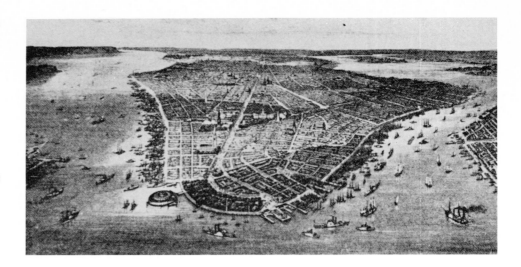

The first phase of metropolitanization in the 19th century was characterized by its densification of the city centre. The transformation of Wall Street in New York, Bay Street in Toronto or Portage Avenue in Winnipeg was achieved through successive generations of ever-denser buildings that shaped and then extruded the volume of the street. In the case of Wall Street or Bay Street, this process mutated "street" into "canyon," which is probably the most distinctive public space type of this initial period of rapid urbanization in North America. Views of Manhattan from 1851 and 1951 show the "growing up" of the city at its greatest intensity (from Percy Johnson-Marshall, *Rebuilding Cities* (Edinburgh at the University Press, 1966))

modern urban space, its fixation with buildings as objects and the degradation of the traditional, but complex, continuum of urban spaces, streets and squares in the historic European city. They argued against technocratic and bureaucratic civic administrations that promoted the provision of utilities and the management of traffic at the expense of the architecture of the city. Through all of this Sitte has become firmly associated with urban historicism.

But Sitte's original text, while clearly critical of the modern practices of his time and clearly obsessed with the nuanced relationship between buildings, monuments and public squares in the Western tradition, calls for innovations to improve modern city planning, rather than the restoration of historic models per se. His attitude toward tradition is dialectical and accommodating, and contrasts sharply with the narrow historical utopia of Leon Krier. In his "Note on Camillo Sitte" for the first English translation of the book in 1944, Eliel Saarinen recognized this quality of

Sitte's work. He acknowledged his personal debt to Sitte for teaching "that the building must be an integral part of an environment [that] is expressive of contemporary conditions, and of no other conditions." He suggested that Sitte helped lay the ground for the rejection of the "super-stylistic Beaux-Arts" and the search for a new form-expression that became widespread for Saarinen's own generation. At the same time, he stated that it was from Sitte that he "learned to understand those laws of architecture that are from time immemorial." Indeed, Saarinen's own work is a testament to a dialectical appreciation of history and to the ongoing confrontation of tensions in the modern condition.

The kind of modernity that is evident in this rereading of Sitte is, of course, quite different from the doctrinaire program of reconstruction associated with the modern movement in architecture, and particularly with the radical statements of CIAM (Congrès Internationaux d'Architecture Moderne) in the 1920s and 1930s. But it is equally distinct from the doctrinaire program of restoration associated with the Kriers. It was in the spirit of this kind of modernity, which seeks an engaged relationship between change and continuity, that the work collected in this volume was launched.

This first volume of the RAIC ANNUAL presents critical reviews of the architecture of public spaces in Canadian cities. It is composed of three parts: a catalogue of an exhibition, the papers presented at a conference, and two commentaries. The voices contained within it express diverse, and at times conflicting, views; the documentation of sites from across the country reveals an equally diverse and often disturbing reality. All of this reflects the complex condition of public space as we experience and construct it today. Our cities are changing dramatically; they are not what they used to be, and to echo Sitte, we cannot turn the clock back. But they are in many ways unsatisfying and improvements are desperately needed. This collection is intended to help prepare the ground for more creative design of public spaces that will be integral to, and expressive of, the fabric of contemporary life.

The Exhibition

The exhibition presents public spaces from nine cities that serve to examine the ways in which urban spaces have been adapted, transformed and mutated by the forces and cultures of the modern metropolis. While it may be said that urban experience in Canada is hardly comparable to that of large urban centres such as Paris, New York, Los Angeles, São Paulo or Tokyo, there are, of course, several cities in Canada of metropolitan scale, but more importantly there are few cities remaining, regardless of size, that have not been touched by the fever of metropolitan renovation. Even small cities now proudly display downtown freeways, high-rise buildings set in empty plazas, internalized downtown shopping malls, elevated pedestrian bridges and historic squares overwhelmed by traffic and refurbished with false histories.

Since the Industrial Revolution, cities have been undergoing successive transformations that have been so radical as to confound the very language used to
describe them. The early industrial city of the 19th century caused such a termino-
logical crisis until writers such as Dickens, Engels and Mayhew adapted the language
and conventions of literature to suit the unprecedented concentration of settlement
and the disintegration of society in what came to be known as the "Great Town" and
later the modern city, or the metropolis.

As a response, in part, to the demand for concentrated settlement and, in part,
to the problems revealed by it, new kinds of urban spaces were generated in
European and North American cities in the late 19th and early 20th centuries. In
Paris, for instance, the chaos and congestion of the suddenly overpopulated medieval
fabric was relieved by carving out a network of broad boulevards with stately buildings and avenues of trees. This remarkable synthesis of efficient vehicular movement
for both civilians and the military, mass sewage provision, urbane residence for the
new bourgeoisie and bucolic promenade became the first public space system of distinctly metropolitan character and scale.

In the United States, the sudden capacity to build tall in Chicago and New York
created the sublime canyons of Lasalle Street and Wall Street, which were direct
extrusions of existing urban forms into the sky. More terrifying, perhaps, than exhilarating were the shadowy realms created by the elevated and subterranean train
systems designed to move the masses through the major centres. And in both
European and North American cities large urban parks were created in the image of
the natural countryside to provide respite and recreation within the confines of the
metropolis. While these new types did have formal antecedents, they were distinct in
their scale, purpose and culture from anything that had preceded the emergence of
the "Great Town." These were the first generation of metropolitan public spaces,
which continue to serve to this day. In the second phase of the metropolis, specialized
suburbs were created on the periphery of the great cities as people of different
income, race, birth and class sought to separate themselves from the chaotic urban
mass of the centre. This flight from the big city into the country shattered the
balance between private and public experience that is essential to sustain a vital
public realm. While the mass suburbs are a metropolitan phenomenon, they have
been overwhelmingly orientated toward private values and have offered little nour-
ishment for public life.

The consequences of suburbanization on the city centre were numerous. Not
only did this migration of people diminish the vitality and economy of urban life, not
only did its service highways encircle the centre like a new city wall, but the applica-
tion of the suburban ideals of mobility, privacy and open space to historic urban districts produced a devastating series of further mutations: the downtown expressway,
the high-rise building set on a plaza or in open space, the separation of cars, transit
vehicles and pedestrians into specialized zones, and internalized quasi-public

In Winnipeg, the broad prairie road of 1872 with its wood-frame buildings developed into an incipient boulevard of Parisian scale, whose most urbane moment may be represented by the photograph of 1922; unfortunately the street's character as transportation artery has continued to dominate while the pedestrian edge has yet to benefit from the civilizing devices of the boulevard with its wide sidewalks sheltered by trees, and punctuated by pedestrian light poles and benches. Despite efforts of the City Beautiful Movement, the European boulevard was rarely achieved in Canadian cities (courtesy Public Archives of Canada)

domains. Unlike the earlier benign mutation of street into canyon or landscape garden into urban park, these more recent attempts at genetic urban engineering have been highly problematic and controversial. For while they respond to the scale, mobility and economy of the modern metropolis, they rarely provide urbane experiences and have not served to create a vital metropolitan public culture.

The characteristics of the modern city in its current phase are complex and still being delineated. Observers have commented on the diffusion and decentring of the city through relentless urban sprawl, long-distance commuting and the revolution in communications technologies. The contemporary metropolis may indeed be seen as a multi-centred "urban field," an intricate service network of transportation, telecommunication and utility systems through which urban experience is available in quasi-urbanized zones. While the idea of the city has traditionally been tied to the idea of place, urbanity need no longer be the exclusive trait of the city dweller. In this process, the value of the historic city centre has, of course, been diminished. While it is no longer universal, many of our city centres have been depopulated and then sub-urbanized to accommodate easier traffic flow and suburban building types, including the ubiquitous shopping centre.

At the same time, there has been a remarkable renaissance of urban culture over the past decade. Where twenty years ago the "crisis of the cities" presented itself as a national imperative in the United States, and where as recently as the mid-1970s New York City was on the verge of bankruptcy, there is today phenomenal investment and energy in the great cities of America, as there is in Canada and around the world. Moreover, with the growth of tourism and the benefits of improved international transit and communication, the global village has developed a fondness for urban culture that embraces the contemporary as well as the historical, the raw as well as the sophisticated.

At the moment, then, cities that have any kind of economic vitality are being intensified at their centres **and** expanded at their edges. Where a sufficient culture of urban life exists, the suburbanization of the city core is being halted and remedied, and the post-war suburbs are being densified and urbanized. The emerging urban field is simultaneously urban and non-urban, centred and decentred, spatial and aspatial, rooted and free. Within the context of this complex and layered history of metropolitan development, the exhibition examines five kinds of mutant public spaces in their current state:

HISTORIC SPACES IN TRANSITION presents spaces inherited from the past, valued for their physical characteristics and their capacity to bind generations, but adapted or transformed to suit the changing economy of cities, the norms of traffic management and the aspirations to renew.

NEW VERSIONS OF OLD TYPES looks at spaces from the post–World War II period that may be seen as mutations of historic urban types — the street, the square and the urban park — in which the deviation is caused by conditions of the modern metropolis, such as increased density, radical fluctuations of use, and connections into regional, if not international, networks of communication, transportation and resource management.

MULTI-LEVEL CITY CENTRES compares the experience of three cities in the creation of underground and above-ground networks of interior quasi-public spaces that are controlled and motivated by private interests and that substitute for the public space of the street.

CENTRES IN THE FIELD examines the condition of the quasi-public interior in the suburbs where recent marketing trends have combined the regional shopping centre and the theme park, while recent urban design trends are transforming the first generation of regional shopping centres into incipient urban centres.

MARGINAL SITES REZONED FOR PUBLIC USE focuses on obsolete zones of the industrial city that once served as vital ports, railway yards and manufacturing districts and are now attractive for their marginality as well as their potential for development.

The presentation of these case studies is not intended simply to praise or condemn, but rather to illuminate the architecture of emerging public spaces in Canadian cities, to facilitate criticism and to act as a catalyst for a gentle metropolis. This exhibition sets a double agenda, on the one hand, to restore and renew historic public spaces as loci of contemporary public life, and on the other, to re-evaluate and absorb the mutations of the metropolis into a positive vision of the emerging city.

The Conference

The ambiguities and contradictions of the current moment reverberated throughout a two-day conference held in Saint John, New Brunswick, on June 9 and 10, 1988, on the subject "The Architecture of Emerging Public Spaces." In trying to measure and evaluate this moment, speakers were alternately seduced or frightened by the present, absorbed by the potential for invention or worried by the failures of recent past.

In his keynote paper, George Baird explored how ideas of mobility, plurality and the historic city have conditioned the architectural debate on urban form in Europe and North America since the end of World War II, and argued that this debate will not be resolved until a fuller understanding of the city as a space of appearance is absorbed into the theory of urbanism.

Several speakers addressed those characteristics of urban form and public places that make particular cities unique. Lance Berelowitz gave an interpretation of Vancouver as a centrifugal city in which the most valued public spaces are at the water's edge and provide platforms for the contemplation of the natural tableau. In contrast, Montreal was presented by Peter Rose as a city of streets with an intensity of street-life unequalled in the rest of the country.

Two contributions from Ottawa touched on the national theme. Following his primer on the Canadian street, Trevor Boddy contrasted several recent projects that defile the form and character of the street with several others projecting a normative vision of the street whose conservative qualities, he claimed, mask its profundity. In a more progressive vein, Nan Griffiths established an agenda for creative work to delineate a distinctively contemporary Canadian urban landscape that would resonate with mythic and cultural significance.

Kenneth Greenberg drove into the suburbs of Toronto to examine that city's emerging subcentres, which are becoming increasingly urban through changes in use, density and the creation of formal public spaces. With suburban Halifax as his base, Tom Emodi suggested that the distinctive qualities of the suburbs should be maintained as new uses and development are introduced.

Phyllis Lambert and J. Michael Kirkland both confronted the implications of urban highways on the potential for public spaces. The garden and park of the Canadian Centre for Architecture in Montreal, now under construction and presented by Phyllis Lambert, are exemplary new public spaces designed to make civil the scars of traffic engineering, relate to the history of the site and the city and provide a delightful and revealing landscape. With Toronto's Gardiner Expressway as his focus, J. Michael Kirkland explored the possibility of absorbing the utilitarian infrastructure of the modern city into a civilized urban realm, but concluded that such efforts would be futile.

The popularity of the ever-expanding world of interior shopping malls and elevated pedestrian walkways in Calgary and Halifax served for Frank Palermo to argue that architects need to develop a more diverse and accommodating repertoire of public spaces than is provided by traditional types. Gerald L. Forseth identified some of the dilemmas inherent in the creation of such *private* public spaces and questioned whether these contributions by private corporations were really in the public interest.

And finally, Donald McKay portrayed a new metropolitan frontier in those territories that do not belong to any of our current descriptive models, be they the historical city, the shadow city of crime and intrigue, or the metropolis itself as network for the movement of goods, people and information.

The discussions that took place during the conference underscored the general ambivalence, and occasional hostility, toward the present state of public spaces in Canadian cities. A lively exchange of views is collected under the heading "Transcripts," in which the audience, as well as the speakers, wrestled with the trauma of traffic, the substance of the suburbs, the problems of privatization, the politics of power and the virtues and vices of metropolitan mutations. With so few unqualified successes in this sphere of design, the construction of a critical discourse remains the order of the day. Commentaries by Steven Fong and Michael McMordie conclude this volume and help to project the discourse beyond the conference.

The exhibition as installed at the
Palazzo del'Arte in Milan, Italy, where
it represented Canada at the XVIIth
Triennale di Milano, "World Cities and
the Future of the Metropolis"
(installation design, Detlef Mertins)

THE EXHIBITION

By documenting public spaces from nine Canadian cities, this exhibition reveals the ways — sometimes benign and sometimes malevolent — in which urban spaces have been adapted, transformed and mutated by the forces and culture of the metropolis.

With drawings prepared by students of architecture from across the country, and with the provocative photography of Robert Bean, Jack Buquet, John Dean, Marc Fowler, Eugene Kedl and Peter MacCallum, it presents
- historic spaces in Ottawa and Quebec City that are much valued, but have been deformed to suit traffic management and the tourist economy
- the modern squares along Toronto's Bay Street
- the quasi-public networks of bridges, interior routes and tunnels in central Montreal, Calgary and Halifax
- the West Edmonton Mall — the largest theme park/shopping centre in North America — contrasted with the emerging Mississauga City Centre, which is slowly transforming a regional shopping centre into an urban district
- the marginal industrial lands of Vancouver's Granville Island that have become the spiritual heart of Vancouver

The presentation is intended to facilitate criticism and to act as a catalyst toward a gentle metropolis — a positive vision of the emerging city, which is simultaneously urban and non-urban, centred and decentred, spatial and aspatial, rooted and free.

Aitken Bicentennial Exhibition Centre, Saint John

Triennale di Milano, Milan

Toronto City Hall, Toronto

Maison Alcan, Montreal

Edmonton Art Gallery, Edmonton

Technical University of Nova Scotia, Halifax

Dunlop Gallery, Regina

Community Gallery, Mississauga City Hall

HISTORIC SPACES IN TRANSITION

Ottawa

Quebec

Throughout Canada, historic public spaces continue to be retained and rehabilitated. Main streets, market halls, urban squares and parks still serve the public life of many communities, and spaces such as Ottawa's Parliament Hill, Quebec City's Dufferin Terrace, and the Niagara Falls Parkway have virtually been enshrined. Yet, at the same time, many historic spaces have been degraded in their spatial quality and landscaping, reconditioned to suit contemporary models of traffic management and marketing, or recodified as separate domains for historic experience.

One of the most dramatic examples of the erosion of urban space in Canada during the recent phase of modernization is Victoria Square in Montreal. Seventy years after its inauguration in 1810, the square had become not only the commercial centre of the city, but one of its finest urban spaces. Tightly contained by monumental buildings, the square itself was intensely planted and adorned. Here, traditional ideas of public space had been adapted to the scale of the early metropolis as in many European cities. During the 20th century, however, urban expansion gradually diminished the vitality of the square and by the late 1960s neglect had turned into outright destruction. Old buildings were demolished and not consistently replaced; new ones were not only banal and overbearing, but broke the spatial order of the square. By the mid-1970s even the landscaping had been removed, leaving only the statue of Queen Victoria as a forlorn reminder of past dignity.

While some urban spaces such as Victoria Square have been stripped of their former significance, others have been recodified. The case study in Ottawa presents three historic public spaces — Sparks Street, Confederation Square and Rideau Street — that have been reconditioned into traffic management types: the pedestrian mall, the traffic island and the transit mall. In Canada, as elsewhere, the period after the Second World War was characterized not only by unprecedented prosperity and urban expansion, but by the introduction of professional planning and the urban models of the modern movement in architecture. Segregated land use zoning was introduced as well as the separation of vehicular and pedestrian traffic.

The reconfiguration of Confederation Square, following the grandiose plan of 1937 by the Parisian architect Jacques Greber, attempted to transform the picturesque and more intimate urban sensibility of Ottawa into the image of L'Enfant's Washington. In the process it served merely to break the continuity from Rideau Street to Sparks Street and to give priority to vehicular traffic flow; rather than consolidating the space as the symbolic heart of the city, the plan created a vast open space encircled by enlarged roadways and led to the diffusion of the space itself.

During the 1960s Sparks Street was further isolated through its transformation into Canada's first pedestrian mall. Following examples from the rebuilding of European cities after the war, several blocks of Sparks Street immediately to the west of Confederation Square were closed to traffic on a trial basis in 1960. In 1967 a permanent mall was established complete with exuberant modern pavilions, light poles, flags and planting. While the "malling" of the street was initially a success, its com-

Two views of Victoria Square in Montreal (1880 and 1988) show one of the most dramatic losses of urban space in Canada (courtesy Public Archives of Canada and Marc Fowler)

Views of Market Slip and Market Square in Saint John, New Brunswick, from c. 1910 and today reveal the extent to which this urban space — part water and part land — has been eroded through demolitions, roadway engineering and poor landscaping

21

QUÉBEC

While Place Royale in lower Quebec City was a vital part of everyday life in this view of 1933, today it has become a domain exclusively for tourists and its image has been purified for this purpose (courtesy Public Archives of Canada)

mercial vitality has suffered during the past decade, confounding merchants and planners alike. Today the pavilions and street furniture of this specialized pedestrian shopping precinct have been renewed to post-modern tastes in a desperate attempt to compete with large-scale, franchised suburban shopping centres.

The situation of Rideau Street has become even more extreme. Reassigned in 1983 as a transit mall servicing the downtown bus system, the street has essentially died. Glass enclosures constructed to shelter the sidewalks from the irritation of the buses have simply served to render the sidewalk as grim and alienating as the roadway outside. The specialization of the street in terms of regional traffic management, its internal fragmentation and the recoding of people into abstract generalizations such as "pedestrians" or "transit users" have led to the wholesale degradation of the urban experience. The diversity of the historic city is neutralized, and even retailing cannot survive.

A different, but no less problematic, form of recoding is evident in the new status of historic urban spaces that has occurred with the growth of mass-market tourism. In sites such as Quebec City's Place Royale, history has been halted and sanitized as the Lower Town has been emptied of any resident population and transformed into a tourist precinct surrounded by roadways and parking lots. Founded in the early 17th century, Quebec City is one of the oldest settlements in North America, and its "Old World" form has lent itself to becoming a popular boutique-filled monument to the past. By isolating the past as a specific locale to be visited but not actively engaged, the modern tourist is endistanced from it and is put, conceptually, outside the continuum of time. As the emblematic loci of our myths of genesis, the historic precincts of our cities compensate for the neutral, unrooted and decentred reality of the everyday world in which the majority of people now live. And indirectly they have prompted the restyling of that environment in imitation of historic garb. The popular consumption of history entails alienation from it and signals a crisis of self-identity.

The preservation of buildings in historic city centres is, in itself, not sufficient to assure the existence of a public domain; and while successful retailing will require good transportation facilities, the effective channelling of traffic is also not sufficient. If these districts are to have any meaningful role to play and vitality in the sprawling urban field, they must once again become places of residence and ordinary life, a locus of active urban culture.

OTTAWA'S CHANGING PUBLIC REALM

Nan Griffiths, Ottawa

Confederation Square

The City of Ottawa revolves around a triangular and monumentally dimensioned space known as Confederation Square, which is not a square at all but an open triangle. Symbolic centre of the nation, physical pivot of the city, it links the two parts of Ottawa once known as Upper Town and Lower Town.

Confederation Square came into being as a result of a process of transformation beginning with the necessity to bridge over the fissure between Upper Town and Lower Town created by the Rideau Canal. The two early bridges were replaced in 1912 with a single bridging platform that is still part of the plaza. Once substantially built upon, destruction by fire and the changing perceptions of civic design have gradually brought the site to its present extreme openness.

In 1937 the French planner Jacques Greber proposed the outlines of the current arrangement with particular consideration for efficient traffic flow. More recently the proposal by Roger du Toit, Associates would absorb it as a major focal point in the new Ceremonial Route of the National Capital. Final approval of their plan to reroute vehicular traffic to a two-way system on the canal side and to join it to the pedestrianized Sparks Street has not yet been obtained.

Past proposals for the Square have been defeated partly by design problems such as the difficulty of resolving the conflict between pedestrians and cars, the peculiar angled relationship with Parliament Hill and a sweeping undefined openness to the north, east and south. The vexing question of spatial containment presents itself as a condition of primary concern. With its one urban edge on the west, the War Memorial's axial relationship with Elgin Street is compromised by the steep slope of the landscape down to the east and Lower Town. The vast organic openness resulting from this is compounded by a traffic pattern that further isolates the triangle from its ordering context, a gridded morphology sheared by the diagonal cut of the Rideau Canal. Urban definition is not easy to establish.

Confederation Square leading to Sparks Street and Wellington Street, with the Rideau Canal below and Parliament Hill beyond; the view shows how both Wellington Street and Sparks Street had been connected to Rideau Street, c. 1917 (courtesy Public Archives of Canada)

The solemnity of the commemorative War Memorial of 1939, the granite bleakness of the plaza and its unremarkable landscaping discourage public use save on Remembrance Day. It is unfortunate that a place of such symbolic and physical importance cannot celebrate the vitality of the country while at the same time commemorate its dead heroes.

Sparks Street

Sparks Street is historically the primary commercial street of Ottawa. Although built after Rideau Street in the 1850s, its development was accelerated by its proximity to the construction of the Parliament Buildings during the 1860s. Since then, the image of town and Crown has been played out between Sparks Street and Wellington Street, the urban edge and link between the town and Parliament.

One of the first "pedestrian malls" in North America, Sparks was part of Greber's vision for the city and by some accounts was the idea of Ottawa architect Watson Balharrie. The three blocks of Sparks Street between Bank Street and Confederation Square were closed to vehicular traffic in the summer of 1960. In June 1967, the "Mall" was officially opened as a permanent precinct, its mainly 19th-century facades overlooking a landscape of trees and shrubs in concrete planters, an abundant provision of concrete and wood seating, exhibition kiosks, restaurant areas, telephones and the like.

The Mall has been a highly successful and popular open-air environment, a significant social and urban space in a fairly dense fabric. It has given a unique identity to the core area and to the image of the city as a whole, and has served for special exhibitions, parades, theatre, dance and musical performance including buskers.

With the construction in the 1980s of a large suburban-type shopping centre in close proximity, Sparks Street began to lose some of its marketing power, and at the same time it was apparent that the 1960s installations had lost some of their sheen. It seemed also that the populist clutter of the 1960s was outmoded and that the time was ripe for a new marketing and urban image.

The objective, therefore, for the major renovation work by landscape architect Cecilia Paine that is now nearing completion was to create a new "upmarket" image for the Mall, an image of "tradition, elegance and distinction" to complement and enhance the heritage of the street. Tree urns and markers establish the entrances off Bank Street and Confederation Square; timed fountains, tree columns, lamp standards and pavilions are orchestrated as one composition that is repeated over the length of the Mall.

Until the extensive system of high-level planting is complete and the summer seating and other animating devices are in place, it is not possible to assess the project. At the present time, however, the pavilions appear overstructured and heavy. They introduce a new scale and, in the narrow space of the street, compete with the existing heritage buildings. The alternation of these compositions from one side to another obscures the vista and the clarity of the street as a linear space.

The frankly nostalgic form of the lamp standards is unfortunate and gives the design some of the imagery of Disneyworld. Informal public reaction to the special lighting fixtures that serve as gates and intersection markers, and which have large, white glass bulbs at waist level, has been ribald, with no pun intended.

Part of Plan for City Improvements by Jacques Greber, Architect, 1937, showing reconfiguration of Confederation Square to terminate Elgin Street in the monumental manner of Washington, D.C. (courtesy Public Archives of Canada)

Rideau Street

Like most main streets in North America, Rideau Street suffered an ever-increasing loss of trade following the development of suburban housing and shopping centres. In an attempt to arrest the decline, the federal government announced plans in 1972 to revitalize the street, thus beginning one of the most complex urban debates in the history of the city. The project, which sprung from the decision to exploit the vacant railway lands adjacent to the canal, reverberated with the political and economic complexities of contemporary urban democracy. The economic focus of the project became the Rideau Centre, a complex that was to have federal offices, a large shopping centre and a hotel. In the final version the movement centre of the entire area was drastically reorganized. The project had become a revitalization for the entire Central Business District.

Rideau Street itself was sidelined in this process, in spite of a number of positive propositions. Its function since 1983 as an exclusive Bus Transit Mall is specific to the larger goal of core area renewal and regional servicing of the Rideau Centre. The three-block transit mall is lined with glass enclosures that provide a climate-controlled pedestrian environment. As might be expected, the shelters are, to some extent, appreciated by some of the public, particularly in the severe winter months. As stimuli to revitalization and growth on Rideau Street itself, however, they have failed to create an environment of growth and their effect on retail has been described by market consultant P. Boname as another "nail in the coffin." The sidewalk enclosures contribute greatly to the sense of discontinuity. The winding, anti-street configuration of the transit lanes and the staggering of the bus shelters present a disorderly and impenetrable vista, especially when filled with "platooning" buses. On dull winter days, the mass of disordered and dirty glass appears particularly unattractive.

Kiosk on the trial pedestrian mall on Sparks Street, 1960 (courtesy Public Archives of Canada). The permanent pedestrian mall was opened in 1967

A recent study by Griffiths Rankin Cook/Griffiths concluded that the dislocation caused by the Transit Mall had a substantial impact on the retail and social environment of Rideau Street and further that it is inappropriate for such an important urban space to function as a bus-only transit station. In September 1987, Ottawa Council voted to remove the existing structures and to open the street to vehicular traffic. The economic, management and design strategies for this are now being developed. The decision has been watched by other cities in North America, including Vancouver, which have similar problems with this type of public space inherited from the 1970s.

25

**Aerial photograph of downtown
Ottawa (courtesy Department of
Energy, Mines and Resources)**

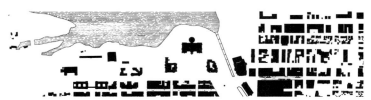

**Figure/ground plan of downtown
Ottawa**

Confederation Square looking north
with War Memorial; Parliament Hill is
on the distant left

PHOTOGRAPHY BY MARC FOWLER

Confederation Square from the canal

**Confederation Square with War
Memorial of 1939**

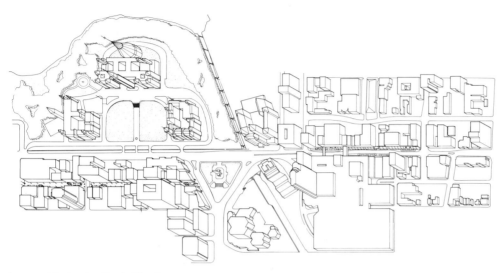

**Axonometric showing Sparks Street,
Confederation Square, Rideau Street
and Parliament Hill**

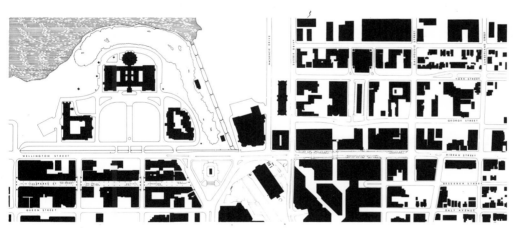

**Plan of Sparks Street Mall,
Confederation Square and Rideau
Transit Mall**

29

**Sparks Street Mall at Bank Street
looking east**

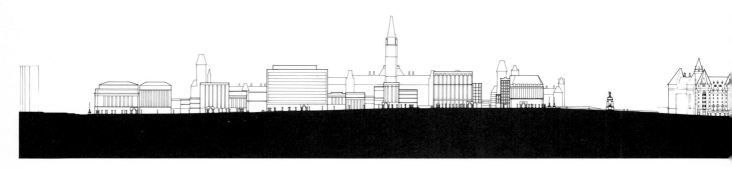

Sparks Street Mall showing current pavilions and street elements

Sparks Street Mall

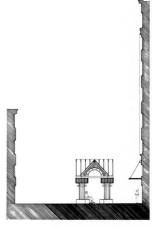

Detail cross section of Sparks Street Pedestrian Mall

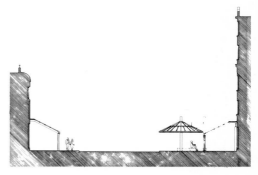

Detail cross section of Rideau Transit Mall

Long section of Sparks Street Pedestrian Mall and Rideau Transit Mall

Rideau Street Transit Mall

Rideau Street Transit Mall from sky-walk bridge

Inside glass-enclosed sidewalks along Rideau Street Transit Mall

Naomi S. Neumann, Quebec City

Place Royale

Place Royale is located in the Lower Town of Quebec City on a narrow strip of land between the St. Lawrence River and the steep cliff of Cap Diamant. The site has a long prehistory as an important Indian trading spot. This was probably the reason for its choice as a location for Champlain's first Habitation in 1608.

Place Royale is a small urban space of intimate scale at which the narrow streets of the Lower Town converge. It was to serve as public space and in particular as the marketplace of the French settlement from the mid-17th century onward.

Because of the limited area of the site, building plots as laid out in the mid-17th century were exceedingly narrow. The buildings themselves represented various French regional models of domestic architecture, which soon showed a gradual adaptation to the constraints of the Canadian climate.

Following a destructive fire in 1682, new regulations led to an increase in the building density and to the replacement of most wooden structures with stone building. The square was completed with the installation of a Louis XIVth bronze bust in its centre and the construction of the church Notre-Dame-des-Victoires on the site of Champlain's Habitation.

Place Royale also played an important role in the defence of Quebec City. Two batteries of cannons on the waterfront were deployed in six successive battles. In 1759 these defences were destroyed, as was the entire Lower Town, following relentless British bombardment.

The reconstruction of the Lower Town after the English Conquest introduced few architectural modifications. The commercial activity of the square was taken up by English merchants replacing the ruined French ones.

In the first half of the 19th century Quebec became the most important port on the North American continent. However, the second half of the century witnessed the economic decline of Quebec and with it the closing of the market in Place Royale. The rebirth of Place Royale dates from the early 1960s. The square and its urban context were designated as the historical quarter of Place Royale. Restoration work was geared toward the conservation, the highlighting and the interpretation of pre-Conquest architectural heritage.

The Place de Paris, south of Place Royale was inaugurated in 1987.

Plan of Quebec City, 1693 (Archives Nationale de Paris & Ministry of Cultural Affairs, Quebec)

Etching of Place Royale after the devastating fire of 1759 (Musée du Québec)

Le Village Normand, Place Laurier, Sainte-Foy

Le Village Normand is an indoor public space located in the large shopping centre Place Laurier in Sainte-Foy, a suburb of Quebec City. Built in the early 1960s, le Village Normand occupies the large covered court on the third floor of the shopping centre. Originally it consisted of small shops and boutiques surrounding the court and inserted stage-set decoration representing Norman village architecture.

The decoration proved insufficient to attract the public to the third floor. The shops' survival was precarious. Le Village Normand was plagued by a rapid turnover and a permanently high vacancy rate.

In 1983 le Village Normand was replanned and redesigned as a space dedicated to the consumption of fast food. The existing decoration was enhanced with a fountain, artificial trees, birds, etc. The result was a highly successful public space.

Hotel Louis XIV with Anglo-turrets prior to restoration, 1966

Commentary

Place Royale and le Village Normand are two public spaces that are in many ways diametrical opposites:

- Place Royale is located in the old city of Quebec in a historically significant site, while le Village Normand is part of a huge modern shopping centre complex in the middle-class suburban municipality of Sainte-Foy.
- Place Royale is an exterior public space, while le Village Normand is an interior one.
- Place Royale has a diffused vocation of historical interpretation. In contrast, le Village Normand has a highly focused function, namely, the consumption of fast food.
- Place Royale lives in the seasonal rhythm of the tourist activity, while le Village Normand has a diurnal rhythm of activities generated by the captive public of hungry employees and consumers of the shopping centre.
- Because of their urban context, Place Royale serves as a parking place during the winter months, but in le Village Normand the leaves of the cardboard trees never change colours, the water in the public fountain never freezes and the menus in the fast-food shops do not offer seasonal variations.
- Finally, the restoration of Place Royale to its 18th-century glory implied a very large public expenditure. Compared to Place Royale, the stage-set decoration of le Village Normand represents a negligible private investment.

Place Royale during the period of restoration work. The buildings on the left have already been completed, while the buildings on the inside corner are shown under construction

Despite all these differences, parallels can be drawn between the two public spaces. This is due to the fact that their histories, although very distinct, intersect in the early 1960s. It is at that date that the importance of the French architectural heritage became a determining factor in the restoration policy of Place Royale, as well as in the stage-set design of le Village Normand. Thus, surprising as this might seem, the reconstructed houses in Place Royale are in fact contemporaneous with the pastiche facades of le Village Normand. This is true despite the fact that le Village Normand can be viewed as the commercial scrounging of collective heritage values.

The parallelism between the two public spaces is even more far reaching if one considers the fact that the decoration of le Village Normand has already been the object of an explicit act of conservation. Thus, the architects who were commissioned to prepare the new plan for le Village Normand in 1983 received strict instructions to conserve the existing stage-set decoration.

Place Royale and le Village Normand represent two extreme examples of the "public space as the stage for urban theatre." The architecture of contemporary public spaces seems geared toward the overemphasis of physical form and cultural imagery at the detriment of public life itself. It is condemned to offer a stage decoration for an endless variety of consumption, from food to cultural values.

Contemporary tourist poster of Place Royale

Detail aerial photograph showing Place Royale on lower left and redevelopment of the port for mass tourist attractions

Aerial photograph of Quebec City
(courtesy Department of Energy,
Mines and Resources)

Figure/ground plan of Place Laurier
in Sainte-Foy

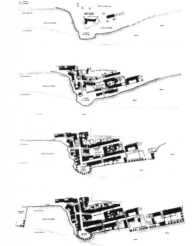

Series of four plans showing the
evolution of the built form of Place
Royale: 1650, 1682, 1715, 1759
(courtesy Robert Cote)

Figure/ground plan of Place Royale
in the Lower Town

36

The Place Royale district of Lower Town of Quebec City is now entirely dedicated to tourism and has no significant resident population

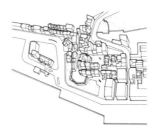

Axonometric of Place Royale

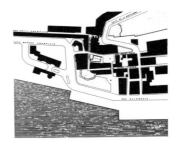

Plan of Place Royale

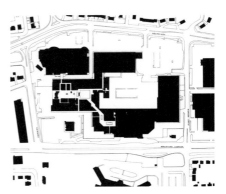

**Plan of le Village Normand in Place
Laurier shopping centre**

**From Place Royale looking toward the
Château Frontenac**

Le Village Normand in Place Laurier
shopping centre in suburban Sainte-
Foy. The historically themed food fair
provides a surrogate public space
and a surrogate history in the suburbs, which have neither

Section of Place Royale

**Section of le Village Normand in Place
Laurier shopping centre**

Detail section of Place Royale showing Notre-Dame-des-Victoires

Like any other major tourist attraction, the periphery of Place Royale is dominated by roadways and great numbers of cars and buses, which effectively isolate the "town" from the river

Detail section of le Village Normand showing the food concessions

A mutated "street" at le Village Normand

NEW VERSIONS OF OLD TYPES
Toronto

In the period since the Second World War, the imperatives of the metropolis as a service system have produced new versions of familiar urban space types: the street, the square, the urban park and the urban belvedere. These new versions of old types respond to contemporary transportation and utility requirements, modes of development and mass-market consumerism. And while they are recognizably related to historical examples, they are more regional than local in their constituency, more independent than integral in their physical context and more specialized than diverse in their primary purpose.

While Montreal has a legacy of grand urban spaces from the 19th century, the public space system of Toronto has been essentially aspatial. The street pattern in the central city is an irregular grid established through land speculation rather than design, and while it is punctuated by civic buildings in prominent locations, there has been no tradition of public squares, linked spatial sequences, grand urban parks or overlooking terraces with splendid views; that is, until recently. Toronto is essentially a post-war metropolis that contains fragments of earlier urban constructions within its bounds. The current scope, form, image and quality of the city centre, including its principal public spaces, were established and developed after the war.

With the construction of the City Hall (1959–64) designed by Viljo Revell of Helsinki, Toronto received a broad and expansive civic platform where none had previously existed. Nathan Phillips Square serves all the traditional functions of a civic square; it is an honorific setting for the City Hall, a vital space of celebration and political demonstration as well as a pleasant open space for use in all seasons. And yet it differs substantially from historic spaces such as Place Royale in Quebec City, and its success is due precisely to these differences. While Place Royale served the life of a tiny community of settlers, Nathan Phillips Square serves a regional municipality of several millions and sits on top of a parking garage for 2,500 cars. While Place Royale is intimate and spatially enclosed, Nathan Phillips Square is monumental in scale, dominated by the City Hall and only tenuously enclosed by a free-standing colonnade. While Place Royale is tied inexorably into the fabric of small streets and buildings in the Lower Town, Nathan Phillips Square sits as an object in space, independent of its neighbouring streets and buildings. Yet in both cases these public spaces are icons for the city, symbols of collective civil agreement.

The Toronto case study that follows presents the modern squares of a modern city. Contemporary with the City Hall, the Toronto Dominion Centre (1962–73), designed by Mies van der Rohe of Chicago, is a group of high-rise office towers and a banking pavilion set within an open plaza, with underground shopping and parking. While the site is privately owned and maintained, it gives a moment of monumental grandeur and repose in the bustling city. The plaza is composed of two interrelated courtyards: one landscaped and facing south, the other surfaced exclusively in granite, facing north and originally centred on a skyscraper from the 1930s now replaced. Much criticized for its wind-swept and empty quality, the space is nevertheless generous, articulate in its context and uplifting in its existential challenge.

Old and new squares: Place Royale, Quebec City, and Nathan Phillips Square, Toronto

Old and new streets: Toronto Street, c. 1900 (courtesy Public Archives of Canada) and Eaton Centre Galleria, Toronto

41

Old and new urban parks: Public
Gardens, Halifax, c. 1900 (courtesy
Public Archives of Canada) and
Ontario Place, Toronto

Following the success of the Toronto Dominion Bank, its chief commercial rival, the Canadian Imperial Bank of Commerce, undertook its own project for a new head office tower at King and Bay streets. Designed by I. M. Pei of New York, the result is known as Commerce Court (1968–72). The project created a new public space internal to the block formed by the bank's 1929 tower restored, a new prismatic tower in stainless steel and two medium-scale buildings in limestone. This is a remarkable 20th-century urban space, a composite of old and new buildings intimately arranged, amenable but dense.

While other opportunities have arisen since for the creation of new public spaces, the more recent examples lack the clarity of conception and deftness of execution of these three. It should finally be noted that this sequence of spaces along Bay Street has a shadow underground. Tunnels now link below-grade concourses from City Hall to Union Station. While these two parallel systems are sustained by the dense and congested daytime population, their interconnections are weak and the underground is organizationally confusing.

The Eaton Centre designed by Eberhard Zeidler of Toronto (1973–81) is a metropolitan-scale interior street, a modern baroque of grand volumes, changing levels, theatrical overlooks and vistas containing a phantasmagoria of displayed goods and people. With its connections to the regional subway system, its massive parking garages and department stores, this quasi-public street has become the principal shopping precinct in the downtown. Like the arcades of European cities, it is descended from the urban street yet is radically different in scale, specialization and ownership.

Similarly, Zeidler's Ontario Place of 1968 offers a mutation of the familiar urban park. Following Montreal's Expo'67, this is a pleasure ground of man-made islands and lagoons that features technologically exuberant bridgeworks and display pavilions, theatres, amusement rides, waterfront drinking terraces and marinas. In comparison with the 19th-century Public Gardens of Halifax, this urban park of the 20th century reveals a similar diversity of landscape types and the ongoing appeal of the pavilion as folly in the landscape and base for entertainment. It differs once again in its spatial expansiveness, commercial motivation and relative isolation.

And lastly, while Quebec City has the promenade of the Dufferin Terrace with its magnificent views of the St. Lawrence River, Toronto has its Gardiner Expressway. Constructed during the 1960s, the expressway provides a route for high-speed movement in and out of the city, and serves as an elevated platform to view the city and the lake. Indeed, the contemporary image of the city is largely formed by its skyline as seen from the harbour and the expressway. Despite its utilitarian and anti-urban conception, the expressway has become a metropolitan belvedere.

Old and new belvederes: Dufferin
Terrace, Quebec City, and the
Gardiner Expressway, Toronto

Steven Fong, Toronto

Although Bay Street begins at Toronto's harbourfront, and goes 3.6 kilometres to the north, it is only the southerly third that has any formal stature. This length of street is the reference for a series of public spaces in Toronto's downtown and, in the portion popularly referred to as "the canyon," is a significant space in its own right. Together, these spaces constitute a recognizable and extensive public domain. Going from south to north, the spaces are:

Ferry Terminal - The entry to the Island Ferry Terminal is at the southeast corner of a space that, in turn, is formed by the water-edge, the backside of the Toronto Hilton Harbour Castle and a condominium tower. The verticality of the latter two buildings provides the space with a powerful directional emphasis toward the horizon to the south. The ground plane is characterized by landscaped mounds of grass and trees, with concrete walkways.

Commerce Court - The southeast corner of Bay and King streets is the site of both the original tower of the Bank of Commerce (1929–31) and the newer tower of the consolidated Canadian Imperial Bank of Commerce (1968–72). The two towers separate a "front-yard" on the street corner and a "back-yard" space called Commerce Court. The mid-block space, approximately 200 feet by 200 feet, has a central, stabilizing fountain and a pinwheeling configuration of connections; the pinwheel connects both to King Street, through a passage between the old and new towers, and to Bay Street with an east–west link.

Toronto Dominion Centre - On the east side of Bay Street and across from Commerce Court, the Toronto Dominion Centre visually conjoins corner and midblock conditions. The corner is occupied by a low, pavilion-like Banking Hall, which in turn allows for the high towers behind it to form the perceived closure of the space. The abstract spatial figure, abetted by very restrained architectural delineation, is a geometrically precise, orthogonal "dog-leg" with two north–south axes, each respectively terminating on the broad sides of towers, and forming a sequential through-block public domain. Each of the parts of the "dog-leg" is approximately 250 feet north–south and 200 feet east–west.

The Canyon - North of King Street, Bay Street becomes canyon-like with separate but continuous towers averaging 200 feet in height and lining the street. This compressed spatial "slot," approximately 60 feet wide and 1,200 feet long, culminates in the tower of Old City Hall. It has an energetic array of buildings that is more the result of common functional parameters than specific design initiatives. In comparison to this space, the "throat" formed by the Old City Hall, the Simpsons Tower and the Thomson Building is dissipated and out of scale.

Nathan Phillips Square - This space, a front to the Toronto City Hall, is, through the agency of a continuous colonnade and series of lawns at the streets, both architecturally controlled and introverted, and at the same time open and accessible. The space and building, void and solid, each have recognizable figural qualities. In turn, both share a common clarity of architectural elements. If conceptualization can

Aerial photograph of downtown Toronto, 1968, looking south showing City Hall, Bay Street and Toronto Dominion Centre (photo Ron Vickers, courtesy Toronto Dominion Archives)

Bay Street looking toward Old City Hall, c. 1940 (courtesy Public Archives of Canada)

Trinity Square (courtesy City of Toronto Archives)

Preliminary sketch of City Hall and Nathan Phillips Square, Viljo Revell, Architect, 1958 (courtesy City of Toronto Archives)

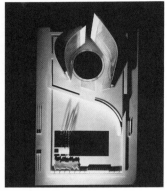

Competition model for City Hall, Viljo Revell, Architect, 1958 (courtesy City of Toronto Archives)

be thought about as either "subtractive" or "additive," then Nathan Phillips Square and the City Hall are clearly additive. The surface of the square is a series of separated concrete slabs whose emphatic gridding is reminiscent of a Superstudio grid.

Trinity Park - The results of a recent competition, the space surrounding Trinity Church has a very private sensibility. In the case of this space, entry and visual access is through one of several adjoining spaces, the lobby of Bell Canada, the galleria of Eaton Centre, Bay Street or James Street. Functionally, this space is seen as both an adjunct to the galleria of the Eaton Centre shopping mall and as a lunchtime "park" for office workers in the surrounding area. Demarcated by street lamps and other urban paraphernalia, its centre is a simple lawn 200 feet square.

Although the six spaces that are related to Bay Street constitute a group by virtue of proximity, they are neither a coherent nor a sequential entity. Instead, the spaces are individual and autonomous, with few apparent collective initiatives. Often, spatial passages are isolated and axes lead nowhere. Nevertheless, the spaces provoke speculation about a series of generic issues related to space-making in the North American city, as well as particular concerns about the public domain in Toronto.

Bay Street spaces may be seen as representing three processes of urban design. These are designs by (1) accident, (2) amelioration, and (3) intention. Cross-comparisons would not be particularly fruitful, as they would tend to only point up the obvious shortcomings of the first two categories.

Models submitted to the City Hall Competition in 1958 assembled as a virtual city (courtesy City of Toronto Archives)

City Hall under construction showing the installation of plaza paving over the underground parking garage and demolition of the Registry Office, 1963 (courtesy City of Toronto Archives)

Accidential Spaces - The "canyon" on Bay Street from King Street to Queen Street is a recognizable space because of the closure afforded by the continuous street-wall of buildings and the axial alignment with the Clock Tower of Old City Hall. However, this accident of real estate speculation does not provide sufficient shelter or depth on the facades to support activities at the bases of the buildings. Street-level amenities are limited to the width of the sidewalks, which hardly invite the intrepid blue-suit-types to linger beyond normal business hours.

Ameliorative Spaces - Many successful North American public spaces are the result of ameliorative efforts to transform residual spaces between autonomous, visually self-referential buildings. Paley Park in New York, with its paving and fountain, is a good example. In Toronto, the equivalent spaces are at the Ferry Terminal and Trinity Park. The former, with its curious mounds of grass and trees, is so obviously disagreeable that it may be immediately dismissed. The latter example responds to a very difficult site where the bulk of available space bears little formal relationship to the neighbouring object building (a small church). The solution to the problem has been to make an autonomous, square lawn. The potential for a discursive relationship, however, between lawn and church, space and object, has been abrogated. Instead, street furniture is the most identifiable characteristic of this space.

Intentional Spaces - Commerce Court, Toronto Dominion Centre and Nathan Phillips Square make an engaging comparison because all three spaces came about through the marshalling of significant resources. It should be noted that the first two spaces are adjunct to private institutions, while the latter is a forecourt to a seat of municipal government.

Opening night of City Hall, 1964 (courtesy City of Toronto Archives)

The relative hierarchy of private and civic institutions is a worthwhile conversation in and of itself, and certainly traditional cities have an order with respect to this issue that has no correspondence in Toronto. However, this is a different discussion altogether, and its brief inclusion here is only to pre-empt the obvious caveat about the curious condition of mammoth private buildings and diminutive public buildings. That aside, we may first look at the two banking institutions.

The configuration of most office towers does not vary from city to city, but is rather based on a set of simple, mathematical parameters. The optimization and standardization of the floor plate for towers is much like that for any industrial product. In the case of the office tower, this entity must then be inserted into an urban context. Toronto's urban block is typically 400 feet deep, which leaves a surplus of space, given the average floor plate dimensions of about 120 feet by 180 feet. So, the tower may occupy the middle of the block with space all around it, or be placed at the perimeter, directly on the street. Both the Canadian Imperial Bank of Commerce and the Toronto Dominion Towers utilize the latter strategy, but with very different results.

Commerce Court is a space formed in the mid-block where the office tower is only one side of a varied spatial perimeter. Two of the other sides are formed by low,

City Hall and Nathan Phillips Square showing the reflecting pool, 1983 (courtesy City of Toronto Archives)

45

From the elevated walkway City Hall seems to be set in a lush landscape of trees, 1985 (courtesy City of Toronto Archives)

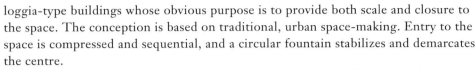

King and Bay streets, 1930, showing Bank of Toronto by Carrere & Hastings, 1911–13 (photo Pringle & Booth, courtesy Toronto Dominion Bank)

Toronto Dominion Centre under construction, from the air, c. 1968 (photo Ron Vickers, courtesy Toronto Dominion Bank)

loggia-type buildings whose obvious purpose is to provide both scale and closure to the space. The conception is based on traditional, urban space-making. Entry to the space is compressed and sequential, and a circular fountain stabilizes and demarcates the centre.

The obvious classicism of Commerce Court is contrasted by the modern space of the Toronto Dominion Centre. The office towers are placed at the north and south extremities of the site and the resulting urban space is a dynamic and fluid entity between the towers. The public plaza and the towers, space and object, are reciprocal conversations where one provides context for the other. However provocative this spatial diagram seems, the urban reality is unnecessarily expansive in a context that lacks sufficient street definition and density. On a windy, winter day this reality is especially cruel.

The proposition about the reciprocal relationship between building and plaza is successful at Nathan Phillips Square. The space allows for the perception of the parts of the building, its base, council chamber and office towers. The base transforms into the colonnade that, in turn, defines the space. Inside the colonnade, the elements of the plaza, including pond/skating rink, are peripheral and the centre of the space remains open for large gatherings. However, because of the scale of the colonnade, this openness at the centre does not result in vacuousness.

If this discussion is to constitute a kind of "scorecard," then certainly Nathan Phillips Square is seen as the superior urban, spatial production. Poignant, highly charged and energetic, it is evidence of a collusive agreement between space and building. Of the other spaces, Commerce Court and the Toronto Dominion Centre are also significant, and in many aspects urban exemplars. However, large private institutions can rarely sustain a protracted and active vision of public life that is the necessary social component of public space. In this context, public space is reduced to being the foreground for the making of skyscrapers, which might be architecturally interesting, but is urbanistically irrelevant. However, if these spaces are improperly animated to coincide precisely with one's perceptions of "public space," then it is clearly not the fault of the architecture, but rather a paucity of public life in the city. Architecture, after all, cannot do everything.

Aerial photograph of downtown Toronto (courtesy Department of Energy, Mines and Resources)

Figure/ground plan at grade of Bay Street district

Architect Sidney Bregman and models of Toronto Dominion Centre being prepared for delivery to first tenants, c. 1967 (courtesy Cadillac Fairview Corporation)

Grey Cup festivities at the Toronto Dominion Centre, 1969 (photo Ron Vickers, courtesy Toronto Dominion Bank)

View looking north from Wellington Street, showing the south garden court, 1982 (photo Ron Vickers, courtesy Toronto Dominion Bank)

Trinity Square looking south to James Street and Old City Hall

View from City Hall at Christmas with Toronto Dominion Centre in background, 1968 (photo Ron Vickers, courtesy Toronto Dominion Bank)

PHOTOGRAPHY BY PETER MACCALLUM

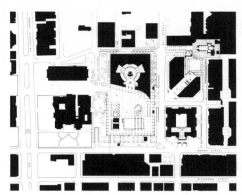

Plan of Trinity Square (Thom Partnership, Architects, with Moorehead, Fleming, Corban, McCarthy, Landscape Architects) and Nathan Phillips Square (Viljo Revell, John B. Parkin, Architects)

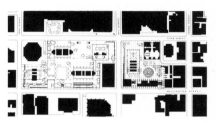

Plan of Toronto Dominion Centre (Mies van der Rohe, John B. Parkin and Bregman & Hamann, Architects) and Commerce Court (I. M. Pei, Page & Steele, Architects)

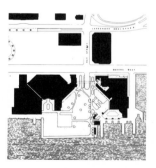

Plan of Harbour Castle Hotel and Condominium with Island Ferry Terminal

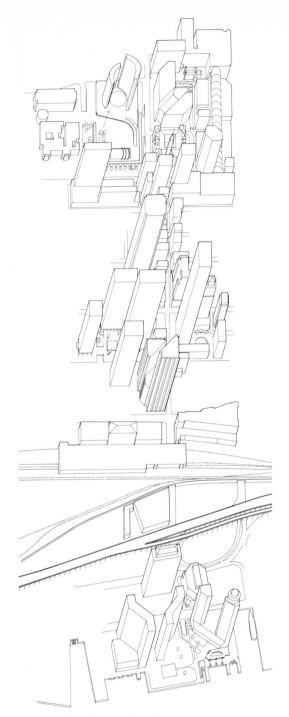

Axonometric of Bay Street showing Trinity Square, Nathan Phillips Square, Toronto Dominion Centre Plaza, Commerce Court and Harbour Castle/Island Ferry Terminal

49

**Trinity Square looking toward Trinity
Church and Eaton Centre**

**Approach to Trinity Square from Bay
Street**

Nathan Phillips Square on Bay Street

**Approach to Nathan Phillips Square
from Queen and Bay streets**

Nathan Phillips Square from under
the colonnade

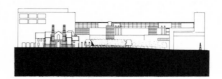

**Section through Trinity Square
looking east**

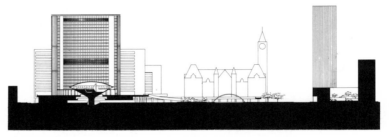

**Section through Nathan Phillips
Square looking east**

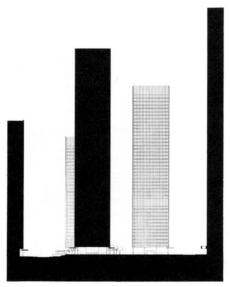

**Section through Toronto Dominion
Centre looking east**

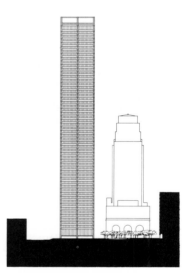

**Section through Commerce Court
looking north**

**Section through Harbour Castle
showing Ferry Terminal**

**Commerce Court from inside new
tower**

Detail section at Trinity Square tree-lined approach from Bay Street

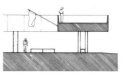

Detail section at Nathan Phillips Square showing colonnade

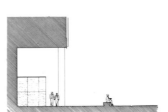

Detail section at Toronto Dominion Centre showing arcade and lawn

Detail section at Commerce Court showing arcade and fountain

Commerce Court showing both old and new towers and courtyard buildings

Commerce Court from King Street looking toward the courtyard

Toronto Dominion Centre looking up
from the garden (photo Ron Vickers,
1976, courtesy Toronto Dominion
Bank)

Toronto Dominion Centre from King Street (photo Panda, 1968)

Toronto Dominion Centre looking toward King Street (photo Panda, 1968)

Waterfront park at Harbour Castle looking north toward the city

Island Ferry Terminal at Harbour Castle, looking toward the water

Waterfront park at Harbour Castle looking south from Bay Street

MULTI-LEVEL CITY CENTRES

Montreal
Calgary
Halifax

Over the past two decades urban designers and architects have largely abandoned the radical ideas of the modern movement for restructuring the city; but while new developments try to restore a measure of urbanity to city centres that suffered massive destruction and distortion during the 1960s, specialized precincts for pedestrian movement and shopping have firmly taken hold underground and in the air. Each successive wave of economic prosperity seems to intensify and expand the labyrinthian network of concourses, malls, corridors, tunnels and/or bridges that lure people in from the weather and noise of the street. Throughout this century utopian visions of the multi-level city in both Europe and North America have offered redemption from the chaos and intensity of the metropolis. In Canada, these visions have been seized upon and built on a vast scale. The emerging underground pedestrian districts of Montreal and Toronto and the elevated +15 networks of Calgary and Halifax are mutations of public space at the scale of the city and are now so expansive as to constitute cities within cities. Interiorized, commercialized and privatized, these second cities ameliorate the harsh climate, create controlled domains for retailing and put into practice early 20th-century visions of the metropolis.

As long ago as 1490, Leonardo da Vinci began speculations while in Milan about a multi-levelled city of canals, subterranean service streets and upper-level *strade nobile*; this sorting out of various kinds of spaces for various kinds of movements had, of course, quite common antecedents in the domestic architecture of the nobility where a strict hierarchy of servant and served spaces informed the structure of the building for reasons of both propriety and efficiency. A version of this kind of city was realized in microcosm in Robert Adam's Adelphi Terrace in London of 1768; a rough and servile lower level opening directly onto the River Thames was ruthlessly segregated from a noble and civil realm above.

With the sudden growth of the early metropolis into a concentrated and congested settlement, the impetus grew for segregation and specialization of various aspects of the city centre. London began construction of its underground tube in the 1860s and Paris followed by 1900. In New York the multi-level Grand Central Station of 1903–13 established an extensive crypto-city as a monumental response to the problem of regional movement. Such examples fuelled the imagination of visionaries like Moses King in New York and the Italian futurist Antonio Sant'Elia. By 1929, the Greater New York Region Plan included numerous visionary proposals for elevated pedestrian systems, interestingly attached directly to the space of the street like giant continuous balconies. And, of course, the principles of modern town planning articulated in the Athens Charter (1933) of the CIAM group codified the separation of pedestrian and vehicular realms in their program of radical deurbanization. Even when CIAM, followed by Team Ten, turned its attention to the withering city centres during the 1950s, they continued to promote withdrawal from the street. With the emergence of large-scale developers in North America, the opportunity for profit in the neglected city centres of North America became the ground for testing these new architectural models.

Sketch by Leonardo da Vinci showing a crypto-city of canals, service streets and upper-level *strada nobile*, 1490

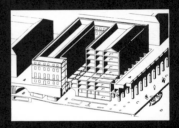

Robert Adam's Adelphi Terrace, London, 1768–74

The London Underground Railway
from *Universal Illustrated*, 1867

Place Ville Marie in Montreal (1958–62), designed by I. M. Pei with Affleck, Desbarats, Dimakopoulos, Lebensold and Sise, created the first extensive interior shopping concourse in Canada underneath a massive office tower. Connected by tunnel to the railway through Central Station and later to the underground Métro, the concourse provided controlled flow of people for retailing purposes. At the same time, it created an interior refuge from the miseries of the street and winter, setting into question the traditional norms of exterior public space on the ground. Regarding its subterranean character, Ray Affleck had these comments in 1967: "This system has sometimes been referred to as an 'underground city' — a notion that seems hardly appropriate to a high density centre city area built primarily over air rights where the 'ground' is in effect where the designer chooses to put it. In effect the notions of 'underground' or 'above ground' involve entirely new criteria. The 'ground' itself has become an artefact."

A deliriously active future envisaged as "Moses King's View of New York," 1911, Richard Rummell delineator

Such projects are radical mutations not only of the ground, but also of the urban block. Unlike the 1929 visions of elevated walkways within the space of the street, the pedestrian domains of new commercial developments have been located in the middle of the block, with the block becoming the basic module of development and turning itself inside out. This internalization has had a devastating effect on the quality of the streets outside, which have become progressively blank and servile, like the lower level of the Adelphi Terrace. At the same time, it has rarely provided interior spaces of sufficient scale, architectural stature and diversity of use to be considered as public places. In Montreal, the only space of such a type is the Grand Hall of Complexe Desjardins. Designed by La Société La Haye-Ouellet in 1967, the Grand Hall not only provides a clear passage through the block at ground level, but also makes a clear spatial connection with the pedestrian system below ground. The mere scale of the space creates a theatre for urban events and a landscape for the restless *flâneur*.

While such developments have been controversial in terms of their effect on the city, even critics of the stature of Melvin Charney have welcomed the emergence of the city within the city. He described it in 1981, with a certain irony, as "a diagram of streets and squares that are at best shadows of their former selves: 'ruins before they have begun to crumble.' However, here among the 'ruins' of a street-wise culture, one is undeniably warm and dry."

In 1967 Affleck, Desbarats, Dimakopoulos, Lebensold and Sise turned their attention on Calgary and initiated a plan for a rationalized redevelopment of its city centre, a plan that was to reshape the city over the next two decades. Selected streets were recast as pedestrian mall and transit mall; parking garages were encouraged on the periphery, high-rise commercial buildings in the core, and a network of elevated pedestrian spaces was intended to resolve the perceived conflict between cars and pedestrians in the street. The plan was a text-book illustration of Team Ten principles as represented, for instance, in the Smithsons/Sigmond plan of 1958 for the rebuilding of Berlin.

Unlike the ad hoc system in Montreal, the +15 pedestrian system in Calgary resulted from a planner's dream and the implementation of a master plan. The intention was not simply to connect buildings, but to create a total pedestrian environment of walkways, bridges and open spaces sheltered from traffic. An upper-level system was chosen for reasons of both amenity and pragmatics.

The system was developed in several distinct versions and is now almost continuous with forty-one bridges and nine kilometres of walkways. It began on the model of open decks between existing buildings and above existing laneways. Then during the early 1970s the City embarked on an urban renewal plan in which new institutional buildings were built in the centre of their blocks, surrounded by landscape and connected by open-air bridges, some with nominal weather protection. While the initial conception was for an open-air system, subsequent generations favoured interior spaces and linkages for comfort during inclement weather.

In the main retail area, new full-block developments such as Toronto Dominion Square created interior retail concourses at the +15 level that connected existing department stores on adjacent blocks. In addition, this project by Skidmore, Owings and Merrill created an expansive interior garden with landscaped terraces under a sloping glass roof. Located at the +45 level, the Devonian Gardens provide a variety of garden spaces for the pleasure of the public. Like many of the skywalk bridges, the garden was built by the developer, but is now operated by the City and open for extended hours. Finally, the system has been incorporated into office buildings where there is no significant merchandising but simply a desire to link into the downtown network.

With the assertion of the +15 as the principal public level, the streets — with the exception of the Stephen Avenue Pedestrian Mall — have become the exclusive domain of traffic and are increasingly hostile for pedestrians. New buildings are penetrable only in their lobbies and otherwise offer blank walls. In a revealing anecdote, the combination of apparent density and the absence of street activity made Calgary the ideal site for the shooting of the *Superman* film series. The films' producers could achieve the appearance of Manhattan without the trouble of having to clear the street of people. The effect is hauntingly unreal.

While Montreal and Toronto begin to confront seriously the challenge of

Chicago's multi-level city with service and vehicles below the street and lift-bridges over the river, c. 1965

Photomontage of proposed upper-level walkways for Manhattan, Greater Region Plan of New York, 1929

Plan for central Berlin showing pedestrian platform net superimposed over roadway system, Smithsons/Sigmond, 1958 from *Team Ten Primer*

making the underground system and the street into complementary systems of pedestrian amenity, Calgary shows no strong interest in the street for anything but transportation. And given that the core is simply the work centre for this expansive suburban metropolis, there would not likely be sufficient density or variety of population to make two levels viable; as it is, one level seems to be challenge enough. Indeed, the Calgary situation gives pause; for while the idea of the multi-level city may become appealing and viable in concentrated urban centres with residency, diverse use and intensive public life, it seems tenuous in the context of suburban diffusion.

A final example from Halifax illustrates the tension between the new interior city and the historic city. Founded in the middle of the 18th century, Halifax is one of the oldest settlements in Canada, and its original plan bears the imprint of the Enlightenment. A grid of small blocks and streets was laid out in a clearing on a hill, facing the harbour and reserving a central place for public ceremonies. The town served the military stationed there, and the military served the town. At its heart, George Street led from the waterfront through the Grand Parade to the Citadel and became not only a main route in the town, but its symbolic axis. Church and town hall still face each other on the Parade and the Legislature still has its side yard on George Street. And while occasionally something new reinforces the street, like the Art Gallery of Nova Scotia renovating a building at its foot, its general physical condition is losing its integrity and its social position has been substantially diminished. New buildings on its edges are architecturally undistinguished and internalized, barely urban let alone civic. And the surfaces, landscaping and public elements of the street — with the exception of the historic wall of the Parade — are impoverished.

New investment has been drawn away from George Street to the west where large land assemblies have facilitated construction of large and inward-looking hotels, commercial complexes and convention centre, all linked internally by means of overhead bridges. Despite their contribution to the economy of the downtown, the isolation and independence of this complex from its urban context has had a divisive and compromising, rather than a stimulating, effect on the rest of the downtown. For Halifax the current challenge is compounded: not only are the interior spaces of the new developments insufficiently public, but the streets around them have been devastated and the historic and symbol heart of the city has been eroded. If the upper-level city is to augment and not replace the historic fabric of public spaces, then the inhabitation of the city centre will have to grow to metropolitan intensity. Without the will to achieve this, the +15 system will simply diffuse the centre and render it a minor incident within the ever-expanding and decentring urban field.

MONTREAL'S VILLE INTÉRIEURE WITH SPECIAL REFERENCE TO THE FRENCH AXIS

Pieter Sijpkes, Montreal

The City of Montreal was founded twice. The first time was in 1642 when forty religious pioneers founded Ville Marie on a spit of land where the St. Pierre creek ran into the St. Lawrence River. The second founding coincided with the opening in 1960 of Place Ville Marie, a high-rise office building that includes an underground link between its shopping concourse and Central Station on the other side of Dorchester Boulevard. While it took almost three hundred and fifty years for Ville Marie to develop into the major urban centre that Montreal is now, "la ville intérieure" has developed at a much more spectacular rate over the last thirty years. It is expected that by 1989, 50 per cent of all merchandising in the downtown will be part of this indoor network.

Carpenter ants can turn an oak chair into a complex warren of tunnels and spaces that are only hinted at by round holes at the surface of the wood; analogously, Montreal has been subject to a frantic level of activity underneath the surface. This underground infrastructure is practically invisible at street level, except for the entrances to the Métro transit system; it can only be grasped in its entirety by looking at the ever-expanding grid of black lines on tourist maps. Like the carpenter ants, the excavators of indoor public space live by the art of subtraction: they burrow into the existing structure of the city. Nowhere is this more evident than in the current effort to slip a three-storey shopping mall underneath venerable old Christ Church Cathedral.

The basic principle of Montreal's indoor city, the "Place Ville Marie formula," is to locate shops where they will be exposed to the natural flow of a large captive audience. The opening of the Métro in 1966 and its subsequent extension into a far-flung system created such an audience and made it possible to establish a "merchandising net" at any of its many access points.

The current indoor environment in Montreal can roughly be divided into three sections, sometimes identified as the English axis, the French axis and the St. Catherine Street axis. The English axis is centred on Place Ville Marie and extends south underneath the Queen Elizabeth Hotel, Central Station, Place Bonaventure and the Bonaventure Métro Station. This system was in place by the late 1960s, and at that time it was decided to create another axis, the French one, farther east to link Place des Arts Métro with the Place d'Armes Station. It is this French axis that has been shown for this exhibition.

The St. Catherine Street axis is the most recent outgrowth of the system. Unlike the previous two systems that are orientated north–south, the St. Catherine Street axis runs east–west and is intended to link the English and French axes in the future.

When the creation of the French indoor axis was contemplated, Place des Arts was already in place. The redevelopment of the block to its south created the first opportunity for the system. Complexe Desjardins was built by the Caisses populaires Desjardins in the early 1970s as a multi-use complex containing office towers, a hotel

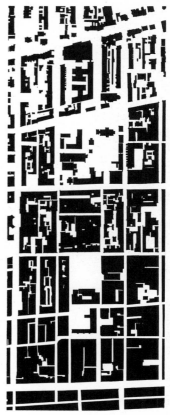

The fine grain urban form of 1922 has been replaced by a few very large building complexes (courtesy McGill University)

**Exterior of Place Ville Marie, 1961
(courtesy ARCOP Architects)**

**Interior of Place Ville Marie, 1962
(courtesy ARCOP Architects)**

and shopping on several levels. A large daylit space forms the heart of the complex and has become the venue for fêtes of the Expos baseball team and the Canadiens hockey team as well as other diverse cultural events.

The federal government's long-standing desire to centralize its employees in Montreal was fulfilled with the building of Place Guy Favreau on the block south of Complexe Desjardins. This mixed-use building includes housing as well as a major interior public space for the government offices, and is linked to Complexe Desjardins by a tunnel.

Finally, the Quebec government chose the air rights over the Trans-Canada Highway as the site for a convention centre, the Palais des Congrès. This building was to demonstrate the possibility of building over the gash of the sunken expressway that isolated historic Old Montreal from uptown.

This quick succession of major building projects has made it possible to walk indoors from the Métro at Place des Arts, through the bowels of Place des Arts, underneath St. Catherine Street, through the "great hall" of Complexe Desjardins, underneath Dorchester Boulevard, through Place Guy Favreau, underneath rue de La Gauchetière, through a tunnel under the plaza facing the Palais des Congrès, across rue Viger and arrive at the Place d'Armes Métro Station. The route oscillates between grand spaces and inhospitable tunnels and, unfortunately, ends at one of the most unpleasant pedestrian spaces in Montreal: a bridge crossing the expressway, underneath the concrete convention centre. This foul-smelling, ill-lit place is continuously subjected to the roar of the traffic below and is compressed by the underbelly of the building above. And while Old Montreal lies just a few hundred feet to the south, its pleasures remain mysteriously inaccessible.

The same walk at street level reveals the high price we pay for this string of large-scale urban interventions. Place des Arts is an unmitigated disaster at street level for all approaches, while Complexe Desjardins offers mainly blank walls (with windows or not) along its outside edges. Place Guy Favreau does have housing on top of an arcade on its south side, but offers little on the other sides. The Palais des Congrès has a public plaza facing the south-side housing that remains largely empty; the majority of visitors arrive by Métro or taxi and approach the building from below. The overall quality of the exterior urban environment invokes nostalgia for the city plan of 1922. Row houses, public institutions with large gardens and street-level commerce squarely faced the street, while the coming and going of streetcars and pedestrians filled these streets with life.

It is true that part of the year these streets were made impassable by snow and sleet; it is true that the overall density has increased; and it is true that the Métro moves hundreds of thousands of people effortlessly along its subterranean tracks. But the bleakness of the streets, the dullness and fake variety of the corporate interiors make a public evaluation of the future of the "ville intérieure" urgent.

Three different areas of concern can be identified:

1. The impact of the indoor network on the regular streets: Will the streets of Montreal be able to keep their lively population of shoppers, tourists and *flâneurs*? Will the enlargement of scale that so far has accompanied every new intervention add to the quality of the city fabric, or do the linked, one-block fiefdoms of Place Ville Marie, Complexe Desjardins, etc., actually impoverish the overall quality of city life with their inward-looking malls and their outward-looking truck docks and garage entrances? What kind of stores on the street will be able to compete with the corporate "boutiques" of the indoor city?

2. The urban quality of the indoor city itself: Will the indoor environment, despite its weather-protected quality, be able to provide Montrealers with the ambience they have historically prized on streets such as St. Catherine, Sherbrooke, St. Laurent or St. Denis? Is the lack of daylight, the absence of landmarks, the oppressive acoustics and the resulting disorientation that are now the rule in most of the indoor city necessary, or is it possible to "open up" the domain by making it more transparent, more spatially satisfying, and more humane?

3. The legal ramifications of the creation of a large domain of pseudo-public space: Visitors to the indoor domain are subject to an ever-changing and ill-defined set of rules that are fundamentally different from the ones that govern behaviour in the public domain. The rules are enforced by private guards whose mandate is to "protect the shopping climate." Is this arrangement the appropriate one for such an important part of the city? Is it unethical that private interests can obstruct and detour the natural flow of pedestrians from the Métro to the street at will in order to guarantee exposure of even the remotest storefront to passers-by?

These questions are complex and cannot be answered by a simple "yes" or "no." To a large degree the answers are political; the current City administration has recently initiated the creation of a master plan by publishing an important discussion paper. Three possible directions for the indoor city are outlined for the citizens of Montreal to choose: to continue the haphazard growth of the past thirty years; to halt the extension of the system; or to put guidelines in place to guarantee that both the existing and future system will serve the needs of Montrealers at large and not just narrow commercial interests.

The last option is clearly the most persuasive. The indoor city is now an important part of the city. Recognizing its positive aspects as well as its limitations in a public forum is a crucial and long-overdue process. Only with full community participation is there any hope that the two Montreals founded almost three hundred and fifty years apart can be reconciled into a complex, integrated urban fabric. It is a delicate balancing act to satisfy the often contradictory demands made by the indoor and the outdoor public domains; it is an act that we are only beginning to learn.

Exterior view of Place Bonaventure, 1967 (courtesy ARCOP Architects)

Christ Church Cathedral on stilts as an underground retail complex is constructed in 1987 (courtesy Derek Drummond)

Place des Arts Métro station

PHOTOGRAPHY BY MARC FOWLER

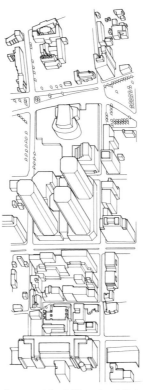

Axonometric of "French axis" above grade

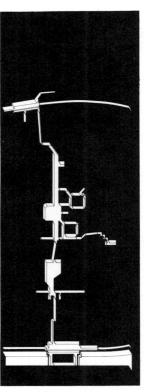

Axonometric of "French axis" underground, from Place des Arts Métro to the Palais des Congrès

Concourse of Place des Arts

Underground link between Place Guy Favreau and Palais des Congrès

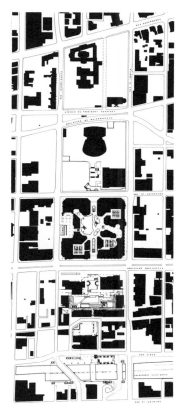

Plan at street level

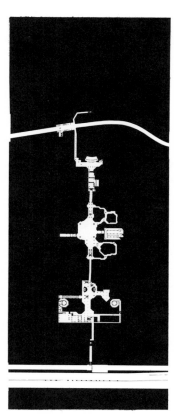

Plan underground

Bridge link from Place Guy Favreau to Palais des Congrès

Great Hall in Complexe Desjardins at
Métro level

Exterior view along rue Jeanne-
Mance

Exit from underground system at
Palais des Congrès

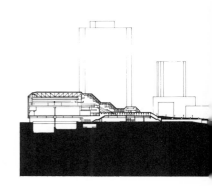

68

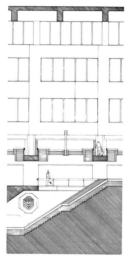

Detail section of stair in Complexe Desjardins leading to tunnel underneath Dorchester Boulevard

Detail section of entrance to tunnel underneath St. Catherine Street from Place des Arts

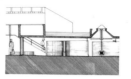

Detail section of tunnel-stair at Palais des Congrès

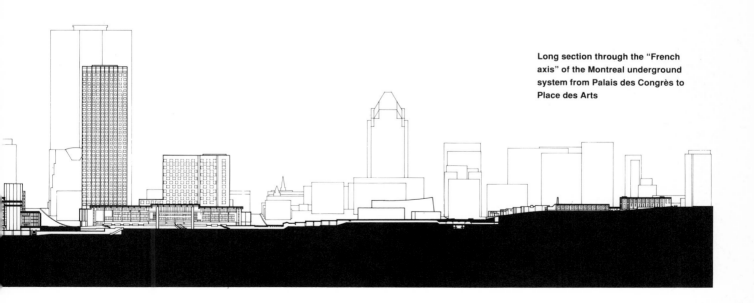

Long section through the "French axis" of the Montreal underground system from Palais des Congrès to Place des Arts

Underground link between Place des
Arts and Complexe Desjardins

Interior of Place Guy Favreau at Métro
level

MULTI-LEVEL CHOREOGRAPHY

Harold Hanen, Calgary

> Too many designers today seem to be yearning for the physical characteristics of the past instead of searching for the abstract ordering principle which the town of the past happened to have and which the modern conceptions of the city have not yet found.
>
> Christopher Alexander, *The City is Not a Tree*

Impact of New Technologies

To deal with the impact of contemporary movement technologies, Calgary has introduced a multi-level and multi-modal movement system in which pedestrians and vehicles are separated. This comprehensive design approach, coupled with the city's rapid growth over the last two decades, provides a unique study of the benefits and pitfalls of weaving three-dimensional pedestrian movement into the fabric of the city.

The +15 system emerged from a 1960s "platform" proposal by architects Henry Migallo and David Kehoe of the City Planning Department to bridge the streets of Calgary's Churchill Park Urban Renewal Project. Then, in 1967 the Montreal firm of Affleck, Desbarats, Dimakopoulos, Lebensold and Sise refined the pedestrian network of the urban renewal scheme in conjunction with senior members of the Planning Department, including Mike Rogers, Stu Round and myself.

The extension of this initial, discrete pedestrian system into an organizing element of urban form that was integrated into the city's overall downtown development process was my responsibility. The image projected for the future was a three-dimensional public infrastructure that would be finer in scale and richer in detail than most cities spawned in the 20th century. It was to be a city that supported the idea of felt space rather than viewed objects.

Photograph of Eighth Avenue in 1915 (Provincial Archives of Alberta)

A comprehensive plan was devised for the downtown core. For vehicular traffic, the narrow street right-of-ways of 66 feet were designated for specific functions; for instance, one was to serve as a public transit corridor, others as one-way streets to meet high capacity needs or two-way streets for slow flows. For both grade and upper levels, a pedestrian system was designed to be extended incrementally over time as needed and as means permitted.

The at-grade pedestrian system included river walkways, two bisecting malls, and block-encircling sidewalks softened by arcades and open spaces. At one, two and three levels above ground, the pedestrian network conceived of open spaces, sheltered or enclosed walkways linking retail, residential, cultural, recreational, commercial, educational activities, parking garages and public transit. Since 1968, the riverbank walkways and approximately two kilometres of grade-level mall have been completed. At the upper levels, forty-one bridge connections and nine kilometres of public easements have been built, making it the world's largest above-grade pedestrian system.

Aerial photograph of downtown Calgary, 1959 (Provincial Archives of Alberta)

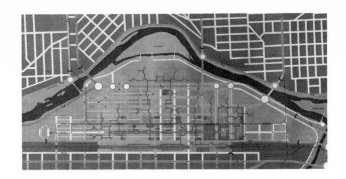

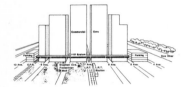

City of Calgary's +15 concept showing links between specialized transportation systems, office buildings and retail core, 1987 (courtesy City of Calgary)

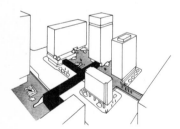

City of Calgary's initial vision of +15 bridges, walkways and mid-block open spaces, c. 1975 (courtesy City of Calgary)

Implementation

In few other post-war downtowns was the planning determination to develop a comprehensive pedestrian system so closely matched to the opportunity to build that was created by the oil boom of the early 1970s. A premise underlying the implementation of the system was that **all** citizens have a vested interest in, and a right of access to, a quality public environment. The challenge was to develop a regulatory mechanism to encourage public and private sectors to participate in the system's total development.

The bonus system, which was developed by planner David Diver and incorporated into the "Downtown Development Guidelines" in 1969, was the heart of the implementation strategy. It established a formula by which developers provided public space amenities in exchange for specific ratios of building density. A project would be granted extra floor area for every square foot of public pedestrian amenity that it constructed at ratios ranging from 5:1 to 30:1.

Visual and Spatial Considerations

The most visible part of the system — its bridges — are also the most dominant element in the streetscape. While the first designs were bland structural expressions, the more recent solutions enrich their contextual settings and, through the rediscovery of the classic ideas of bridges, heighten the experience of place, arrival and departure.

Calgary's movement channels are organized on the typical prairie gridiron. Grid patterns have advantages for vehicular movement, but the view from the sidewalks are down open-ended and scaleless vistas to infinity. Upper-level bridging does two aesthetically satisfying things: it arrests the boring views for the driver and the pedestrian at grade, and it creates memorable visual experiences at the upper level. As one emerges at right angles from the typical block, above the flow of the streets, a heightened and central vista bursts open down the dynamic canyons of the city toward the Rockies beyond. The result is not only aesthetically pleasing, but provides a reassuring sense of place in the regional context.

+15 Versus Ground Level

The simple argument that elevated pedestrian systems sterilize the street environment has had little validity in Calgary's experience. On cold winter days, one sees streams of office workers in short sleeves and dresses moving along upper levels of shops, restaurants, theatres, banks, apartments and fountained garden atriums. On warm days, the same promenaders pour out of doors to the ground-level mall and

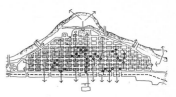

plazas. The issue is not an either/or proposition, but the creation of environmental choices appropriate to our special climate and our citizens' needs.

Social Opportunities

Perhaps the most significant and unexpected benefit of the +15 system is the increased social connection fostered by bridging. Calgary, like many cities, was being reshaped to accommodate the proliferation of automobiles and high-rise buildings. Sidewalks were narrowed and open spaces filled in. Many of the downtown buildings were turning inward, away from congested streets that were saturated with vehicular noise and gaseous smells and covered by the cold shadows of skyscrapers. The sensual hostility of the street and the emphasis on corporate territory created a feeling of alienation and rejection in many people.

The +15 system penetrates the private realm and encourages the lowering of traditional territorial barriers. An example of this is its influence on the lives of downtown Calgary's older residents. Several senior citizen housing buildings are now linked through the +15 to hotels, government offices, performance centres and museums. In their daily outings the residents come into direct and intimate contact with a unique montage of social opportunities.

Public Rights

Public control is critical to the achievement of true public space. In some separated pedestrian systems and many North American shopping centre malls, control of access and use of spaces commonly perceived to be public is retained and exercised at the discretion of the private owner. Calgary's +15 system is neither exclusively private nor exclusively public. It is built by private developers, but use and access is controlled by the City through individual contractual agreements.

The Future

As cities become more complex and people become less satisfied with fragmented and reductive approaches, new urban ordering and implementation strategies must be devised. I believe in a holistic, multi-level conception of the public inner city, one that supports richer choreographies of urban movement, new standards of safety and comfort, and can play an instrumental role in the evolution of a more humane 21st century.

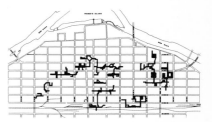

Four plans showing the incremental development of the +15 pedestrian system from 1970 to 1982 (courtesy City of Calgary)

Open plaza at +15 level, from early 1970s (photo Detlef Mertins, 1987)

Covered skywalk of the Court and Remand Centre, 1974 (photo Detlef Mertins, 1987)

Entrance atrium of Petro-Canada Building, 1985 (photo Detlef Mertins, 1987)

Aerial photograph of downtown Calgary (courtesy Department of Energy, Mines and Resources)

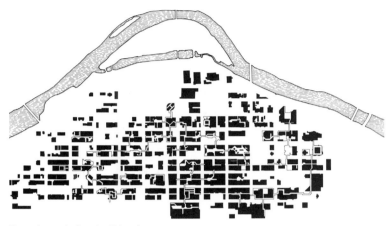

Figure/ground plan at +15 level, downtown Calgary

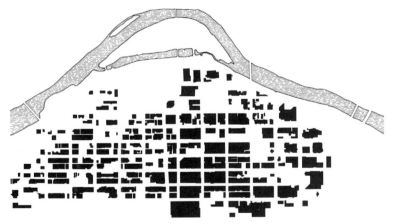

Figure/ground plan at grade, downtown Calgary

Typical signage system identification installed beginning 1987 (photo Detlef Mertins, 1987)

Current condition of link waiting for redevelopment of the other side of the street (photo Detlef Mertins, 1987)

Aerial view of downtown Calgary
showing Eighth Avenue Pedestrian
Mall and the concentration of high-
rise commercial buildings

View of downtown Calgary from the
suburbs. Since few people reside in
the centre of the city, the high-rise
core area is largely a commuter
destination

PHOTOGRAPHY BY JOHN DEAN

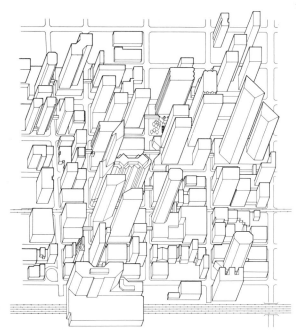

Axonometric of central area of Calgary

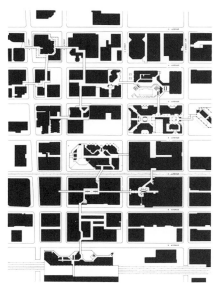

Plan of central area of Calgary at the +15 level

View of Seventh Avenue Transit Mall, Calgary

**Interior view of Esso Plaza at +15
level, Calgary**

Exterior view of Esso Plaza, Calgary

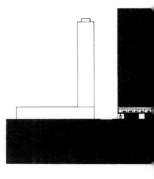

**North/south section through central
area showing Esso Plaza and Toronto
Dominion Square**

View of skywalk bridge from Esso Plaza to Bow Valley Square, Calgary

Detail section of typical new skywalk bridge using suspension structure

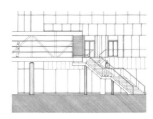

Detail elevation of Esso Plaza skywalk bridge

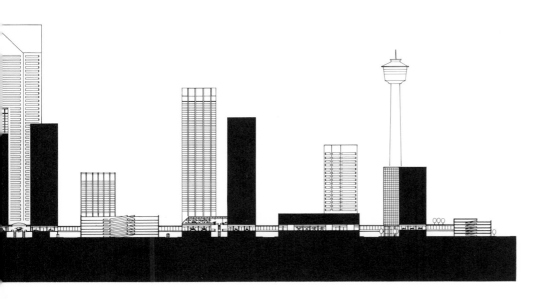

Interior view of Devonian Gardens at
+45 level in Toronto Dominion
Square, Calgary

View of skywalk bridge from Toronto
Dominion Square over Seventh
Avenue Transit Mall, Calgary

Interior view of lobby of Toronto
Dominion Square, Calgary

Frank Palermo, Halifax

Policies in the Halifax City Plan clearly indicate the importance of the George Street district. The Plan designates George and Barrington streets as the axes of the central area and acknowledges the Grand Parade as the symbolic city centre. It also seeks to promote George Street as an important east–west pedestrian route linking Citadel Hill, the Grand Parade and the waterfront and providing access to many buildings and features of historic and architectural interest, including the Town Clock and Province House.

Like most east–west streets in the city centre, George Street climbs abruptly from the waterfront to the foot of Citadel Hill. The street ascends almost 100 feet over a distance of about 1,500 feet. Like a few other streets downtown, the view of the water remains relatively unobstructed. Punctuated by the Town Clock, bisected by the Grand Parade and flanked by Province House, George Street is unlike any other street in the downtown. While the street is typical in dimensions, gradient and block pattern, its end points and monuments give it distinction.

Views of the water at one end and the Town Clock at the other act as effective reminders of the city's history and context. The sense of history, permanence and civic stature is reinforced by City Hall and St. Paul's Church, which front onto the Grand Parade. The Parade Ground itself interrupts George Street's climb up the hill with an elongated open space that serves as a setting for quiet contemplation as well as noon-hour concerts and parking lot as well as a ceremonial stage set.

The historic and ceremonial aspects of the street have been compromised by intensive redevelopment, particularly on the north side. New office buildings, convention centre, hotels and shopping centre have dramatically altered the street in their scale and by introducing an elevated walkway system that runs generally parallel to George Street and provides a climate-controlled connection from the waterfront to the foot of Citadel Hill.

Locally, George Street is looked upon fondly; it is imbued with mythical qualities and revered as a significant place in the city. The following critique attempts to distinguish intentions, wishful aspirations and fleeting recollections from the reality of the artefact. Its concern is with George Street as it is, not as we would idealize it. Our selective memory, in this instance, is much more powerful and appealing than the "facts." While analysis might be seen as cold and dispassionate, it is intended as a series of reflective and constructive observations. The views that follow are structured around three key issues: the notion of centre, the nature of the end points and the workings of an important street.

The Grand Parade

Halifax has a long and rich history that has affected the nature of the entire country and touched the lives of many individuals. From here, soldiers set sail determined to return. Here was the first line of defence and the last sight of land. Halifax is a capital

View of Halifax, 1750: a clearing in the wilderness, a grid of streets and blocks on a hill, and a place reserved for the Parade (courtesy Public Archives of Canada)

Plan of Halifax, 1835 (courtesy Public Archives of Canada)

city and a regional centre. Its influence extends far beyond its size. Are George Street and the Grand Parade an appropriate centre for such a city? Does this spatial sequence adequately reflect collective aspirations? Does it reasonably serve as the focus of public ceremony, express civic pride or symbolize the city and the Maritimes?

Buildings on the north side of George Street bear testimony to the modern movement's pervasive influence. The attitude to city form is decidedly anti-street. Structures assert their individuality rather than forming a common public realm. They pay little homage to the style, materials or scale of the street or the Grand Parade. The notion of centre seems to be equated not with public ceremony, civic pride or collective memory, but rather with intensive redevelopment potential. This conflict in values reduces the centre to a not-so-grand public place. The relative insignificance now ascribed to the Grand Parade is further dramatized by its use as a parking lot for city officials and its barren and underutilized presence during the winter months.

It could certainly be argued that the designation of centre might be more appropriately applied to Scotia Square, a large shopping complex in the adjacent block. It is in this shopping centre, for all its uninspired dreariness, consumerism, exclusivity and detachment from the city fabric, that teenagers "hang out," the elderly sit and watch, and office workers have a quick meal. This is the current setting for concerts, sidewalk sales, informal gatherings and community events.

The Waterfront and the Clock

The most successful aspect of George Street is the memorable quality of its two end points. The water and the Town Clock serve as landmarks in the city's physical context and reminders of its history. They orientate shoppers and attract tourists. The imagery is powerful and comprehensible. But under more detailed scrutiny, both the Town Clock and the waterfront prove rather disappointing. The Town Clock is not a very significant structure, is detached from both the city fabric and the work-ings of the Citadel and appears precariously balanced on the lower slopes of the Hill. It is no more than a carefully placed "public" billboard, an advertisement, a stage set and backdrop for nostalgic post-card views.

At the other end there is little ambiguity about the waterfront, from a distance. Sunlight reflects on the water. Sailboats, fishing vessels, navy and cargo ships cruise by. Fortunately, efforts in the 1960s to install a major road between the city and waterfront did not materialize, and unlike many other cities, Halifax remains easily connected to the water. But once again, the distant view is much more meaningful than that revealed on close inspection.

The area between Water Street and the water's edge is ambiguous and ill-defined; it is grass and gravel, park and parking. There is little definition of it as a place. The traditional pier buildings that remain have been domesticated, retained in thoughtless reverence to dinosaurs. At the same time, there is little evidence of the emergence of a new order of building. The view of the water seems preserved more by accident than by design. The evocative and promising view down the length of George Street terminates in a rather dismal array of unfocused gestures.

City Hall on the Grand Parade, 1907 (courtesy Public Archives of Nova Scotia)

George Street

Halifax is characterized by an orthogonal street grid. Within this skeletal structure, it would seem that George Street is intended to play a pivotal role, as an "axis" and an "important east–west pedestrian route." Like Regent Street in London or the Via del Corso in Rome, George Street is special by virtue of its location and relationships. But unlike these examples, it is not a "designed object," but rather the inevitable by-product of disparate generations of building. It might be argued that the clash of attitudes represented by new and old forms of architecture and urbanism might result in fertile territory, filled with energy and scope, both provocative and compelling. But the result is mundane, confusing and ambiguous. While George Street occupies a special position, the promise is unfulfilled. It lacks form, a sense of place and drama.

The uninspired building response to topography, block length and climate further compromise George Street as a significant urban element in its own right. The steep, sloping topography makes the walk up from the waterfront difficult and uninviting. Buildings along the street struggle to cope, but generally result in blank facades, elevated plazas and the utilitarian side walls of buildings that actually front on the "flat" streets intersecting George Street.

Finally, adverse climatic conditions typified by rain, slush, snow and more rain often make walking along George Street decidedly unpleasant. Buildings along the street make no effort to provide cover or any element of relief. The situation is aggravated (or relieved, depending on your point of view) by the adjacent enclosed, elevated walkway system. Though circuitous and uninspiring, this system provides a well-used alternative connection from the waterfront to Citadel Hill.

We can easily conjure up unsullied images of a splendid George Street filled with pleasant sounds, actions, ceremonies, concerts, theatre, comings and goings, the meeting of friends and all that typifies a significant street. It deserves to be such a place and has undeniable potential. The current reality, however, falls far short.

Looking east on George Street with the ground of the Legislature to the left, the Grand Parade, Clock Tower and Citadel beyond, c. 1920 (courtesy Public Archives of Canada)

Aerial photograph of central Halifax
(courtesy Department of Energy,
Mines and Resources)

Figure/ground plan of the George
Street district

Inside the Citadel, which is now used for public events as well as being a historic site

PHOTOGRAPHY BY ROBERT BEAN

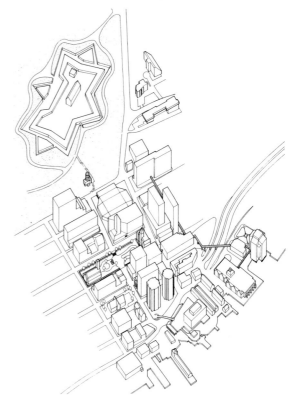

Axonometric of central Halifax

**George Street looking toward the
Citadel with the introverted World
Trade Centre on the right**

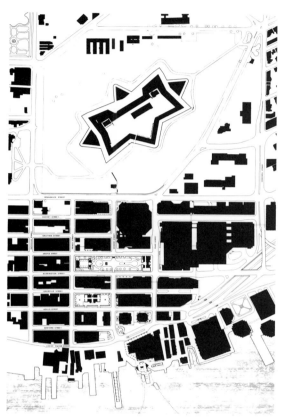

**Plan of George Street at grade
showing the Citadel, George Street,
the Grand Parade, the waterfront and
new developments to the west**

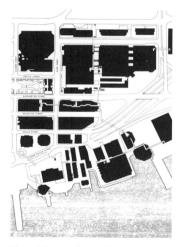

**Plan of George Street above grade
showing the interior routes of the
new developments**

George Street south of Barrington Street with Province House on the right

The foot of George Street with pedestrian bridge leading to elevated plaza of the Law Courts

Central Halifax from Upper Water Street looking south showing skywalk bridges between recent commercial developments

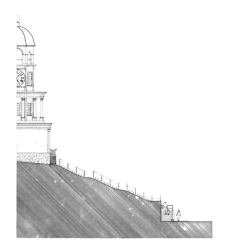

**Detail section at the base of the
Citadel showing the Clock Tower**

**Detail section at the entrance to the
Grand Parade**

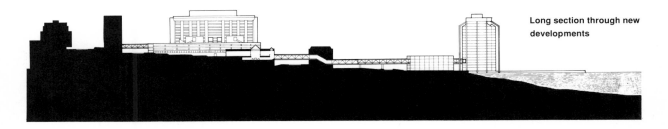

**Long section through new
developments**

89

George Street downhill from the
Clock Tower is not nearly as grand a
street as its image would have it

Long section through George Street

The Grand Parade showing the City
Hall. The public space is now spoiled
by the asphalt driveway with its oil
stains and parked cars; the planting
is also much deteriorated

Seen from above along Barrington
Street, the Grand Parade seems over-
whelmed by the new commercial
high-rise developments

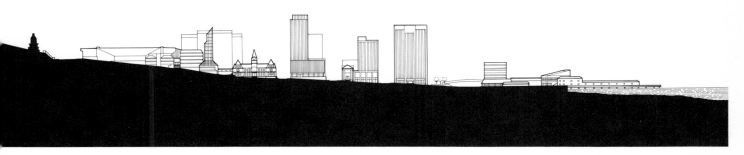

Historic Granville Street from
pedestrian bridge

One of the "public" entrances to
Scotia Square

Pedestrian bridge through Canadian
Imperial Bank of Commerce

Pedestrian bridge between buildings
on the waterfront

CENTRES IN THE FIELD

Edmonton

Mississauga

The pedestrian shopping mall was introduced in rebuilding cities such as Rotterdam after the Second World War

One of the most dramatic events in the post–World War II period, of profound urban as well as cultural significance, was the debut of the big regional shopping centre. Of course, small neighbourhood shopping centres with limited retailing had been built prior to the war in ways both ad hoc and idealized as centres of garden suburbs. But suddenly in 1950 regional shopping centres emerged transforming anywhere from 50 to 150 acres of peripheral farmland into groupings of over 100 stores and services, including giant department stores.

As use of the private car became commonplace and high-speed freeway systems expanded, vast numbers of people moved to the suburbs. At the same time, increasing population, rising incomes and the demand for consumer goods fuelled a retail boom. And with the resulting congestion in the traditional shopping districts of the city, the situation was ripe for the emergence of the large-scale suburban retail centre. Experimental and risky for both architects and developers, the first centres became highly successful and spawned countless clones and variations.

A high-school dance at the Midtown Plaza, Rochester, New York, Victor Gruen, Architect, 1963. In the context of boundless suburban space, shopping centres have served as places for public events and entertainment, but have stopped short of allowing political activity (courtesy Victor Gruen)

The impact of the regional shopping centre has been felt on almost every aspect of contemporary life. Consumer habits changed as shoppers abandoned the congested downtowns in favour of safety, traffic-free access and ample free parking of the suburban shopping centre. Graced with amenities such as landscaped open spaces, park benches and children's playgrounds, these innovative centres promoted themselves as marvellous, new entertainments where shopping was less a chore than a pleasurable, leisure activity. The effect on downtown retailers was devastating, and led many cities to respond with new development strategies that would attempt to replicate the conditions of the shopping centre in the heart of the city.

The main retailing concept of the shopping centre, offering everything for "one-stop shopping" was based on an analogy with the downtown. So too was its physical plan with its simulated streets, squares and parks. Of course, this was a reformed downtown where parking was separated from shopping and where the primary space was a pedestrian mall, familiar by then from the example of Rockefeller Center, the rebuilding of European cities such as Rotterdam, and the proposed pedestrianization of Main Street in towns like Rye, New York, during the 1940s.

The regional shopping centre was initially designed, in Victor Gruen's words, as "a thoroughly practical affair," with attention focused more on problems of site planning and parking than on architecture, which was often relegated to a minor role. However, proponents such as Gruen saw in them the seed for the redemption of the shapeless, sprawling megalopolis and the creation of a new social, cultural and recreational "crystallization point." His earliest shopping centres were conceived from the outset as the hub for other buildings housing offices, hotels, theatres, institutions and community services. Nevertheless, its fundamental purpose, whatever else it might have claimed to be — as entertainment, cultural, or budding civic centre — remained merchandising.

As the number of regional shopping centres increased during the 1960s, as customer mobility increased and competition became keener, shopping centre design became more subtle, psychologically and aesthetically, and greater attention was devoted to customer comfort and visual appeal. By the late 1960s the rising value of suburban land encouraged compactness in new designs while concern for customer comfort encouraged weather protection in the main spaces of the centre.

With the introduction of skylit malls, the regional shopping centre developed additional allusions to compound those borrowed from the city, namely the myths of the Crystal Palaces of the 19th century, those magical domains in which the bounty of the world was displayed. The general outlines of this version of the shopping centre had been projected by utopians of the 19th century, Charles Fourier in France and Ebenezer Howard in England. In his highly influential *Garden Cities of Tomorrow* (1898) Howard proposed that one of the features of his new garden city be a ring-shaped Crystal Palace to serve as a shopping centre around a central park. "Here manufactured goods are exposed for sale, and here most of that class of shopping which requires the joy of deliberation and selection is done. The space enclosed by the Crystal Palace is, however, a good deal larger than is required for these purposes, and a considerable part of it is used as a Winter Garden — the whole forming a permanent exhibition of a most attractive character."

The West Edmonton Mall is the current culmination of this trajectory toward the Crystal Palace as microcosm and fantasyland. Located in the boundless periphery of Edmonton, Alberta, the West Edmonton Mall is the largest shopping centre in the world. The *Chicago Herald Tribune* has said "one must see it to believe it," and the *Los*

Angeles Times calls it "a world apart, a world with its own experiences, free of the mundane struggles with weather and boredom...5,200,000 square feet of neon and marble, of cockatoos and fast food, of miniature golf and Cartier diamonds. And more." First opened in 1981 and completed in 1986, with an estimated current value of $1.2 billion, the mall includes 800 stores, 100 food outlets, an amusement park, a seven-acre wave pool, an NHL skating rink, 120-room hotel and nightclub, 30 aquariums containing 1,000 specimens, ten aviaries, two submarines, a life-size replica of Columbus's galleon and 58 entrances. It attracts over six million visitors a year. And while there are many sceptics about the financial viability of so costly an infrastructure for public entertainment, and its effect on the economy of the downtown, the marriage of shopping centre and amusement park has already produced numerous offspring.

In contrast, the Square One Shopping Centre in suburban Mississauga is now undergoing a poignant transformation into a city centre. Conceived by its original developer during the early 1970s in the spirit of Victor Gruen's "crystallization points," Square One was built with several office towers clustering around it, as well as the local City Hall. Following the formalization of this rural/suburban district into a city, the area of the shopping centre was designated in 1974 to become the city centre and a plan was made that combined British models of new towns (Milton Keynes) with North American developer densities. This hybrid plan foresaw a new grid of roads around and into the shopping mall with a separate mid-block system of pedestrian spaces elevated at +15 level. Subsequently redirected by the urban design work of Baird/Sampson, Jones & Kirkland and Roger du Toit, the emerging city centre is now informed by the neo-Rationalist resurrection of traditional urban space types — the street, the square, and the urban park. The grid remains, but the +15 has been abandoned and the mid-block routes have been demoted, giving priority to the making of the street. The cycle of appropriation has come full circle, as the shopping mall — itself an urban form once removed — is mutated into a kind of urban fabric. What the specific characteristics of this fabric will be and whether this urbanization of the suburbs will sustain an active public culture remains to be seen.

Plan of English new town Milton Keynes, c. 1972 (courtesy Derek Walker)

Canadian exhibits in the Crystal Palace, London, 1851

These two examples from the ubiquitous urban field present two opposing directions. The West Edmonton Mall accepts its isolation from any immediate context or public space system, as well as the status of its location as simply one of numerous shopping centres sprinkled about according to statistical marketing analyses and land opportunities. Like an ocean liner at sea, it is a self-sufficient commercial utopia, without history or civic purpose, a time-warped simulation of a reality more akin to television than any actual place. On the other hand, while Mississauga's New City Hall (Jones & Kirkland) is literally in a field, this incipient city centre promises to subsume the shopping mall into a structure of diverse buildings, uses and public spaces and thereby to constitute an urban realm that will have its own history, civic structure and myths of place. It demonstrates the reassertion of ideas of place and centre and the will to create the essential tissue of the city in the suburban frontier.

Photograph from the dance floor of the Crystal Garden, Victoria, British Columbia, 1925, F. M. Rattenbury, Architect. The Crystal Garden was an early 20th-century pleasure palace, combining swimming pool, dance hall, restaurant, winter garden, lounge and political forum (courtesy Crystal Garden Preservation Society)

THE FABRICATION OF PLEASURE

Detlef Mertins, Toronto

"Places to go and things to see." "A journey into the unknown." "The latest and greatest." "The experience of a lifetime." Amusements and thrills. Fantasy and delight. The exotic and the bizarre. These are the worn-out promises and clichés of amusement parks now applied by the Ghermezian Brothers of Edmonton to the mass-marketing of consumer goods in the suburbs. Something to do on a Saturday afternoon; buy sneakers and catch the side show.

In hindsight it seems inevitable that the boredom of the ubiquitous shopping centre should be relieved by the culture of artificial stimulation. Having killed the retail economy of the downtown by simulating the form of the shopping street in the desert of the suburbs, it was both necessary and straightforward as a second step to construct a synthetic version of urbanity.

While the ideal of the early suburban shopping centre was to provide a gentle landscape for calm and leisurely shopping — an antidote to the chaotic experience of shopping downtown — restraint has turned to boredom in the media and tourist-based culture of the 1980s. Something else was urgently needed. Most of the early malls, if they still exist, have been interiorized and climate-controlled for comfort; some have invested in flamboyant architectural flourishes (Square One in Mississauga, for instance, now sports extravagant entrances and skylight arcades). And a few have embraced the techniques of animation. Of these, the West Edmonton Mall, in a quiet suburb of Edmonton, Alberta, is the largest and most aggressive.

Instead of the rich diversity of activities and spontaneous urban theatre that have been characteristic of cities, the new shopping centre/amusement park offers the entertainment of exotic wildlife, fashion shows, practice-sessions of the Edmonton Oilers and concerts, as well as the disorientation of carnival rides and the distraction of submarines, mini-golf and countless fountains, including one that squirts fire and another that is timed to the theme from *The Pink Panther*. Two giant arcades provide

Interior of HUB showing the interior arcade employed for student residences, University of Alberta, Diamond & Myers, Architects, 1973 (photo Detlef Mertins, 1987)

97

hundreds of video games where thousands of teenagers congregate. There's the all-day night-life of Bourbon Street, the refuge of the all-season wave pool with its sun-bathing decks, and the titillation of theme rooms at the Fantasyland Hotel. The West Edmonton Mall is audacious in its conception, absorbing in its scale, and delightful in its incongruities.

But what about the shopping? When it opened in 1981 the mall was large with 225 stores targeted at the residents of the immediate vicinity and the affluent neighbourhoods along the North Saskatchewan River valley. After its initial success, it was expanded in 1983 to 450 stores and became Canada's largest shopping centre. But still it was just like any other mall, except bigger. Even now, with 800 stores and food outlets, including eight major department stores, the retailing is all very familiar, consisting of chain stores some of which even have several outlets within the mall. Except for the car dealerships and the post office, the merchandise of the mall is utterly commonplace and browsing is generally unrewarding.

While the West Edmonton Mall is a major conceptual and financial feat, its architecture is as unambitious as its merchandise. Standard frame structures with brick exteriors, flat roofs and off-the-shelf galleria roofs house conventional shopping centre storefronts, ceilings and floors. Only the extensive use of mirror glass and glass balustrades with tivoli lights distinguishes the architecture of this mall from any other. Indeed, its entrances are the most two-dimensional openings imaginable. Clearly, neither the investment nor the attraction is in the architecture but in the clutter of animation that the building contains.

Yet the complex seems to be successful (although no one but the mysterious owners really know for sure) and tourists come from great distances and foreign countries to visit and enjoy its virtual pleasures. Edmonton has never had a better tourist attraction. The shopping centre has become a destination in the tourist landscape of hyperreality described with irony and eloquence by Umberto Eco. It has been absorbed into the world of wax museums, Madonna Inns, Disneylands, and enchanted castles, participating in the culture of the New, the Absolute Fake, and More for the purpose of retailing common goods.

In its simulation of realities, histories and fantasies that were once actively made it turns them all into generics, the environmental equivalent of pulp fiction. Clearly there is no point in arguing for a solid foundation to reality, which is after all a social construction that is constantly changing and being interpreted. Nor would one want to deny a legitimate place for the culture of pleasure in the public realm. Indeed, in the recognizable public life of past societies, the pursuit of pleasure was

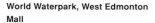

Fantasyland, West Edmonton Mall

one of the central dynamics of public life, as in the baths of ancient Rome, the plea-sure gardens of 19th-century capital cities and the hotels of the early American metropolis. And, of course, the arcades of the 19th-century city were magical cities within the city, surprising realms of filtered light for the coveting of marvellous goods. And yet accepting the necessity of artifice, the fabrication of pleasure present-ed in the West Edmonton Mall is still problematic.

In terms of retailing, the mall is the latest step in a long trajectory described by Richard Sennett in his book *The Fall of Public Man* as the shift from an interactive marketplace to passive consumption. Until the introduction of mass-manufactured products, haggling over price was an essential aspect of shopping; people were actors in the public theatre of the city. The stimulation of choosing from a wide variety of goods presented in a department store replaced bargaining during the 19th century. And as novelty assumed ever-greater importance, the display of goods became more exotic, mysterious and enticing. Today large shopping centres try to hold their cus-tomers by making spectacles of themselves. Continually renewed forms of stimulation keep them coming back to the highly controlled and manipulative environment of the malls.

What is at stake here is not so much the coupling of shopping and fun, nor the scale of the complex, both of which are potentially marvellous. One is simply over-whelmed by the singularly unimaginative nature of the enterprise and the mind-numbing effect of the experience. Aside from its scale and bravura, the frightening contortions of its roller coaster and the occasional performance of Wayne Gretzky, it offers nothing that really impresses or engages. And even these features do not sustain attention for long. In its present state the mall relies on an audience that is unworldly, untravelled and illiterate. It effectively reduces everyone to the level of a child. And while that state may be appealing for a moment, it cannot sustain a vital culture of pleasure, let alone a vital public realm.

As a place of fantasy and a utopia of pleasure, the mall is a poor imitation of its models. In comparison with Disneyland or the Madonna Inn, it is uninventive in its conception, crude and underdeveloped in its orchestration and celebration of experi-ences, and insubstantial in its fabrication. While the tension between the convention-ality of the building and the charged quality of its attractions is aesthetically provocative, in its present state it simply serves to diminish the effect of the attrac-tions. Never mind that there is no critical discourse, no art, no architecture and no politics. Where's the novelty? Where's the pleasure?

The relaxations of the baths in ancient Rome supported discourse; the urban parks of the 19th century provided fragrant settings for the display of self and the viewing of others. More locally, the Crystal Garden of Victoria, B.C. (1925) was a West Coast fairyland social condenser with its popular swimming pool, ballroom, tea

Roller coaster in Fantasyland, West
Edmonton Mall

terrace and promenade.

While there is something teasing about the gigantic and kaleidoscopic nature of the West Edmonton Mall, in order for it to nurture a metropolitan culture it will have to go another step toward becoming like an ocean liner or a casbah of sensual delights in which the experiences themselves are more enticing, people are on display and there are possibilities of action and interaction as well as consumption. While it does not need to be any bigger, it should offer a greater diversity in its retailing, and greater opportunity in its architectural and landscape settings as well as its cultural program. At the moment, only the skating rink forms a public space for public spectacle, which is rather specialized and still lacks an architecture for the audience. Like the amusement park in its heyday, a more ambitious and creative mall could serve as a laboratory of the unconscious, responding to shifts in the phenomenology of perception and seeking new satisfactions for changing cultural aspirations.

The West Edmonton Mall has undeniably become a place of public experience. With a 30 per cent market share of retailing in Edmonton, the mall has virtually supplanted the downtown as the image of Edmonton. And while the downtown struggles to redefine, renew and revitalize itself for retailing, its prospects remain precarious in the absence of a downtown population and a downtown urban culture. If such a culture were to exist, then the downtown and the mall would be two completely different kinds of places. One would be lived in, spontaneous and urban; the other would be visited, contrived and commercial. It is interesting to note that the West Edmonton Mall has had no real effect on its distant cousin, the HUB student union building at the University of Alberta. This interior galleria street, by Diamond & Myers, with its diverse combination of residences, shops and lounges, continues to serve the needs and public life of its active local constituency.

While the fantasy-mall may have a legitimate role to play in the culture of the metropolis, it is hardly likely to become central for street-culture, despite the fact that teenagers hang out there to find out where the parties are. And unlike the shopping centres of the 1950s or the HUB, the fantasy-mall does not even aspire to fulfil this role. The possibility exists that such places could be entertaining parts of a larger public realm, and that in their popularity they could actually help to renew the theatre of urban experience. But for the moment, let's just buy some sneakers and catch the side show.

Souvenir images of the Hotel Fantasyland, West Edmonton Mall

**Aerial photograph of Edmonton
(courtesy Department of Energy,
Mines and Resources)**

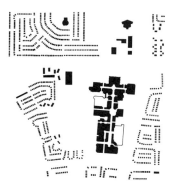

**Figure/ground plan of West
Edmonton Mall**

**Deep Sea Adventure Area, West
Edmonton Mall**

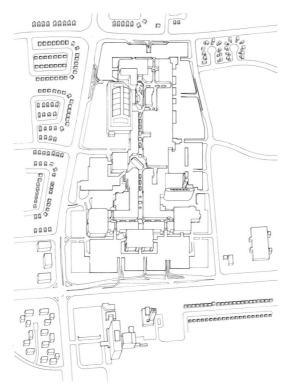

**Axonometric of West Edmonton Mall
with roof removed**

**Ground floor plan of West Edmonton
Mall**

**Roof of West Edmonton Mall with
downtown in the distance**

PHOTOGRAPHY BY JOHN DEAN

Ice Palace

Ice Palace from the second floor

Long section of West Edmonton Mall

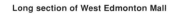

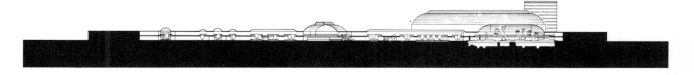

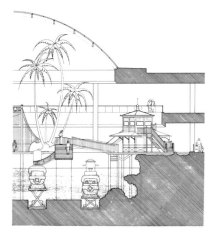

Detail cross section of Deep Sea Adventure Area

Deep Sea Adventure Area with its underwater submarine ride and dolphin shows

Replica of Columbus's galleon in the Deep Sea Adventure Area

MISSISSAUGA CITY CENTRE: TOWARD A MODEL OF URBANISM

Ryszard Sliwka, with Rob Lefebvre, Waterloo

The city as an institution is a representation of ideas and values, and as such its creation and ongoing transformations are critical acts, commentaries in themselves and in relation to the past. Situated on the periphery of Metropolitan Toronto, the City of Mississauga was incorporated in 1974 and consists of several previously independent towns and their environs as well as extensive rural, suburban and industrial precincts. It owes its status as a City more to the act of amalgamation than to the evolutionary growth of a single nucleus as experienced in other cities.

With a population of about 400,000 people, Mississauga is a territory of 287 square kilometres. Several orders of settlement exist simultaneously as layers over one another. The colonial township grid continues to form a net-structure of principal roads and concession blocks, although it has been superseded in the road hierarchy by the expressways that cut through the city. The farm landscape remains in fragmented form. The towns and villages are being reappropriated as cultural heritage and as foci of community identity. Infill developments of the 1930s and 1940s dot the concession roads as they criss-cross the landscape. And finally the most recent order of residential enclaves, industrial parks, shopping centres, office towers and high-rise apartment buildings is being extended and intensified. Within the context of this settlement structure, the plan and development of the City Centre is a strategic departure from ubiquitous suburbanization toward the realization of an integral city.

Throughout the history of Mississauga radical shifts have occurred not only in the form of settlement, but in the fundamental relationship between public and private domains. Three models may be discerned — the rural, the suburban and the urban — each of which has its own particular vision of public space.

Rendering of a typical Mississauga farm, *Historical Atlas of Peel County*, 1877

1954 BUILT FORM

1964 BUILT FORM

1970 BUILT FORM

1980 BUILT FORM

**Plans showing development of City
Centre from 1954 to 1980 (courtesy
Kleinfeldt Mychalowycz, Architects)**

The Rural Model

The early settlement of the land was structured through a survey, completed in 1806,
of orthogonal concession roads at intervals of one and a quarter miles with a subdivision of linear farm lots in-between. Settlers cultivated the land and improved the
road allowance along their property. Farm buildings were arranged typically with the
house set back from the road facing south toward the lake, the main water-route
leading back to England and the symbolic front of the township.

Throughout the 19th century, as intensification of this settlement pattern
occurred both sides of the concessions roads became occupied. The development of
Main Streets in villages serving the farming community reinforced the increasing
importance of the road. It was in the combined interest of local farmers and village
merchants to develop and maintain the roads for their social and economic benefits.
The road became more than a means of communication, serving as the main public
space in both the rural districts and the villages.

The Suburban Model

During the economic boom that followed World War II, a new suburban model of
development was applied to the landscape of Mississauga and radically altered the
conception of public space. In this model the private values of both developers and
consumers came to dominate over traditions of collective and civic space.

In the 1950s individual businesses acquired large parcels of farmland in anticipation of economic opportunities. During the 1960s and 1970s suburban residential
subdivisions, industrial estates, shopping plazas and office towers rose from farmers'
fields. With these new buildings, the space and force of the public realm was diminished and reassigned. The road became a traffic artery linking sites rather than a
space of address and inhabitation.

When it was opened in the early 1970s, the Square One Shopping Centre was the largest centre of its kind in the Toronto region. It consisted of three department stores and a supermarket linked by an interior mall of 170 shops arranged in a diamond shape. The mall enclosed an open court that served for recreation and entertainment. The total complex was 1.5 million square feet and was surrounded by a ring road that gave access to surface parking all around the mall. Unlike most shopping centres, Square One was conceived from its outset as part of a more diversified and comprehensive development. Office buildings and the original City Hall were built along the ring road, like sentries looking down on the shopping centre.

In the suburban model, the diverse functions that come together in a traditional urban fabric have been separated and formalized as discrete precincts. As a result, the public spaces of these precincts are associated with singular activities, either shopping or work or housing. And as the buildings are focused inward as well, public spaces become not only one-dimensional, but also empty, and public life is all but lost.

The Urban Model

One of the distinctive characteristics of Mississauga over the past decade has been its relentless drive to become a city rather than remaining a bedroom suburb. A series of very interesting shifts toward a more urban model of development have resulted from this initial proposition.

To begin, there was a debate about the suitable location for a City Centre. While traditionalists argued in favour of developing the former Town of Cooksville, the progressives and the largest local developer were successful in having the area around the Square One Shopping Centre chosen. A plan was commissioned from the British planners Llewelyn-Davies, Weeks who were responsible for the plan of Milton Keynes new town in England.

Similar to Milton Keynes, the Mississauga City Centre Plan consisted of a grid of roadways serving low-density developments with a second grid of elevated, mid-block pedestrian routes superimposed. It absorbed the existing buildings into a complex matrix that called for new public buildings and open spaces as well as more commercial and housing developments. In its final form as the City Centre Secondary Plan, the infrastructure based on the Llewelyn-Davies, Weeks plan was coupled with more conventional development densities, and urban design requirements were established for a certain degree of spatial definition of the public domain. The public space system was divided into utilitarian roadways and pedestrian zones.

Before any major private redevelopment had occurred, the City initiated its planning for a New City Hall and Civic Square. In his capacity as professional advisor of the national design competition for this public building, architect George Baird began a slow process of adjustment to the Llewelyn-Davies, Weeks model in which the primacy of the street as public space was reasserted, and the pedestrian system was brought back to the ground and normalized as parks and squares.

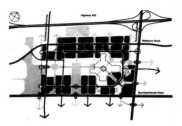

Llewelyn-Davies Master Plan Proposal for City Centre of 1974; a reworking of the Milton Keynes New Town Plan in England, complete with separated movement systems

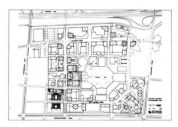

The current urbanization plan of Square One Shopping Centre by du Toit, Allsopp, Hillier proposes more traditional streets and blocks

As the winners of that competition, Jones & Kirkland have recently completed the construction of the New City Hall and Civic Square, a project that has not only acted as a catalyst for more development in the area, but has also established a model of urban design for the City Centre. In this new model there is a reciprocity between building and public space. Today the building still stands among former farmfields, a part waiting for a larger whole.

Recently, the principal landowner in the City Centre has put forward a development plan by Roger du Toit, Associates that extends these principles over a vast part of the City Centre. The plan is characterized by urban blocks in a grid of streets engineered to suburban scale, but boulevarded and landscaped for pedestrian use. Buildings spatially define the street and take their address from it. Parking will be internalized or constructed underground.

Future Prospects

Two possible futures can be seen for the Mississauga City Centre. In the event of economic stagnation the momentum toward an urban fabric may be lost. The incompleteness of the fabric would result in isolated buildings that would have to continue to operate in a suburban way, and this in turn might stabilize as an acceptable status quo. The second scenario would be the continuation of the current plans that both developers and city planners seem to favour. If the market is strong enough and the density of development is sufficient, parking lots will be built underground at a cost-effective financial level. This is the key element to achieve the continuous fabric of buildings and the diverse urban experience that is envisaged.

At the same time, the envisaged form of the City Centre will be unlike any existing urban fabric. It will have to serve a far-flung suburban municipality. Its scale will be larger in accommodation of vehicular traffic standards, and it will still include a dominant retailing centre with its imperatives of internalization. While the specific form of its public spaces and the patterns of use that they will engender remain uncertain, the emerging City Centre of Mississauga is promising in its renewal of the will to create urban centres.

**Aerial photograph of Mississauga
City Centre (courtesy Department of
Energy, Mines and Resources)**

**Figure/ground plan of Mississauga
City Centre**

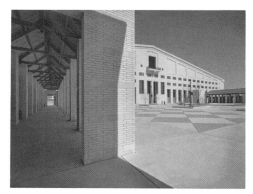

**Civic Square with colonnade, Jones
& Kirkland, Architects**

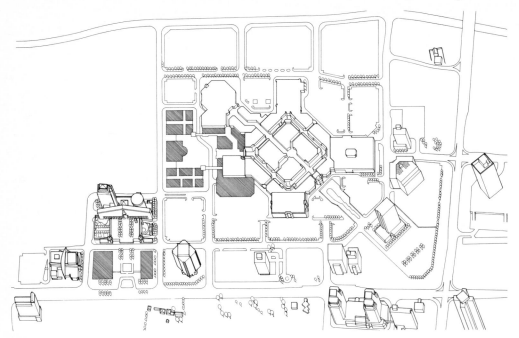

**Axonometric of Mississauga City
Centre**

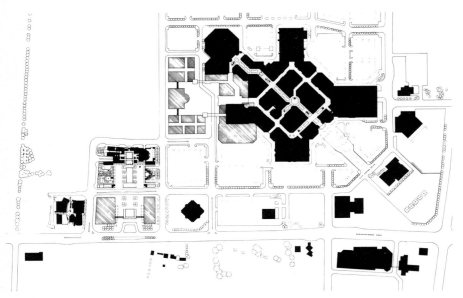

**Ground floor plan of Mississauga City
Centre**

City Centre Drive at entry to Civic
Square and City Hall

Main entrance to Square One and bus
terminal from parking lot

Urban expansion to Square One
under construction, with City Hall in
the background

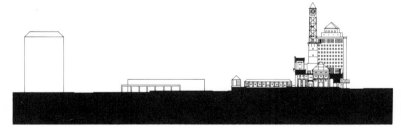

Section through Mississauga City
Hall and Civic Square, Jones &
Kirkland, Architects

Section through Square One
Shopping Centre, Murray Marshall
Cresswell, Architects, Yabu
Pushelberg Retail Interiors,
Consultant

111

Main entrance of Square One
Shopping Centre with new street-
related building under construction

Central atrium in Square One
Shopping Centre

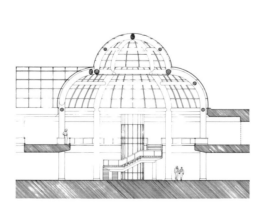

Detail section of central atrium of
Square One Shopping Centre used
for fashion shows and performances

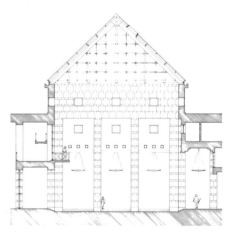

Detail section of Great Hall of
Mississauga City Hall, Jones &
Kirkland, Architects

MARGINAL SITES REZONED FOR PUBLIC USE

Vancouver

Halifax Harbour, 1911

Mutations of public space are also discernible in the marginal industrial zones of the early 20th-century city. Here many of the railway lands, shipping harbours and manufacturing districts have become obsolete for economic or technological reasons. These sites have become attractive for both their redevelopment opportunity and their marginal, historic and sublime qualities. In cases from Halifax to Montreal to New Liskeard, tensions have arisen between these two sets of opportunities. For most models of development, the residue of the industrial landscape seems awkward to reinterpret, costly to maintain and at odds with the image of the new. As a result, spectacular structures such as grain elevators have been lost as developers, both public and private, have scraped clean these once robust sites.

In Halifax, controversy surrounding the future of the central waterfront prevailed throughout the 1960s. Plans for a sewage outlet, a southward extension of a harbourside expressway and new public buildings placed the historic port in jeopardy. Citizens who valued the historical and architectural character of the area, however, opposed the sacrifice of the old warehouses to this modernizing agenda. By the early 1970s both civic and federal governments were committed to retaining a limited area of warehouses now known as Heritage Properties. Bounded today on one side by the new Law Courts with its raised podium and overhead bridge, and on the other by a large hotel disguised as a historic building, the old warehouses have been renovated into tourist boutiques and restaurants. While the buildings have certainly been retained, their meaning has been distorted; the sublime qualities of the raw industrial zone have been rendered commercially palatable but weakly picturesque.

Since 1972 Toronto's central harbour has been the site of similar tensions. Under the auspices of a Crown corporation, some of the historic piers and warehouses have been adapted for commercial, residential, cultural and community uses. While many other structures have been demolished to make way for new condominiums, parking garages and hotels, and the structure of built versus open spaces has been radically altered, a residue of the industrial past remains.

The most challenging reuse of such a site is found at Vancouver's Granville Island. Built in 1917, this man-made island provided inexpensive sites with water frontage for small and intermediate manufacturing operations. For four decades the island was a hub of industrial production, noisy and raw. With tight physical

Toronto central waterfront and railway lands in 1969 when these industrial zones were still in use

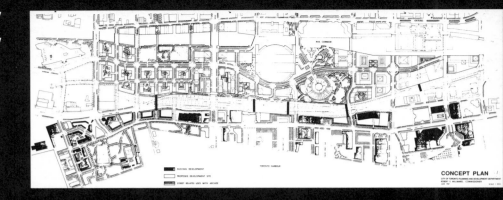

Concept plan for the railway lands by the City of Toronto, 1987. The plans show a proposed urban fabric of new streets and blocks that will link the city to the waterfront. While the industrial landscape will be lost, some landmark industrial buildings, like the round house, will remain for new public uses

boundaries at the water, limited access from the mainland and the Granville Bridge overhead, the experience of the island was spatially as well as actively intense. However, by the 1960s the location and conditions of the island were no longer suitable for expanding and modernizing operations. Disuse, fire and lack of maintenance turned the island into a derelict zone, posing a considerable dilemma for the City.

After a decade of political haggling, land swapping and studies, Granville Island was designated a "public place" and slowly the enterprise of reinterpreting it began. Early in the process, the decision was made to keep and refurbish as much of the industrial fabric as possible. New public uses such as a market, theatres, marinas, an art college, artists workshops, tennis courts and playgrounds were eventually woven in and among the existing structures and machinery. As well, limited commercial enterprises were introduced including a hotel, restaurants, shops and a brewery. While not originally built for such purposes, the buildings and open spaces of the island provided a generous and stimulating setting. Several production operations remain — boat building and cement making — and complement the more genteel activities. Railway lines, cranes and other artefacts of the industrial past also remain as an informal museum of industrial archaeology. While cars have access to the island, there are still no sidewalks or curbs, reinforcing the spirit of coexistence between people and machines and posing a quiet challenge to the conventions of traffic engineering. Like the city itself, the island has no single centre, but many centres; its public space system is diffuse yet generous, fluid yet memorable. In less than a decade Granville Island has become the spiritual heart of Vancouver and a model site of urban theatre and romance in the metropolis.

It is a poignant sign of our times that we are drawn to inhabit the industrial wastelands of the recent past. As the officially endorsed urban environment becomes increasingly diffuse, sanitized and simulated, derelict warehouses, railway lines and machinery begin to resonate with an undeniable and intense reality. What is at stake in the redevelopment of these lands is not merely the creation of economic opportunity, but the very integrity of culture and its capacity to redefine itself in the face of the often grim/banal conditions of the metropolis, both past and present.

THE INDUSTRIAL BRICOLAGE OF GRANVILLE ISLAND

Joel Shack, Vancouver

The man-made Granville Island shortly after its original formation in 1917 (courtesy Vancouver Public Library)

As a set of public spaces, Granville Island is the most vital urban theatre in all of Vancouver. Its success does not come from importing models of grand formal squares or boulevards, but rather from a site-specific reinterpretation of the historic industrial fabric of the island. This waterfront maze of quays, docks, industrial basilica sheds and outdoor working spaces is Vancouver's equivalent of the "faubourg" of European cities, looser settlements like the Left Bank of Paris that grew up just outside municipal authority.

What may have been discounted in another time as an industrial waterfront mess was declared a heritage site by the federal government in the mid-1970s. This faubourg place, a seedy labyrinth of abandoned industrial facilities isolated under the Granville Bridge and along the polluted False Creek, was redefined through reasserting the value and honour of workplaces and the industrial vernacular. In most Canadian waterfront developments the industrial urban fabric has been obliterated while selected buildings of "substance" have been preserved. Toronto's Harbourfront and Montreal's Old City waterfront are cases in point.

In maintaining industrial lots and street patterns as well as existing shed structures and marine services, Granville Island attains the scale and complexity of bricolage. Bricolage has been described by the anthropologist Claude Lévi-Strauss as a way of working imaginatively with "what's-at-hand" to create assemblages of diverse elements. This idea was adapted to architecture and urbanism by architectural critic Colin Rowe in his book *Collage City*.

Vancouver with Granville Island in foreground left (courtesy Vancouver Image Finders)

The original industrial development of Granville Island occurred in a piecemeal way over several decades and may be seen as an unself-conscious bricolage, a highly animated texture in which the relationships between elements are as important as the elements themselves. In cultivating an incremental approach to growth, designing responsively and planning individual pieces within a loose framework, the architects of the island's renewal, Hotson & Bakker, have self-consciously added to and elaborated the bricolage.

The new Granville Island buildings are least successful where they have been made as literal reproductions of the past or where existing buildings with thin corrugated steel sheathing have been imitatively tarted up. In such instances, public spaces approach a cute, Disney-like cartoon version of the original and raise the larger issue

of how to deal with the romanticization of an existing fabric. Examples, however, can be found that suggest we need neither freeze history, as we do by preserving only the shells of heritage buildings, nor imitatations of it. The palace of the Roman emperor Diocletian at Spoleto was provocatively reused, reordered and reinterpreted into a city during the medieval period and demonstrates that it is possible to transform artefacts of the past into evocative memory through the echo of time of a "ruin" reused.

In places where complementary oppositions exist between ruins and contemporary additions, Granville Island is a truly evocative public place. Where shed structures have simply been reproduced and gayly painted, a low level of urban drama results. The setting gains depth of time when ruins become metaphorical through **abstraction**, meaning **extracting the essence** of the former place and making it more evocatively memorable.

The same memorable evocation is essential in the reshaping of the "ground" of the island, its seawalls, landfill, quays, docks, streets and service courts, which also gather meaning in the archaeological bricolage. False Creek is here framed by two overhead city bridges, creating the most amazing "water square" in Canada. The Granville Island Market is dramatically centred here, but its water-edges still only suggest the theatrical potential of harbour amphitheatre and pier. Other water-edges similarly provide great vantage points for views and performance, but the forms do not yet match the potential of the setting. Again one wishes for the depth of time that could be cultivated in playing the durability of the seawall against the fragility and urgency of boats and docks.

Greater success is attained landward in the "working squares" of the island. Conventionally we tend to use idealized forms of Baroque and Beaux-Arts squares and gardens when we think of models for Canadian public spaces. The life of Granville Island's outdoor spaces is more in character with contemporary working use of European city streets and squares, which sustain parking, markets, pedestrian life, service access and street celebration in the same spaces. Whereas in Rome the circumstantial medieval fabric was reinterpreted and responsively reshaped by Baroque architects, so too the island's circumstantial industrial fabric has now been incrementally tuned with Hotson & Bakker's "streetworks." The streetworks are essentially an infill of trees, lamps, benches and arcade posts, all treated as if they were bollards in an interlocking concrete pavement that stretches wall to wall.

Thus is created an informal car-pedestrian-service realm of ambiguous front–back formal order that seems to suit the **ease of access** that most Canadians value in urban settings. This realm has a hybrid quality that is unlike conventional suburban or urban complexes. It has multiple centres and multiple axes and is an

116

open-ended form in which each small outdoor court or square is supported by an adjacent public market hall, theatre or restaurant. The core of Canadian public life takes place in such indoor public spaces, and even in Vancouver's temperate climate, seasonal vitality is sustained by keeping outdoor spaces appropriately small with generous openings to indoor gathering places.

The lessons of Granville Island may be broadly applicable. The industrial vernacular of buildings as well as urban fabric is vital to the culture of Canadian architecture and public space. The bricolage of such settings has appealing romantic qualities, but more important, can be interpreted in design as a means to reconcile diverse oppositions of form and language while maintaining the vividness of original meaning, scale and time. A greater open-endedness of urban theatre results and is reinforced by the multiplicity of allowable roles in authentic working spaces.

Granville Island

Terrace at Granville Island (courtesy Vancouver Image Finders)

Aerial photograph of downtown
Vancouver (courtesy Department of
Energy, Mines and Resources)

Figure/ground plan of Granville
Island in downtown Vancouver

Water's edge from above

Typical street from above

PHOTOGRAPHY BY JACK BUQUET

Granville Island from the Granville
Bridge

Water's edge under Granville Bridge

Old structures and new uses

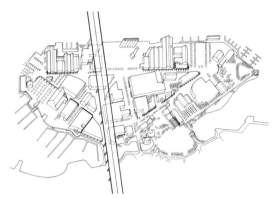

Axonometric of Granville Island

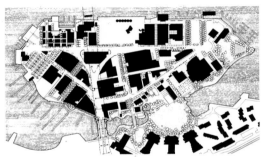

Plan of Granville Island

Tennis court with industrial shed

**Approach to Granville Island under
Granville Bridge**

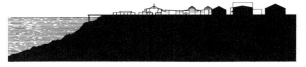

**Section through Granville Island,
showing Market**

**Section through Granville Island,
showing Duranleau Street**

**Tough streetwork improvements
make subtle "public" encroachments
on the industrial site**

Detail section of Market Building

Plaster caster in artist's studio

COMPARATIVE DRAWINGS

COMPARATIVE DRAWINGS

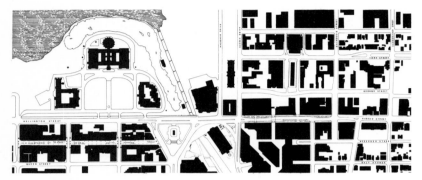

Sparks Street, Confederation Square, Rideau Street, Ottawa

Le Village Normand Food Fair, Place Laurier, Sainte-Foy

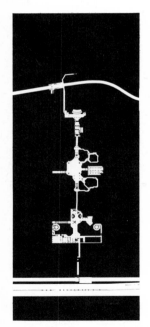

Underground pedestrian system, Montreal

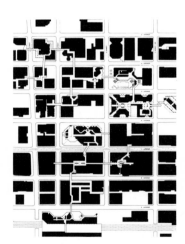

+15 pedestrian system, Calgary

George Street, Halifax

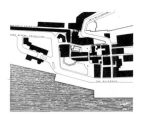

Place Royale, Quebec City

West Edmonton Mall, Edmonton

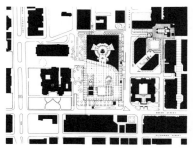

Trinity Square, Nathan Phillips
Square, Toronto

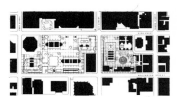

Commerce Court, Toronto Dominion
Centre, Toronto

Harbour Castle, Toronto

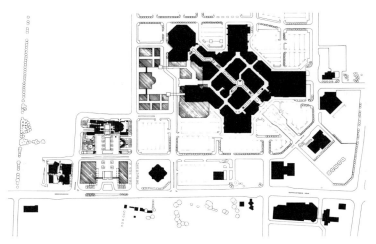

Mississauga City Centre

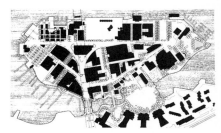

Granville Island, Vancouver

SECTIONS

**Sparks Street, Confederation Square,
Rideau Street, Ottawa**

Place Royale, Quebec City

**Le Village Normand Food Fair, Place
Laurier, Sainte-Foy**

**Trinity Square,
Toronto**

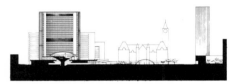

Nathan Phillips Square, Toronto

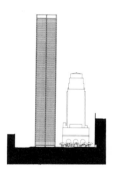

**Commerce Court,
Toronto**

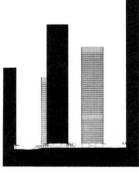

**Toronto Dominion Centre,
Toronto**

Harbour Castle, Toronto

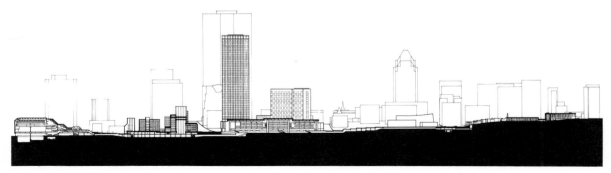

**Underground pedestrian system,
Montreal**

126

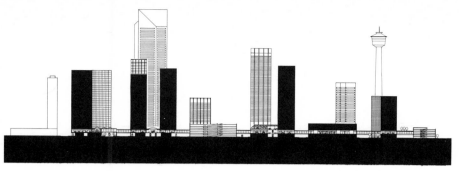

+15 pedestrian system, Calgary

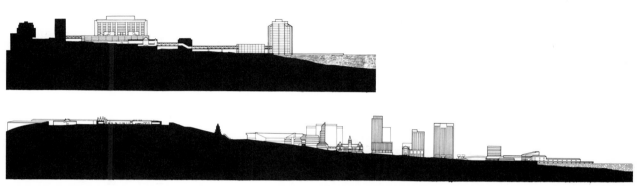

George Street, Halifax

West Edmonton Mall, Edmonton

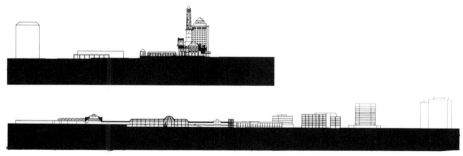

Mississauga City Centre

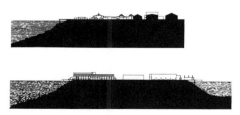

Granville Island, Vancouver

DETAIL SECTIONS

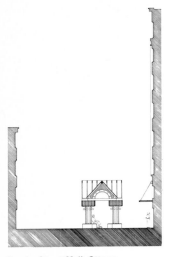

Sparks Street Mall, Ottawa

Rideau Street Transit Mall, Ottawa

Trinity Square, Toronto

Nathan Phillips Square, Toronto

Toronto Dominion Centre, Toronto

Place Royale, Quebec City

Commerce Court, Toronto

Le Village Normand Food Fair, Place Laurier, Sainte-Foy

Complexe Desjardins, Montreal

Stairway to underground, Place des Arts, Montreal

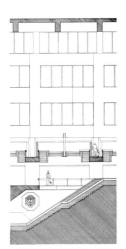

Bridge to Palais des Congrès, Montreal

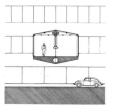
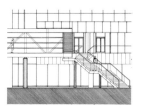

**+15 bridges at the Esso Plaza,
Calgary**

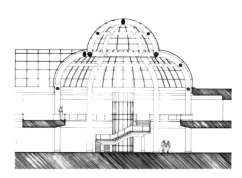

**Market on Granville Island,
Vancouver**

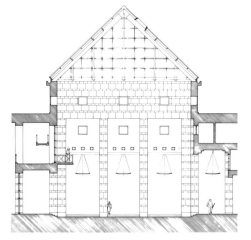

**Great Hall, Mississauga City Hall,
Mississauga**

**Centre in the Square, Square One
Shopping Centre, Mississauga**

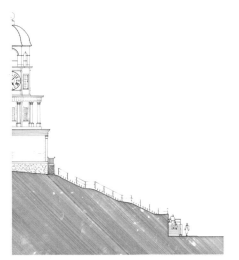

Clock Tower, Halifax

Grand Parade, Halifax

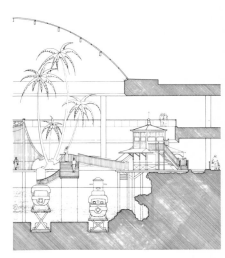

**Deep Sea Adventure, West
Edmonton Mall, Edmonton**

THE CONFERENCE

Saint John, New Brunswick
June 9 and 10, 1988

(top row, left to right) Trevor Boddy, Donald McKay, Michael Kirkland, Terry Williams
(middle row, left to right) Kenneth Greenberg, Peter Rose, Nan Griffiths, Frank Palermo, Gerald Forseth
(bottom row, left to right) Detlef Mertins, Lance Berelowitz, Phyllis Lambert, George Baird, Brigitte Shim, Tom Emodi

THE SPACE OF APPEARANCE[1]

George Baird

> Wherever you go, you will be a "polis": these famous words became not merely
> the watchword of Greek colonization, they expressed the conviction, that action
> and speech create a space between the participants which can find its proper loca-
> tion almost any time and anywhere. It is the space of appearance in the widest
> sense of the word, namely, the space where I appear to others as others appear to
> me, where men exist not merely like other living or inanimate things but make
> their appearance explicitly.[2]

This passage from Hannah Arendt's 1959 book *The Human Condition* appropriately
sets the stage for reconsideration of the meaning of "public space" in the second half
of the 20th century. According to Arendt, the term "public" signifies two closely
interrelated, but not altogether identical phenomena:

> It means, first, that everything that appears in public can be seen and heard by
> everybody and has the widest possible publicity. For us, appearance — something
> that is being seen and heard by others as well as by ourselves — constitutes reality.[3]

Second, Arendt continues:

> The term "public" signifies the world itself, in so far as it is common to all of us
> and distinguished from our privately owned place in it. This world, however, is not
> identical with the earth or with nature, as the limited space for the movement of
> men and the general condition of organic life. It is related, rather, to the human
> artefact, the fabrication of human hands, as well as to affairs which go on among
> those who have it in common, as a table is located between those who sit around it;
> the world, like every in-between relates and separates men at the same time.[4]

Moreover, for the great German-American political philosopher, the fact that the
world "relates and separates at the same time" is one of the profound manifestations
of "plurality, the basic condition of…action." As she puts it:

		TITRE I										TITRE II	
		10.	11.	12.	13.	14.	15.	16.	17.	18.	19.	20.	21.
LES 4 FONCTIONS	HABITER 1												
	TRAVAILLER 2												
	CULTIVER LE CORPS ET L'ESPRIT 3												
	CIRCULER 4												
	DIVERS 5												

Un modèle de la Grille CIAM   Habiter (1) = vert / Travailler (2) = rouge / Cultiver le corps et l'esprit (3) = bleu / Circuler (4) = jaune

1. The CIAM Grid of Functions

If men were not equal, they could neither understand each other and those who came before them, nor plan for the future and foresee the needs of those who will come after them. If men were not distinct, each human being distinguished from any other who is, was, and will be, they would need neither speech nor action to make themselves understood.[5]

Now these ideas of the public and of appearance within it yield a view of the modern city whose implications are as yet far from realized — even at this late date toward the end of the 20th century. But be that as it may, the idea of public life, in all its shades and shadows portrayed here, has formed an implicit backdrop to a whole series of discussions of urban space that have proceeded in architectural circles since the Second World War, and which, in my view, remain unresolved. Moreover, Arendt's conception of "plurality" points to a major underlying theme of debate during that period. The forms of modern life being what they are, contemporary plurality must be seen to manifest itself in "diversity," which in turn is closely linked to "mobility" — another chief hallmark of our age. Finally, Arendt's conception of the "human artefact," which constitutes the world men have in common, also points to the profound significance of the historical form of the existing city.

It is these three ideas — plurality, mobility and history — that have implicitly conditioned the form of the architectural debate on urbanism in Europe and North America since the end of the Second World War. Broadly speaking, it may be said that this debate has occurred in three stages, between 1945 and the present, and that each of these stages has taken the form of an argument between an older and a younger generation. To begin with, we may note how, in the years immediately following the cessation of hostilities in Europe, the architects of the Congrès Internationaux d'Architecture Moderne (CIAM) had an unprecedented opportunity to implement the urban ideas that they had been developing since the 1920s, and which, in the wake of the defeat of the Axis powers in Western Europe, were newly welcome to governments seeking to rebuild their cities. Between the end of World War II and the middle of the 1950s, city after European city developed proposals for reconstruction following the principles of CIAM: the segregation of the four urban functions — work, living, recreation and circulation; the abandonment of the street in favour of extensive new areas of landscaped open space and rationalized systems of circulation; etc. The momentum of implementation of CIAM's urbanism was so powerful, in fact, that it continued until the mid-1960s.

But, it is my purpose here to trace in particular detail the specific evolution of ideas in respect to urbanity per se, as they were debated by various generations of protagonists among the modernists, from 1945 to the present. For while the principles that had been developed by the members of CIAM prior to World War II formed the point of departure for post-war developments, certain limited modifications of the basic ideas of CIAM did occur. Thus the four basic functional postulates

136

of urbanism according to the Athens Charter of 1933 were expanded at CIAM conferences after the war. In 1949 at Bergamo, for example, the concept of the "historic centre" was put forward for consideration, and in 1951 at Hoddesdon, the theme was the "urban core." Here, for the first time, the group devoted itself to a consideration of the phenomenon of the core, be it the core of a new town such as Le Corbusier's St. Dié or Stevenage in England, or alternatively of an existing city such as Coventry or Basel. By 1951, the views of the CIAM group had moderated to the point that they were even prepared to qualify the imperatives of the old functional grid, and to concede that a **mixture of functional activities** was appropriate to this part of the urban territory. In his introductory comments to the 1951 meeting, the then president of the organization, José Luis Sert, went so far as to cite the famous quotation on the city from Ortega y Gasset's *The Revolt of the Masses:*

> So, the "urbs" or the "polis" starts by being an empty space, the "forum," the "agora," and all the rest are just means of fixing that empty space, of limiting its outlines. The "polis" is not primarily a collection of habitable dwellings, but a meeting place for citizens, a space set apart for public functions.[6]

2. A plan of 1748 showing the nine-square grid of central New Haven

Still, it remains true that despite this revised interest in public space, CIAM did not (as of 1951) come seriously to grips with the issues of the historic fabric of existing urban cores, or of the growing phenomenon of mobility, let alone of the more elusive social concept of plurality. Examples of proposals from the 1951 meeting illustrate how high-handed the group remained in regard to such questions. Taking the case of historical fabric, we may examine a project for New Haven prepared by a group of students at Yale University. The deference to history proposed by the group consisted in the retention of the three churches on the green, as well as a series of houses — 18th-century ones only — facing it. Everything else on two entire sides was proposed to be removed. What is more, new construction was proposed which actually penetrated into the green from one edge, eroding the clarity of its original nine-square geometry. Indeed, the whole emphasis of the New Haven proposal is on the segregation of pedestrian and vehicular traffic, with all vehicles being proposed to be removed from the central nine squares and diverted instead to a peripheral ring road.

3. The Yale student project for central New Haven, from J. Tyrwhitt, J. L. Sert, E. N. Rogers, eds., *The Heart of the City: CIAM 8*, 1952

    This growing inclination to deal with the expanding use of the automobile by segregation acquired a reasonably ready reception in Europe, where, of course, the historic cores of cities had been developed without any consideration of the use of this yet-to-be-invented device. But the 1950s generation of CIAM applied it as well to the proposals for such cores as those of "new towns" throughout Europe and even (the case cited above) in North America, where resistance to the idea remained quite strong, since

    (a) pre-automobile urban cores were less common;
    (b) the post-war increase in the use of the automobile had been most
    rapid; and

(c) the suburban model of urban development outstripped the abilities of
European-orientated planners and architects to contain it.

In the early 1950s, the proponents of CIAM were still only tentatively beginning to
face the challenges entailed by the implementation of the 1930s generation's thinking
in a world that was changing. On account of what they saw as failure by the older
generation to respond to these new challenges, younger observers at CIAM conferences from 1951 onward grew increasingly restive. They not only saw a failure to live
up to the original vision of "the Radiant City," as it had been depicted in the 1930s by
Le Corbusier, but they also wanted to put new issues on the agenda for discussion.

In 1955, for example, Peter and Alison Smithson published in the magazine
Architectural Design a text in which they deplored the "mechanical" limitations of the
modern movement as it had developed in the 1930s. By the mid-1950s such a
"mechanical" approach no longer seemed adequate. Even the amendments to the
original CIAM grid seemed to the young to be less than the situation required.
According to Reyner Banham, "The young were for root-and-branch rejection of all
the Athenian categories which they had frequently damned as 'diagrammatic.'"[7] By
1956, the progressive revolt of the young had grown so powerful that the entire organization simply collapsed in the face of their challenges, with the reformers establishing a new international congress known as Team Ten.

Following 1956, the members of Team Ten were in a position to promote their
revisionist ideas with new effectiveness. In a text published in 1956, the Smithsons
summed up their view of their professional responsibilities:

> We are still functionalists and we still accept the responsibility for the community
> as a whole, but today the word functional does not merely mean mechanical as it
> did thirty years ago. Our functionalism means accepting the realities of the situa-
> tion, with all their contradictions and confusions and trying to do something with
> them. In consequence, we have to create an architecture and a town planning
> which — through built form — can make meaningful the change, the growth, the
> flow, the "vitality" of the community.[8]

With this talk of "change" and "growth," the Smithsons introduced concepts that had
had little or no recognition in the precepts of CIAM into the discourse of modern
urbanism, and these new concepts were to set in motion a decade of new urban
experiments, which eventually came to be known under the names of "the New
Brutalism" and "metabolism." For the moment, however, I want only to note that
such concepts, while not exactly constituting plurality as intended by Hannah Arendt,
certainly pointed toward a more malleable and heterogeneous urban form than had
characteristically been associated with the work of CIAM. This interest in heterogeneity can be traced in the development of the Smithsons' own ideas to the 1953
exhibition entitled "A Parallel of Art and Life," which they had organized with the
photographer Nigel Henderson and the sculptor Eduardo Paolozzi. In this celebrated

4. A view of the exhibition "A Parallel of Art and Life," 1953

event, Paolozzi's and Henderson's own works were exhibited in a fashion that paid homage to the so-called "anti-art" of such painters as Jackson Pollock in the United States and Jean Dubuffet in France. Indeed, the terms "art brut" and "art autre" were being employed at the time to characterize these efforts to escape the orthodoxy of modernism, and to declare a highly charged, "angry" and ironic *parti pris* in respect to such ephemera of modern life as advertising, American consumer products and comic books.

But if a nascent evidence of plurality can be seen in these important preoccupations of the 1950s, interests in mobility are much more visible. In the 1956 text cited above, the Smithsons went on to specify the nature of the new urban propositions that they were developing:

> The general idea is the concept of the Cluster. The Cluster — a close-knit, complicated, often-moving aggregation, but an aggregation with a distinct structure. This is perhaps as close as one can get to a description of the new ideal in architecture and planning....
>
> It is traditionally the architect's job to create the signs or images which represent the functions, aspirations and beliefs of the community, and create them in such a way that they add up to a comprehensible whole. The cluster concept provides us with a way of creating new images, using the techniques for examples of road and communications engineering. Many solutions have been put forward to deal with the problem of traffic — motorways joining population centres, urban motorways within communities, peripheral controlled parking round the old centre, out-of-town shopping centres, off-motorway factories and residential dormitories; solutions which either disperse the energies of communities or integrate them in an entirely new way.[9]

Here, we can see the issue of mobility come strikingly to the fore. For the Smithsons themselves, these ideas crystallized in their famous entry to the 1958 competition for the rebuilding of Berlin, the so-called "Hauptstadt" or elevated city; the new plan accepted as givens both the existing road network on the ground, as well as a proposed new expressway network intended to create the kind of ring road around the core described in the above text. What was so noteworthy about the project was that it laid over both the existing and proposed road nets an entirely new, multilaterally continuous upper-level walkway system; this sytem, moreover, assumed a rather free-form geometry, departing from the rigid CIAM geometries that the Team Ten members had long deplored. And this was still not the end of the new image of mobility. As Reyner Banham noted:

> The "image" of "Hauptstadt Berlin" was not only an irregular network of upper pedestrian walks as seen on plan...it was also the means of vertical circulation that connected the old, ground-level grid with the new one above it. This was to be an

5. Proposal for "Hauptstadt Berlin" by Alison and Peter Smithson, 1958

6. Collage of proposal for Golden Lane Housing by Alison and Peter Smithson, 1952

escalator city, in which vertical transportation was to be almost more the norm than horizontal movement. This was both the image of the new elements, and the image of the old that had been transformed, for the urban meaning of the streets at ground level would clearly be quite different now that the main circulation of the city had moved up in the air.[10]

Closely related to the concept of the "cluster" for the Team Ten group was the concept of the "street." Not the street of historic European urban form, to be sure. The opposition to this, which had so forcefully been made by Le Corbusier in the arguments of "the Radiant City," still held sway. But Le Corbusier himself, in his "Unité d'Habitation" at Marseilles (1946, one of the early icons of Brutalism) had put forward the idea of a new sort of street, a "rue intérieure," which was intended to play a key role as "social condenser" within the larger ensemble of the building as a whole.

In their 1952 competition entry for the Golden Lane Housing project in London, the Smithsons took Le Corbusier's rue intérieure and moved it to the outside edge of the building to become the "street-deck," which influenced housing projects around the world for a decade. When, in turn, the concept of the street-deck was linked to the concept of the cluster, there then resulted the further new urban idea of "grain." This concept is probably best represented in two projects for universities in Germany by the Smithsons' colleagues in Team Ten, Candilis, Josic and Woods. These projects are the competition entries for Bochum University of 1962 and Berlin Free University of 1964. In both of these cases, a three-dimensional "urban" grid was created as the structure of the complex, which allowed for a considerable degree of growth and change within the interstices of the system.

Team Ten's concept of grain was a very powerful one. Perhaps the most telling evidence of this is the fact that it had a formative influence on a late design by the first-generation modernist who had most significantly influenced Team Ten itself: Le Corbusier. In his project for the Venice Hospital of 1964–65, Le Corbusier saw fit to adopt the principles of grain and to employ them in a project that constituted quite a significant change of direction for him.

Thus "cluster," "street" and "grain" all pointed in the direction of growing concern for the issues of mobility and plurality in the evolution of modernity within Western European society as a whole. However, as of the mid-1960s, the issue of history and the status of the existing fabric of the historical cities of Europe had still not become a critical issue for Team Ten.

7. Plan of competition entry for Berlin Free University by Candilis, Josic and Woods, 1964

For most of the first half of the 1960s, discussion continued to revolve primarily around the accommodation of mobility, growth and change and their implications for evolving views of appropriate urban form in the modern city. Perhaps the culmination of Team Ten's activities was the realization of a project for a new city of 100,000 population, the competition for which had been won in 1962 by Candilis, Josic and Woods. This was Toulouse-le-Mirail, a vast undertaking that created, between 1964 and 1971, a satellite city to the existing city of Toulouse in southern France. At Toulouse-le-Mirail most of Team Ten's urban ideas were implemented. An elevated pedestrian deck formed a spine that constituted the functional and symbolic organizational scheme of the entire settlement; within a vast ring-road vehicular movement system, street-deck housing blocks lined the edges of the elevated deck, and secondary pedestrian walkway systems led onward to lower-density housing neighbourhoods and to special functional buildings such as schools and recreation buildings.

8. View of Toulouse-le-Mirail as built by Georges Candilis, Alexis Josic and Shadrach Woods from 1964 to 1971

As a built realization of Team Ten's ambitions, Toulouse-le-Mirail could hardly have been more complete. Thus when, only a few years after its occupation, it became a sociological controversy, it put the urban theories of this generation under severe critical scrutiny. But this, too, is anticipating events.

For, it is important to note here, during the same period that the Candilis, Josic and Woods project was being conceived and constructed, even greater divergencies were beginning to be evident between the European and American members of the same generation, in respect to the great issues of mobility and the public realm. As noted above, the principles of vehicular/pedestrian segregation, which had been among the principles taken over by Team Ten from CIAM, had been very slow to take hold in North America where the free movement of the automobile had been associated with individual initiative for so long. Only Victor Gruen's incorporation of such segregation into his early 1950s concept of a new building type — the regional shopping centre — gave the idea any significant North American currency. But in this form, of course, the idea grew extremely powerful over the course of the 1950s and 1960s. Indeed, the result of the hybridizing of such segregation with the economic function of merchandising and the urban social role of a "centre" made the shopping centre the most consequential typological innovation in urban architecture during the 20th century.

9. Aerial view of Northland Shopping Center, Detroit, Michigan, 1954, by Architect Victor Gruen

Moreover, it is not unimportant that in the early development of their own ideas of "clustering," Peter and Alison Smithson paid explicit homage to Victor Gruen's early ideas on neighbourhood planning and vehicular pedestrian segregation for Fort Worth, Texas. But as the phenomenon of the shopping centre grew in complexity and in social and economic power, the twin notions of social centre and of mass-scale mobility began to radically outstrip those of "cluster" and of "grain." And this fact, combined with the central function of the shopping centre as a mechanism of consumption, began to trouble European observers.

10. "Today We Collect Ads"; image selected by Peter and Alison Smithson, published in their book *Ordinariness and Light* in 1970

To be sure, even in the early 1950s when the Smithsons' interests in American consumerism were at their peak ("today we collects ads," 1955) this interest had been a rhetorically endistanced one. And social attitudes that were uncritically accepting of American mores had always met a harsh reception in Team Ten circles. Indeed, the only American architect to escape altogether the scorn of the Team Ten moralists was Louis Kahn. But by 1964, this divergence was formally recognized by both sides in the famous publication by Team Ten member Colin St. John Wilson of his "Letter to an American Student":

> I do not wish to go on raging at the latest phase of architecture in the United States. It seems that by now the conflict in judgement between European and American critics upon this subject needs understanding rather than exacerbation; and certainly as I sat and listened to the contributors to the Columbia symposium (Architecture in the 1930s, Columbia University, School of Architecture, Spring 1964), I began to understand for the first time that there is a fundamental difference between American and European interpretation of the role of architecture in society. For the modern architecture of which these contributors spoke was almost unrecognizable to me. It was supposedly defined by some point of purely stylistic maturity called the international style deeply indebted to Neo-Classicism and quite detached from the problems of its society. No Athens Charter, no "îlot insalubre," no echo of the cry "architecture or revolution," nothing of the search for new standards, of the fervour of groups such as CIAM and MARS to bring architecture to the attention of the people: art for art's sake, amen.

> Now in Europe, the notion of a new architecture was always a polemical one, in which, for better or for worse, a whole body of ideas was at stake, all elements from door-handle to city plan were so bound together that the form of a chair could even project implications for the form of the city. Stakes of this order demand a kind of Hippocratic oath, and this is to be exercised in a realm hard to define, which borders simultaneously upon aesthetics, morality and politics, and can best be described by the word "probity."[11]

Wilson's demurral was soon seconded by Reyner Banham, and by a host of other European commentators who took severely to task the stylistic innovations being promoted by Philip Johnson, Eero Saarinen and others. Then too, just as this new European critique was taking shape, American attitudes to "the public realm" were moving off in a direction that would prove even more troubling.

In 1955, Volume 9/10 of *Perspecta: The Yale Architectural Review* was published under the editorship of a then young American student, Robert A. M. Stern. As one might expect at that date, the work of Louis Kahn loomed large in this issue. But even more pertinently, for my present purposes, the second article in the issue was by Charles Moore, entitled "You Have to Pay for the Public Life." Moore had been asked by the editors of the journal to prepare a commentary on architecture of the American West Coast from the perspective of "monument" and "place." As he put it:

> *Perspecta*'s editors suspected, I presume, that I would discover that in California there is no contemporary monumental architecture, or that there is no urban scene (except in a sector of San Francisco), or, more probably, that both monumental architecture and the urban scene are missing. Their suspicions were well founded; any discussion from California in 1964 about monumental urban architecture is bound to be less about what we have than about what we have instead.[12]

Interestingly enough, Moore even cited the same quotation on urbanity from Ortega y Gasset that had been cited by José Luis Sert at the 1951 CIAM conference noted above. But insofar as he was prepared to concede to East Coast prejudice that his discussion of California public space would revolve around "what we have instead," he nevertheless refused to concede that public space simply didn't exist there. Indeed, having commenced a detailed critique of the "placelessness" characteristic of recent modern work in the state by Ernest Kump and others, he took a strategic turn in his argument:

> Even in the few years of Yankee California's existence, this kind of placelessness has not always been characteristic. During the 20s and into the 30s, with what was doubtless an enormous assist from the Hollywood vision in the days of its greatest splendor, an architectural image of California developed which was exotic but specific, derivative but exhilaratingly free....What came of this was architecture that owed something to Spain, very little to the people who were introducing the International Style, and a great deal to the movie camera's moving eye....The act of recalling another quite imaginary civilization created a new and powerful public realm.[13]

Moore then went on to discuss in some detail what he saw as the virtues of two key examples, Shepley, Rutan and Coolidge's old campus at Stanford University from 1887, and William Mooser's Santa Barbara County Courthouse from 1929. Reaching the climax of his argument, Moore continued:

> More recent years have their monuments as well. Indeed, by almost any conceivable method of evaluation that does not exclude the public, Disneyland must be regarded as the most important single piece of construction in the West in the past several decades. The assumption inevitably made by people who have not yet been there — that it is some sort of physical extension of Mickey Mouse — is wildly inaccurate. Instead, singlehanded, it is engaged in replacing many of those elements of the public realm which have vanished in the featureless private floating world of southern California, whose only edge is the ocean, and show center is otherwise undiscoverable (unless by our revolution test it turns out to be on Manhattan Island). Curiously, for a public place, Disneyland is not free. You buy

11. The Santa Barbara County Courthouse by William Mooser

143

12. "Main Street U.S.A.," at
Disneyland, published by Charles
Moore in his 1966 essay "You Have to
Pay for the Public Life"

tickets at the gate. But then, Versailles cost someone a great deal of money, too.
Now, as then, you have to pay for the public life.
Disneyland, it appears, is enormously important and successful just because it re-
creates all the chances to respond to a *public* environment, which Los Angeles particularly does not any longer have. It allows play-acting, both to be watched and to
be participated in, in a public sphere.[14]

These inflammatory remarks then led to a detailed commendatory commentary on
Disney's creation, as well as to the first extensive portfolio of photographs of
Disneyland in any serious architectural magazine. With this encomium of a major
enterprise of American consumerism, Moore brought European/American critical
tensions to a new height, which has not altogether abated up to the present day.
Hardly at all ironical in his attitude, Moore flew directly in the face of the kind of
continental dismay that was increasingly felt in Europe at certain strong tendencies
in the evolution of architectural culture in the United States. But not only that.
Insofar as the shopping centre had been the link between new urban theories in
Europe and North America in the early 1950s, then the inevitability of the evolution
from the shopping centre to the theme park put new stress on European convictions
about the respective roles of pedestrians and vehicles in urban centres in the first
place. And finally, in its characteristically Californian shamelessness about style,
Disneyland brought stunningly to the forefront of discussion the relationship of the
difficult new concepts of plurality and mobility to the third term of the emerging cultural crisis, that of history. For above all else, Moore argued, Disneyland successfully
reconnected the popular American imagination to mythic past, just as the movies had
already done.

While the course of events did not run precisely parallel, the fact of the matter
is that during the late 1960s and 1970s, the gradual growth of concern for history in
Europe led to yet another full-fledged intergenerational crisis about the form that
urban life should take.

One may trace the emergence of this crisis to a figure who was pivotal in the
evolution from Team Ten to the younger generation that eventually attacked it, the
European Rationalists. This figure is O. M. Ungers, who was slightly younger than
the members of Team Ten proper, but had already been important in Germany in the
late 1950s and 1960s before his move to the United States. In 1959, for example,
Ungers constructed a house for himself in Cologne that placed him in parallel ranks
with the Smithsons and James Stirling in Britain in respect to their shared admiration
for, and influence from, the Maisons Jaoul in Paris of Le Corbusier (1952–54).

By the mid-1960s, notwithstanding his regard for his seniors in Team Ten,
Ungers's position began to shift. In an influential series of student projects under his
leadership at the Technical University of Berlin, Ungers began to promote a strong
current of formality and a sharp urban definition, which contrasted noticeably with

13. Axonometric of project for
Grünzug South by O. M. Ungers, 1964

the then extant "open aesthetic" of visual informality being promulgated by the Smithsons. In a key project from 1964 done with a team of associates, which included the then young Rob Krier, Ungers even went so far as to elaborate a scheme of types, organized together to create a formally distinctive and highly recognizable morphology for the Cologne district of Grünzug South. After his move to the United States, Ungers became first the teacher of, and then collaborator with, the young Dutch architect Rem Koolhaas. By the early 1970s, Ungers had moved to a position sufficiently distinct from that of the old generation to be included among the new, and largely younger, generation coming to be known as the Rationalists. In 1969, in another significant European linkage, Rob Krier's brother Leon went to work for James Stirling, and in the years during and after Krier's stay in the Stirling office, Stirling's work too shifted ground. Projects such as Derby Town Centre began to manifest an increasingly strong preoccupation with history, both in the form of recognizable, if subtle, historical references and in an increasingly deferential attitude to existing urban fabric in the vicinity.

By the late 1970s, the delicate European consensus around the emerging issues of plurality, mobility and history exploded completely, and full-scale generational controversy ensued again. Probably, the battle can be said to have been launched with Maurice Culot's compendium of 1978, *Rational Architecture*, with its highly polemical subtitle "The Reconstruction of the European City." In this important document, a younger generation turned dramatically on its seniors and challenged the ideas that had sustained their vision of the city. Where the Team Ten generation had accepted the motorway as a new dimension of urban form, the Rationalists fundamentally challenged it. In a preface to a series of proposals for Stuttgart, for example, Rob Krier compared the damage done to that city by "land speculation" and by "motorway construction" with the damage done to the city by Allied bombardments during the war. Where Team Ten had developed a metaphor of the street, in connection with its idea of the street-deck, the Rationalists reasserted the primacy of the historical street **in its literal form** as the primary organizational principle of urbanism. Where the generation of Team Ten had conceived of the metaphor of urban "grain," the Rationalists argued for the primacy of the actual fabric of the historic European city and argued that new interventions should defer to it. Where Team Ten had argued for the development of an "open aesthetic" of building that was informal, subject to change and randomness, the Rationalists reasserted the importance of formality in the urban vision, rejecting the traditions of both Team Ten and CIAM, and arguing instead for re-examination of the urban philosophies of such ignored pre-modern thinkers as Camillo Sitte, Otto Wagner and Eliel Saarinen.

Indeed, the Rationalists put forward a series of propositions that were radically conservative by comparision with those of the immediately preceding generation. They argued strongly for the importance of the principles of historic European urban morphology, and they claimed that the historic forms of the street, the square and the

14. Project for Siemens AG Munich by James Stirling, 1969

15. Illustration from "Section V: Dialectical Elements of the Urban Morphology," in *Rational Architecture*

KAPITEL 3

REKONSTRUKTION
ZERSTÖRTER STADTRÄUME

AN
BEISPIELEN
DER
INNENSTADT STUTTGARTS

16. Frontispiece from Chapter 3 of Rob Krier's *Stadtraum in Theorie und Praxis*

block were fundamental to it; they argued that the public spaces of the city should be conceived in the first instance in purely formal terms, and following the principles of Sitte, put forward new lexicons of such spaces.

They argued that the primary obligation of housing design was not individual dwelling amenity, but rather the overall urban relationship of unit type to local urban morphology; they argued that the form of new housing in existing neighbourhoods should be determined by the existing morphology of that neighbourhood. Finally, they reasserted what they saw as the absolute primacy of the urban monument, perceived in a dialectical relationship with the fabric of the city.

Now, this dramatic, internally consistent and conservative series of propositions constituted the most important challenge to the ascendancy of the Team Ten generation that had occurred. Moreover, it was a challenge that coincided with the growth of public scepticism about the long-term social effectiveness of such major works of the previous decade as Candilis, Josic and Woods's Toulouse-le-Mirail in France, and the Märkisches-Viertel in West Berlin by Werner Düttmann, Hans Müller and Georg Heinrichs. By this time both of these major projects had been completed and occupied for some years, and grave evidence of urban ennui and alienation was becoming evident.

Citizen dissatisfactions fanned the flames of dispute between the older and younger generations of architects. And the late 1970s and early 1980s saw a series of increasingly acrimonious quarrels in which the young accused the older generation of betraying the long-standing traditions of European civilization in the creation of unlivable urban precincts, while the old retaliated by accusing the young of betraying the principles of modern liberal democracy, and of seeking a return to the traditional social and political structures of pre-war Europe. But leaving aside the grosser political allegations that were hurled back and forth, it was nevertheless true that the proposals of the young did indeed cast a whole new light on the relationship between plurality, mobility and history, which had formed such a continuous substratum of debate since the end of the war.

For the Rationalists, of course, history, which had received the least attention from Team Ten, was now placed in a position of absolute priority. As for mobility, it was seen as one principal rationale for the destruction of the European city, which had been so extensive in the 1950s and 1960s. Thus it was radically displaced from the higher priority it had enjoyed in the urban theories of Team Ten. Indeed, the attitude of the Rationalists to mobility, and to the phenomenon of the automobile, remains obscure to this day.

Finally, we come to the most elusive of our three interrelated themes, that of plurality. Interestingly enough, this idea had always been somewhat elusive in the work of Team Ten, never receiving the attention that mobility had. Similarly, for the Rationalists, plurality per se had not been an issue as the historical form of the city

17. Interior of the Insurance Headquarters Building in Apeldoorn, Holland, by Herman Hertzberger, 1972

surely had been. To be sure, seeking for fragmentary evidence of consideration of plurality in the debates of the past thirty years, it would probably be fair to place the Smithsons' early interest in the heterogeneity of London street-life and in the aleatory provocations of Dubuffet and advertising alongside Leon Krier's pleas for the reconstruction of the "quarter" as a new and potentially provocative basis of everyday urban life.

But striking evidence of the difficulties faced by the two generations may be demonstrated in a comparative discussion of two projects of the 1970s by representatives of the opposing factions, Herman Hertzberger and Leon Krier. The two projects in question are Hertzberger's Insurance Headquarters Building in Apeldoorn, Holland, from 1972, and Leon Krier's competition entry for housing for Royal Mint Square, in London, England, from 1974.

Hertzberger himself is an interesting intergenerational figure, having been too young to have been a member of Team Ten proper, but having been for some time a protégé of Aldo van Eyck, who was a member. By the mid-1970s, Hertzberger had developed his own significant position as representative of the Team Ten affiliated movement, Dutch Structuralism. And the office building in Apeldoorn, Holland, would generally be regarded, both by the architect and such critics as Alan Colquhoun, as being his most accomplished project up to that date. Basically, the building is an office building to house the administration of a government insurance organization. Given his strong social orientation to architecture, Hertzberger was very interested in the potential programmatic symbolism of the building. But of course, this symbolism was necessarily for him far more poetic and elliptical than institutional and monumental. Indeed, Hertzberger's almost psychoanalytic orientation to the creation of built form was so individualistic in its point of departure that he saw it as the obligation of his building to be anti-institutional and to establish its intended systems of social meaning exclusively from the individual outward, as it were.

Thus, the form of Apeldoorn is a cellular system of modules, grouped roughly into four, and canted to forty-five degrees, so that a fractured edge of a series of working trays abuts to a multi-storey route moving diagonally through the building

147

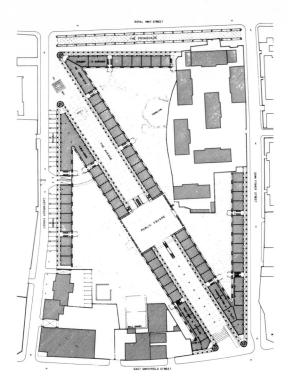

as a whole. Now it is this route, of course, that belongs to the Team Ten tradition of the street-deck, and is surely in some deep historical sense intended as a "social condenser." But, of course, for its author, the route is not conceived of as having any overriding collective symbolic force. Rather, its fractured profile, its character as the resultant of a cumulative series of cellular modules butted against it, and the manifest circumstantiality of the conditions of overlook created, are all intended to preclude any such overriding meaning.

For Hertzberger, the constitution of the public realm can only proceed from the individual act cumulatively outward to the *resultant* collectivity. According to his politics, any preconstituted collective image would necessarily be authoritarian. So we should not be surprised either, then, that the external profile of the complex is an even more circumstantial resultant than the interior profile of the trays against the route. Indeed, the honeycomb reading of the exterior presents no unified reading to the exterior world at all. In sum, we have, it seems to me, growing out of the Team Ten tradition, a commitment to the constitution of a human plurality that is radically individualistic and decentralist, and that cannot tolerate any predetermined representation of collectivity.

Krier's proposal for a housing precinct at Royal Mint Square in London is, of course, not an institution at all, but an extensive insertion into, and in large measure the creation of, a residential quarter. Like Hertzberger's scheme, Krier's also involves a diagonal route across the plan form of the proposal; but where Hertzberger's strives to the maximum degree to eschew collective symbolism, Krier's sets out equally deliberately to achieve it. In his case, the diagonal route is quite formally and axially organized and the fabric of the adjacent housing is formally welded together to monumentalize the route. As well, at the midpoint of the route, Krier locates a collective focal space to serve the new quarter created by the project as a whole. And, according to his poignant description of the project, the opposite faces of the formally defined square are created by facades for community institutions that **do not yet exist**. Thus

148

the political commitment to plurality and to the public on **this** designer's part
commits him to rely on the pure iconographic power of the facade, so as to constitute
a new public realm, for which the institutions do not yet exist.

In Hertzberger's case, we may conclude, the power of architecture to symbolize
"the human artefact" **in itself** is consciously eschewed, while in Krier's, such power is
surely invoked, but in a manner that limits itself to pure iconography, thereby forsak-
ing any possibility of human action in spontaneous terms, independent of a conscious
intellectual appropriation. Given Benjamin's apt characterization of architecture as a
phenomenon generally "appropriated by a collectivity in a state of distraction,"
Krier's exclusively iconographic gesture toward the "res publica" seems excessively
disembodied to be fully effective. Thus, these two key projects taken together crystal-
lize a crisis of symbolic representation of "the public," which must be seen to be
quintessentially characteristic of their period.

Perhaps a certain historical distance on the recriminations of the Team Ten and
Rationalist generations will eventually permit such a reconsideration to occur. For
the moment, however, one is compelled to conclude this account of the intergenerational disputes since World War II by returning to North America, and noting a
further evolution of just the sort of hybridizing of ideas that led to the
European/American recriminations of the 1960s. I have already noted how powerful
the twin European ideas of pedestrian/vehicular segregation and of "centre" became
in North America when they were combined by Victor Gruen in the form of the
generic shopping centre. I have also noted the inflammatory fashion in which Charles
Moore linked the ideas of "history" and of "public life" in his complimentary account
of the phenomenon of Disneyland.

Now in the past decade or so, we have witnessed a further hybridizing of types
in which the generic shopping centre, conceived by Gruen, and the theme park,
invented by Disney, have **themselves** been combined. The controversial Canadian
example of the West Edmonton Mall is only the best known and largest of this
increasingly ubiquitous new metropolitan phenomenon. Moreover, if we see a new
generic hybrid of "shopping centre" and "theme park" emerging, then a further by-
product of Disneyland also seems evident in which the shopping centre is calculatedly
hybridized to a Disney-like model of urban history. This mutation has generated such
well-known precincts as Paneuil Hall in Boston and South Street Seaport in New
York City.

Criticism of these enclaves as ersatz and inauthentic is already beginning to be
familiar, and one would not be surprised to see a reprise of the kind of transatlantic
dispute represented in Wilson's 1964 lament, cited above. But I should like to conclude by noting that I begin to discern the prospect of yet another, perhaps even
more contentious typological mutation, one which, even if the "history" based centre
hasn't done so, is almost certain to precipitate new Europe/America recriminations.

This mutation as I see it will be the result of a commercial North American seizure of the Rationalist concept of the "quarter," so lovingly rendered and justified by Leon Krier in his many urban polemics of recent years. The "quarter" will then be hybridized with the history-based centre to create a new urban type, which will be shopping centre, theme park, and neighbourhood **all at the same time**, and without any necessary anchor in a particular, real historical setting. Such a conception is likely to have sufficient market appeal to develop some of the social potency of the shopping centre as it evolved in the 1950s and 1960s. Then, too, it will no doubt precipitate a torrent of social critique as well, since its lack of any justifying historical reference will open up any number of new marketing possibilities of "theming" and thereby of angry imputations of false consciousness.

Perhaps, at this juncture, a new and more supple consideration of "plurality" will come to the fore, since it seems to me that only on some such philosophical plane as the idea plurality necessarily brings into play will the angry debates that can be expected be able to be rationally articulated. Were one to attempt to rehearse such a rationalization, it seems to me one would need to return to a further consideration of "action" as it has been characterized by Arendt, and by such recent commentators as Richard Sennett. Indeed, the very nature of the anticipated dispute puts one in mind of the historic 18th-century argument between Diderot and Rousseau, which Sennett has recounted in considerable detail in his book *The Fall of Public Man*.

For Diderot, as Sennett characterizes the argument, the concept of "man the actor" arises out of earlier social analogies between "the world" and "the stage" such as that put forward by Henry Fielding. To quote Sennett:

> If, in general, man as actor relieved himself of the burdens of innate sin by divorcing his nature from his acts, 18th Century common sense concluded that he thus could enjoy himself more. Tied in public neither to the realm of nature nor to the Christian duties of the soul, his playfulness and pleasure in the company of others could be released.[15]

But Diderot pressed the matter further, and argued that insofar as one spoke of "acting" as theatrical performance, "playfulness and pleasure" could hardly be considered adequate motivations. To quote Diderot himself:

> If the actor were full, really full, of feeling, how could he play the same part twice running with the same spirit and success? Full of fire at the first performance, he would be worn out and cold as marble at the third.[16]

This led the great French philosopher of the theatre to conclude that "acting," in this sense, must be considered an entirely artificial and repeatable construct, "a work of Art, planned and composed — a work which is built up by degrees and which lasts."

Sennett then outlines how, taking off from Diderot's argument for the necessary "artificiality" of acting, Rousseau mounts a major indictment of the idea of "city as theatre." For if it were true that the emerging urban setting of the 18th century really was a "stage," and that "acting — not just performance on stage," but by extension "visits in cafés, walks and promenades, etc." really were entirely artificial, then for Rousseau, the great 18th-century city was

> an environment wherein you cannot tell what kind of man a stranger is in a given situation by finding out how he survives. The situations, indeed, in which you are likely to meet him are those in which you are not meeting for some functional purpose, but meeting in the context of nonfunctional socializing, of social interaction for its own sake.[17]

And this, in turn, led Rousseau to see his fellow citizens as increasingly preoccupied — through the sheer pleasure of contact with others in public — to become "actors" of a special sort:

> In a big city, full of scheming, idle people without religion or principle, whose imagination, depraved by sloth, inactivity, the love of pleasure, and great needs, engenders only monsters and inspires only crimes; in a big city, where *moeurs* and honor are nothing because each easily hiding his conduct from the public eye, shows himself only by his reputation...[18]

Thus Rousseau is led to conclude that

> the trouble with the great city is that there is *too much* community. The values of the community, whatever they are, count for too much, because people try to win reputation from others by acting out these values. The small town has better values, survival virtues....It permits more isolation, it permits people to ignore the community's standards and search out their own hearts to "see whatever there is, just to see."[19]

Now it seems to me that the debate on the new urban hybrid that I foresee might well benefit by proceeding from a new consideration of the strange dual meaning of "acting," which is brought to the fore in this discussion. For Arendt, with whose ideas I began, acting constitutes in the first instance "the affairs which go on among those who have (the world) in common." In this sense, she is allied with Diderot, in sensing a certain artifice in the experience whereby "I appear to others as others appear to me." Yet her conception of action nevertheless stops well short of the sort of pure artifice represented by Diderot's characterization of theatre. As she puts it:

> In acting and speaking, men show who they are, reveal actively their unique personal identities and thus make their appearance in the human world....This disclosure of "who" in contradistinction to "what" somebody is — his qualities, gifts, talents and shortcomings, which he may display or hide — is implicit in everything somebody says and does. It can be hidden only in complete silence and perfect pas-

sivity, but its disclosure can almost never be achieved as a wilful purpose, as though one possessed and could dispose of his "who" in the same manner he has and can dispose of his qualities. On the contrary, it is more than likely that the "who," which appears so clearly and unmistakably to others, remains hidden from the person himself, like the daimon in Greek religion which accompanies each man throughout his life, always looking over his shoulder from behind and thus visible only to those he encounters.[20]

This future argument must necessarily eschew the grosser forms of attribution of "false consciousness," which seem highly likely to occur. For the ambiguous idea of acting that is implied by the line of argument from Diderot to Rousseau to Arendt suggests that no protagonist is going to be able to claim "authenticity" unquestionably for himself. Indeed, while it is likely that many manifestations of the new urban hybrid will readily be able to be dismissed as "inauthentic," this dismissal will not succeed in legitimating any puritanical, Rousseauesque retreat from rhetoric or from commercialism, any more than Hertzberger's disavowal of symbolic collective form has been able to do. Instead, the way forward will lie in seizing the forms of rhetoric and commerce themselves for symbolic representations, the precise meaning of which we will not be able to predict in advance. Indeed, following Arendt, we may expect as architects not to be able to see clearly the consequences of these efforts of our own, and will have to rest confident that they will "appear clearly and unmistakably to others."

Notes

1 This essay is a shortened version of a text, currently in preparation, on a series of theoretical debates within modern architecture during this century.

2 Hannah Arendt, *The Human Condition* (Garden City, N.Y.: Doubleday/Anchor Books, 1959), p. 177.

3 Arendt, p. 45.

4 Arendt, p. 48.

5 Arendt, p. 155.

6 José Ortega y Gasset, *The Revolt of the Masses* (New York: W. W. Norton, 1960; Spanish original, 1930), p. 151.

7 Reyner Banham, *The New Brutalism* (London: The Architectural Press, 1966), p. 71.

8 Alison and Peter Smithson quoted in Banham, p. 72.

9 Alison and Peter Smithson quoted in Banham, p. 73.

10 Banham, p. 74.

11 Colin St. John Wilson, "Two Letters on the State of Architecture: 1964 and 1981," in *The Journal of Architectural Education* (Fall 1981), Vol. XXXV, No. 1, pp. 9–11.

12 Charles Moore, "You Have to Pay for the Public Life," *Perspecta 9/10: The Yale Architectural Journal* (New Haven: Yale University Press, 1965), p. 58.

13 Moore, p. 60.

14 Moore, p. 65.

15 Richard Sennett, *The Fall of Public Man* (New York: Knopf, 1977), p. 110.

16 Diderot quoted in Sennett, p. 111.

17 Rousseau quoted in Sennett, p. 118.

18 Sennett, p. 118.

19 Sennett, p. 121.

20 Arendt, p. 159.

REMNANTS AND TRANSFORMATIONS

Peter Rose

This paper is about Montréal, which is my home and place of work, a city that I passionately care about and sometimes hate, a city about which one cannot be indifferent. It will present an argument for Montréal as a traditional city, and take a straightforward look at its traditions of urban space, which are still valid and should form the background for current considerations about emerging public spaces. It will not deal with the new spate of developments, projects and civic plans; rather, it is important at this critical period in Montréal's history — a period of regeneration following twenty years of Mayor Drapeau's authoritarian megalomania and ten years of political and economic struggle — to start by simply describing those things of value in the existing urban fabric, in order to establish a base for these new discussions.

Montréalers are now trying to articulate what their city is about. We have a new civic government and a new generation of planners and architects who are thinking about Montréal and its future. An outline of a new urban plan was released this spring, and public hearings began in June. The City asked for public response to its plan, which is very vague at this stage, and received so much interest that the first hearings went on for ten days.

Public space is at the heart of what is significant about Montréal. Like many **European** cities, it has a powerful and intensely used public domain. Public life in Montréal is a **phenomenon**; the city has a dynamic public presence. Montréalers are, more than most North Americans, apartment dwellers rather than owners of private homes. They tend to eat in restaurants with great enthusiasm and great frequency. They shop more than Canadians elsewhere in the country. They go out to clubs of all sorts every day of the week and stay into the wee hours of the morning. There is something about Montréalers that causes them to derive pleasure in traffic jams at midnight on a Thursday night on rue Ste-Catherine.

Montréal curiously supports an enormous number of festivals, year after year. These festivals literally jam the streets and theatres and seem to get bigger and more popular every year. In the case of the fireworks festival, for reasons that are difficult to grasp, twice a week throughout the summer people walk long distances to completely fill Jacques Cartier Bridge and watch countries send explosives into the air; all this with little damage to the bridge and themselves, but with vast consumption of liquor and resultant activities that are explosive in themselves long after the fireworks die down.

The significance of these festivals goes beyond the event itself. The jazz festival, for example, jams several blocks of rue St-Denis and rue Ste-Catherine in the evening for more than a week. Yet, Montréal is in no sense a jazz city; there are two or three clubs where you can hear jazz during the rest of the year. But there is tremendous enthusiasm for public events per se, even though they are ephemeral and occur mostly in the summer.

Montréalers live in their streets, their squares and their parks. Although these public spaces look inhospitable at first glance and have suffered civic neglect, developer greed and bad design, they survive and thrive. Like the strange forms of plant life that grow in the cold climate of Québec, these little pieces of street suddenly appear on the urban landscape and live despite the obvious difficulties. However, while the phenomenon of public life is strong in Montréal, better care must be taken of the city in the future than has been the case in the recent past, or the qualities of the city that are most attractive will disappear forever.

The following pages will present three typologies of public space in Montréal — streets, squares and parks — along with a brief discussion of their history, morphology, function and possible significance for the future.[1]

2. Figure/Ground Plan of downtown Montréal. This plan shows only the imprint of the buildings on the ground and major topographic features. The city began at the harbour on the St. Lawrence River where Old Montréal still remains largely intact from the late 19th century and is quite extraordinary. It has a distinctly European kind of urban form — narrow streets and tightly bounded squares on a sloping ground. The irregular outline of Mount Royal Park and the trapezoidal outline of Lafontaine Park are the major urban events at the northern limit of the central area. The city proper is essentially located between the river and the mountain. There is a dramatic contrast between the older fine grain fabric of small buildings, which front onto streets and have private backs in the centre of the block, and recent developments, which appear as large black blobs on the plan and are single building complexes that consume entire city blocks. Finally, the empty zone that separates the lower and upper parts of the city is the line of the Ville Marie Expressway, a major source of discontinuity and rupture in the public space system of the city.

Peter Rose

1. Montréal, a city between River and Mountain. View from Mount Royal, c. 1901 (photo William Notman, McCord Museum Collection)

3. THE STREET NETWORK. Only the public spaces of streets, squares and parks are shown in black. The street grid to the north of the Old Town is not the result of urban design, but rather is the product of surveyors laying out farmland in the 18th and 19th centuries. The north–south streets are simply persistent marks of the divisions of land into farm plots, while the east–west streets tended to follow the base of the Mountain, provided access to those farm plots or had some other topographical or agrarian genesis. The irregular location of minor streets reflects the attitudes and circumstances of different landowners during the early period of development.

4. The original subdivision of the land. Plan of Montréal, 1825

6. Rue St-Jacques

7. Rue St-Laurent

8. Rue St-Denis

9. Rue Ste-Catherine

10. Rue Sherbrooke

5. MAJOR STREETS. This plan highlights the buildings along Montréal's major streets and thereby reveals the degree of spatial continuity and the scale or grain of buildings along them. Rue Notre-Dame appears intact in the central area of Old Montréal, but falls apart as it goes west. Rue St-Jacques was the financial district of Montréal in the late 19th century, and while it no longer serves this purpose, its buildings are preserved. It is a great place to stroll. It would be a wonderful place in which to work or to go out at night.

Boulevard René-Lévesque (Dorchester Boulevard) has never had strong spatial definition or a clear identity; even now it is the subject of intense discussion. Above it is rue Ste-Catherine, which has been a shopping street with major buildings since the late 19th century. While its form and function have not changed much, it has been taken apart, trees have been removed and terrible lights added. Nevertheless, it remains the essential heart of commercial Montréal; there are traffic jams in the middle of the night and pedestrians fill it even in the coldest part of the winter. Rue Sherbrooke is the grand Park Avenue of Montréal, but is very discontinuous at present. At its best moments it has some wonderful encounters with religious and educational institutions that provide generous views and landscape. The big apartment buildings, the churches and the Ritz Carlton Hotel are still all there.

Of the north–south streets, St-Laurent is the best; one can spend days on this street and be fascinated by it. Often called the Main, it was the main street that forged north from Old Montréal when the city grew. The warehouses and shops that line the street have not changed much and have been humming at a continuous pace for more than a hundred years. To the east is St-Denis and to the west is avenue du Parc, both of which were originally residential but are now major commercial streets. The width of the streets allowed for tree planting and provided a grand scale and leisurely pace; but these characteristics have now given way to six lanes of traffic, no trees and tiny sidewalks. In spite of the difficulties, they remain wonderful streets for restaurants, shops and strolling. All of these streets have been destroyed as they approach Old Montréal to the south. Nevertheless, they defy the odds and demonstrate the Montréal phenomenon that creates life where nothing would be expected to grow.

11. MAJOR SQUARES AND PARKS.
Only the buildings that surround the most important squares are shown on this plan. Notre Dame is the great square of Old Montréal. Its church was once located on the centre of the square, symbolic of its role in the society of that time. In the 19th century the church was put on the side and the Bank of Montréal by McKim, Mead and White was added on the north. It is a very compelling urban square, full of memory, and with some imagination is capable of much greater vitality than its current use for tour buses and tourists. Also in Old Montréal, Jacques Cartier Square is no longer a market, except for popcorn and velvet paintings — a delightful remnant waiting for a new use and subtle transformation. Dominion Square is still relatively intact although each new generation of buildings does a certain damage to it. Victoria Square, at its inception, was the hay market just outside the walls. Under English rule it became a genteel Victorian square where one could stroll in leisure, work or live. As some of these activities relocated, the stature of the square declined and more recently the city traffic engineers decided that it was important to be able to drive diagonally through it and thus wiped out the landscape. And now the Ville Marie Expressway runs underneath it and has contributed a huge ventilating shaft. There is simply no square left and it may be impossible to retrieve;

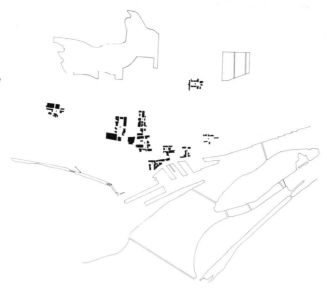

at the least, it will require a major and very skillful transformation.
Viger Square has the Bruce Price Building on it and was a wonderful park and garden, destroyed by the construction of the Ville Marie Expressway. While it has received various new things, it no longer has the characteristics of an urban space, nor does it connect uptown and Old Montréal as it once did so beautifully. Today it is a barrier.
St-Louis Square was originally the site of a reservoir and, like rue St-Laurent, is substantially as it was a hundred years ago.
Mount Royal is Montréal's Central Park and, like the classic New York urban park, was designed by Frederick Law Olmsted. While it needs to be more actively maintained, it is a large, vigorous and monumental "rural" landscape retreat in the centre of the city. It is now more remote from the downtown than it was when the funicular connected it directly. Instead of being able to walk there at lunch time, one is now obliged, by and large, to use a car. To the east of Mount Royal, the rectilinear-shaped park with the angled south end is Lafontaine Park. Its elegant greenhouse with flower gardens is no longer there.

12. Notre Dame Square, c. 1930

13. Jacques Cartier Square, c. 1920 (photo Notman Collection, McCord Museum)

14. Victoria Square, c. 1920

15. Viger Square, c. 1900

16. St-Louis Square, c. 1895 (photo Notman Collection, McCord Museum)

18. RESIDUAL SPACE. This plan shows empty sites and the spaces left over around buildings, waiting to be transformed into buildings and public spaces

157

17. Lafontaine Park

19. The recent reclamation of the old port as a linear public space

In conclusion, a figure/ground study of a 20th-century North American city — although a lovely idea — does not provide the same results that it gave Giambattista Nolli when he drew Rome in 1748. There is simply too much missing on the ground and too much added in the air to be able to describe fully the present architectural condition of the city in plan.

Nevertheless, it is clear that the urban form of Montréal does not require major rethinking or invention. It has a network of streets that works, in spite of discontinuities and disrepair. Making them continuous and repairing them with a higher quality of design than has been the case of late would go a long way toward giving the public life of the city even greater vitality. The leftover space that has been the result of large-scale projects by various transportation agencies or so-called urban renewal ventures now provides a vast territory of developable land through which the current ruptures and barriers may be remedied.

While Old Montréal is now too much of a tourist attraction, with a slightly different program of activities it could come back into the life of the city proper, like other neighbourhoods have. Throughout the city, the squares are still there, more or less. Some need simply to be restored or given new uses. Those that have been heavily damaged are opportunities for creative transformations. There are enough parks, and although they are run down, they present no major conceptual problem.

I am optimistic that the current thrust of civic and urban planning will be sensitive to the extraordinary urban history of Montréal and to the vitality that is there. Montréalers need only to look at themselves to see who they are.

Notes
[1] All drawings have been prepared by Peter Rose, Architect.

PLACES AT THE EDGE:
Public Space as Platform for the Contemplation of the Natural Tableau

Lance Berelowitz

1. Plan of central Vancouver (courtesy Art Gallery of Vancouver, *Vancouver Revisions*)

"Sous les pavés, la plage…" [1]

In Vancouver the beach is not far beneath the paving. Indeed, the famous 1968 rallying cry of the student protests in Paris found a deep echo in the collective psyche of Vancouver, one which continues as a powerful impulse in the city.

The complex symbolic relationship between the quintessentially urban and the profoundly natural as represented in that Parisian battle cry had its counterpart in the West Coast's *back-to-nature* movement, although in Vancouver's case, it may be said that it was more a case of staying **in** nature than getting back **to** it. This is a young city and for many of its residents the city is actually an excuse for the place, a necessary inconvenience on the natural landscape; it is a means to an end that has little to do with urban living, but a great deal to do with the private pursuit of nature and leisure. And this, of course, is the opposite of what is conventionally understood as the basis of a public domain. The following discussion of public space in Vancouver will account for this still-powerful impulse and describe the effect it has had on the nature of public space in this city.

2. "Sous les pavés, la plage …" rallying cry of student protests in Paris 1968 as rioters tore up the city's cobblestones

In another context, Gertrude Stein once remarked, "There is no there there." However, she might well have had Vancouver in mind, for I can think of no phrase that more aptly summarizes the dilemma of this city. Born as it was of a set of accidental imperatives and nurtured more as an ideal or a state of mind, rather than an economic entity, Vancouver is the ultimate vanishing trick. At a distance the city appears as a nascent Manhattan, rising sheer out of the surrounding sea: tall, dense, complex and urban. But the more one looks at it and the closer one gets, the less of a city it seems to become. It dissolves into a series of idealized images that create a formidable and emotionally charged chimera. There is no there there.

3. In Vancouver the beach is not far beneath the paving

One and a half million people live spread over the deltoid lower mainland, and for most of these people the symbol and focus of the city is still the downtown peninsula. But downtown is perceived more as something to be looked **at** from a distance or, for those actually living or working there, as something one looks **out from**, rather than the more common civic phenomenon of the city as a place to be **in**. The city is constantly reflecting upon itself in a kind of collective narcissism. This is the genius loci of the city. Born as the Pacific terminus to the transcontinental railway, Vancouver looks outward by definition. It has always been an outpost without a hinterland, an extension of central Canada and ultimately the British Empire. It is significant that Vancouver was not colonized from the sea, but from the land, unlike super-ficially similar places like Sydney or Cape Town. Vancouver is the last stop on a route beginning, metaphorically, in the British Isles and, geographically, in southern Patagonia where the transamerican coastal highway begins a route that finally runs out at 49° 17' north. It is at this point— the last latitudinal minute, as it were, before the continent plunges into the sea — that we find the last city in the West Coast lit-toral. Vancouver has always been the city at the end of the line: Terminal City.

When one combines an overwhelming topography that lends itself to — even demands — contemplation, a climate benign enough as to require very little shelter, which is the more usual first demand of built urban form, and the soft materiality of a city built in the first instance of wood, then an urban ethos peculiar to Vancouver begins to emerge. It is a soft, low-density city that is open to the environment and revels in its stunning natural setting. It is easy to describe it as anti-urban, but it may be more interesting to define it as a particular kind of urbanism in which the city acts as a kind of mirror, or a vast display case for the aesthetic consumption of Nature. In this context, it is interesting to note the changed role of the voyeur in society as he has moved off the boulevards of the Old World onto the freeways of the New; Baudelaire's Parisian public *flâneur*[2] has been transformed through Chandler's L.A. private eye[3] into the near mystic voyeur of Nature in Vancouver. In this metamorpho-sis from the street-orientated and centripetal urban model to the outward looking Centrifugal City, activity intensifies toward the edges. The centre is stilled.

This distortion of public space, where man is supplanted by Nature as the primary actor in the public domain, is very much in evidence in what is supposedly Vancouver's central public space. Robson Square was carved out of two blocks in downtown Vancouver to become a unique hybrid of Law Courts Building, terraced landscape and urban space.[4] Under the overbearing metaphor of the building and the urban space as landscape, it is difficult to actually see where Robson Square **is**. In the usual meaning of that term, there is no square. Rather there are a series of intercon-nected platforms and token tableaus of Nature in a labyrinthian sprawl across, over and under two city blocks. The closest thing to a square is an ice-rink-cum-plaza sunken beneath Robson Street and serviced by a subterranean food fair, reminiscent of the now ubiquitous suburban shopping mall.

In the process of creating Robson Square, the old Provincial Court House was converted into the Vancouver Art Gallery. In the absence of anything better, the open space in front of this building had served for many years as the city's only public gathering place. While it always did have some problems in functioning as a central place for public rituals, being spatially weak at its corners and surrounded on three sides by some of the busiest and widest streets in the city, it nevertheless did have a sense of enclosure, a suitably civic monument as its focus and some fairly fine facades surrounding it. In the conversion, the main entrance on the square was closed in favour of a new main entrance facing Robson Street, thereby downgrading the space to a back-yard.

160

4. Born as the Pacific terminus to the transcontinental railway line, Vancouver looks outward by definition

Looking across the space from the now dysfunctional courthouse entrance, Robson Square encompasses, in a miniaturized form, the idealized image of Vancouver as a city of Nature; it is a Lilliputian representation of the Natural idyll. As an iteration of the Pacific landscape, Robson Square is a measure of the myth of the city, but as a public space it fails entirely. And despite its degraded state, the Old Court House space is still preferred for public gatherings. At midnight on last New Year's Eve, it attracted over ten thousand people for the year-end countdown. It was exciting, even metropolitan. This not-quite-square, with its chain-link fences, manicured planting beds and enigmatically phallic fountain structure almost seemed to work as a focus for public life, in a way that Robson Square will never do.

Preoccupied with the experience of Nature, public space in Vancouver is reduced to serving private experience: the public *flâneur* becomes the private voyeur. Of course, the transformation of public man from performer to consumer of spectacle (in this case of nature) has had a profound effect on the forms of public culture. This effect is best epitomized in Vancouver in what may be called the Cult of the View. The Cult of the View, in turn, has been a powerful imperative in the creation of a distinct typology of public spaces in the city: Public Platforms for the contemplation of the Natural Tableau.

Before considering the specific cases of this urban typology in Vancouver, it is worthwhile recalling the wealth of historical precedence. From Camillo Sitte's description of the Piazzetta San Marco with its "splendid view across the grand canal toward San Giorgio Maggiore,"[5] to Frederick Gibberd's reference to the "open fourth wall" type of space,[6] the public space that draws the landscape into the city is well documented. Gibberd cites Michelangelo's Piazza del Campidoglio as the classic example of the type, but refers to the fact that this typology recurs often in history.

In *The Design of Cities* Edmund Bacon emphasizes this enduring phenomenon in numerous Italian examples, and indeed this urban type abounds in the hill towns of Italy in which the quintessentially urban is tied into a wider geographical whole. Similarly, Colin Rowe's atemporal, catholic collection of favourite stimulants in *Collage City* includes, under the category of "splendid public terraces," Florence's Piazzale Michelangelo and Vicenza's platform of the Monte Berico, which he compares to the terraced promenades of London's Adelphi, Baden-Baden's Friedrichspark and Algiers's waterfront.

And while thinking of port cities, an attenuated version of the platform type becomes evident: the Promenade. Examples of the waterfront promenade could include lesser known, but perhaps more directly comparable examples such as the Sea Point promenade in Cape Town, the heroic hard-edge seawall encompassing the old town of Syracuse in Sicily and, of course, Venice's Riva della Schiavoni.

From all of this it becomes clear that far from being unique to Vancouver, the platform type of public space that draws the countryside and town together is a well-established part of the urban vocabulary. What remains unique about Vancouver, certainly in the Canadian context, and perhaps even on the global scale, is the extent to which the surrounding natural landscape, as opposed to the built form, is the source of inspiration in the creation of urban form. There is a strong sense in this city, almost a "moral" sense, that unsullied Nature is superior to human artefact and that the urban construct is an intrusion on, and not a complement to, the landscape.

There is something two-dimensional about this sensibility when stated in such a binary way: the city as Experience opposes the land's Innocence. And this is directly reflected in the polarized political dynamic of local politics. One is either a preserver of the sacred ways or a builder of the Socred Way. It is difficult to carve out any middle ground, politically as much as in the design of public spaces.

The formal equivalent of this binary polarization may be interpreted as the opposition of static and dynamic spaces. The static platform has an overriding quality of passivity and contemplation, while the dynamic platform would serve the unpredictable collective act. In the case of the static platform, nothing much public, let alone revolutionary, is going to happen; with Nature as the prime actor, we have little to fear from the public now rendered as passive spectator.

A classic example that illustrates the limitations of this polarization is the recently completed CRAB Park.[7] This park was vigorously promoted on behalf of downtown working-class residents with the admirable aim of giving them access across the railway lines to the waterfront. Located on the central waterfront to Burrard Inlet, the park is a curious example of the pastoral set in the heart of the city. Public space has been distorted, once again, into a token representation of Nature. It includes a token beach, a token hill, token rocks, token planting, even token water. And the formal focus of the entire park is the inevitable Viewpoint with its token sculpture, a trivialized version of native Indian art. Nowhere does the design of the park acknowledge the immediate proximity of the adjacent fishing port, a real and active part of the city; its visibility is ignored in favour of the distant, proscribed Natural view. The irony of the park is that this thin strip of token Nature is still largely inaccessible. It does not connect back to the city streets and to the people whose lives it was meant to ennoble: a misplaced arcadia stranded between port and railway track. The tokenism of CRAB Park represents the worst of both extremes in a polarized society where there is no shared urban vision.

If public space is where homogeneity breaks down, where civic rights and rituals are exercised, then what Richard Sennett[8] calls a Public Geography — that is, a coming together of the Crowd in Public Space — has a tenuous foothold here. Vancouver is endowed with a number of spaces in which the public is rendered passive. Indeed, this is the dominant typology and a large number of examples can be observed, ranging from central spaces such as Leg-in-Boot Square on False Creek to the suburban pocket platforms along the Point Grey peninsula.

A sequence of platforms also exists along the Burrard Inlet edge of the downtown peninsula, where the focus is as firmly on the Natural Tableau as in the previous

5. CRAB Park is a misplaced arcadia stranded between port and railway track

162

6/7. Portal Park, a classic example of the passive platform, an urban type for the contemplation of the Natural Tableau

suburban examples. Here the surfaces are harder, but the Natural is still clearly venerated. In this diffuse sequence of platforms, bridges, arcades and lookouts, the focus is clearly on the Distant, not the immediate.

This sequence culminates in the recently completed Portal Park[9] at the foot of Thurlow Street overlooking Burrard Inlet. Portal Park is a classic example of the platform type. It faces outward, turning its back to the city, which in turn does not address the space. There is no public activity in the space, save for the contemplation of Nature. The View function is reinforced by the formal Lookout at the cliff edge. Just in case you missed the point, a large and rather crude pavilion shelters an inlaid map representing Vancouver's so-called "neighbours" around the Pacific Rim. It is surely significant that the only built structure in the space does not shelter any public activity, but rather enshrines the Distant. Here, we are definitely at the Edge.

This platform reflects the significantly anti-urban and centrifugal nature of the public space in a city in which activity constantly tends toward the edges. Nothing **happens** in these spaces; they simply exist. While public life requires collective activity, these are platforms for private consumption. The tourist pointing his camera here at the panoramic view beyond is really focusing on his home across the Pacific.

The other kind of platform space, the dynamic space, is rarer in Vancouver, although it does exist. The dynamic platform has an overriding quality of active space; while still celebrating the urban escarpment, it is here that public life may take hold. The Natural Tableau remains just as spectacular, but in this variant it becomes a backdrop against which such daily rituals of urban interaction as may remain in the North American city are acted out. Perhaps the best example of this type is the square beside the Granville Island Public Market overlooking the waters of False Creek.[10] The setting and views are dramatic, but there is a multiplicity of public activity, by no means confined to consumption of the Natural Tableau. Nature is displaced in this case by food!

The West End's Alexandra Park with its bandstand that overlooks the bath-houses of English Bay is another example. The bath-houses themselves form an active built-edge to Beach Avenue and provide both an extension and enrichment of the beachfront promenade activity below it and a platform to beyond. With its terrace section, the bath-house structure forms a connection between the city and the sea, supporting a range of uses that connect the active and the passive.

8. The linear promenade has now become the *sine qua non* of all waterfront development in Vancouver

The linear promenade is an attenuated version of the dynamic platform type. The edge platform in its most stretched, idealized form becomes a continuous waterfront strip. This formal distortion of public space is reflected in a parallel distortion in public activity. The linear promenade has now become the *sine qua non* of all waterfront development in Vancouver. You cannot currently contemplate a new waterfront project without its automatic inclusion. The boardwalk has become a sacred cow in this city, and its citizens ardent worshippers. Everything happens at the edges of Centrifugal City.

9/10. Stanley Park Seawall, at ten kilometres long and three metres wide, is the ultimate public space as viewing platform

The most heroic exemplar of this type, the apotheosis of public space as viewing platform, is surely the Stanley Park Seawall. Begun in the 1930s, it took master stonemason James Cunningham thirty years to complete. Ten kilometres long and some three metres wide, it may qualify as the narrowest and longest public space of any city in the world. It is probably fair to say that, here, girdling the western perimeter of the downtown peninsula, Vancouverites come closest to enacting the rites of *Passegiata*, that quintessentially urban form of public passage. But an interesting paradox arises when the most active public life of the city happens not at its urban centre, but at its edges. In the case of the Seawall, a rich lexicon of public forms can be discerned, albeit in ways distorted from the more conventional sense of urban public space.

Where the grid of city streets melts into the park, the Seawall appropriates the role of the street sidewalk, beginning the displacement of the public street-life from the city. Following the curves of the shoreline, the Seawall forms a distinct edge to the land, a sinuous delineation in granite of the public domain, much as would a medieval street.

As one moves along its length, a set of public typologies is revealed: the Intersection, the Terraced Connection and the Lay-by. A series of public nodes, such as where routes intersect service facilities, form the major foci for civic activities. Here, the civic architecture is enhanced, much as it would be in a public piazza. All the while, the natural tableau is never far away; but as you move farther out, the city itself begins to enter the natural backdrop, engaging and, indeed, even usurping it at points. There is drama in the detail and clarity in the sweep, which are admirable conditions of any cityscape.

The rigour of the route is implacable, in places carving through the rockface like a Roman road, in others turning a corner to reveal another exemplar of heroic civic engineering, such as the Lions Gate Bridge. The mythology of the rain-forest is clearly acknowledged in certain places, such as in the case of a creeper-clad caveway into the green underworld, an entrance to the park's interior that is reminiscent of the Italian villas of Bomarzo or Lante.

Swinging around from the depths of the forest, the simple and powerful forms of the Seawall become increasingly stylized as it approaches the city again, until it disappears completely beneath the manicured recapitulation of Nature in the city. The public promenade has come full circle, its strength melting again as it is repossessed by the city, in perfect expression of the paradox of a city whose most active public life is at its edges.

The quest then should be for a combination of the obvious virtues of setting with the equally obvious ones of urbanism. It ought to be possible to live at the doorstep of Nature, yet participate in a collective public life. Vancouver, it seems to me, has just this opportunity, and if so developed, could be one of the most rewarding urban experiences anywhere. The conjunction of natural topography and formalized city could result in a sequence of powerful urban spaces that are part of the natural context while enhancing the urban context. The Seawall gives a clue as to the power of the possibilities. It ought to be possible to bring the Seawall back to town.

The final section of this paper discusses a site that presents just such an opportunity, in which the Cult of the View might meet the Culture of Congestion.[11] It is an opportunity that, one ventures to suggest, would have long since been developed in any European city. The site consists of a sequence of spaces along the northern edge of the downtown peninsula, between Howe and Richards streets, at just about the point where the early city street grid shifted toward the burgeoning west. This rotated grid became in time the dominant downtown street grid, leaving a relatively small fragment of the original settlement grid remaining as today's Gastown.

More through serendipity than any grand vision, a sequence of interconnected interior spaces and public platforms can be experienced or almost experienced. Starting from the recently redeveloped Sinclair Centre block, it is possible to walk from one urban room through a first public platform (Granville Square), into a second urban room (the CPR Station), and on to a final public platform overlooking the harbour, albeit unrecognized as such. In the process one has moved through the equivalent of four city blocks.

The sequence begins in the Sinclair Centre,[12] a city block comprising four discrete buildings that have been knitted together by enclosing the alleys between buildings. Passing through a public square carved out of its middle, one moves out onto a rather weak bridge structure that leads to Granville Square. Built over the railway tracks as a podium for the Port Authority office tower, Granville Square currently sports a motley collection of "Parks Board" paraphernalia — potted plants and scattered woodsy seating boxes — but nevertheless forms a strong, hard-edged platform to Burrard Inlet. It occupies an impressive position at the foot of the city's major shopping street and forms a vital connection between the city and the Station Building. The old CPR Station Building[13] has an entry here which begins a major axis of movement through this renovated building. Inside, the Station has been very successfully adapted to serve as an important nexus in the city. It is a junction of routes, connecting buses, the Light Rail Transit System, and the seabus across Burrard Inlet. It is also one of the finest urban rooms in the city forming an interior counterpart to the external platforms.

Passing through this space, one approaches a putative public space that may optimistically be called Station Square. Currently used for surface parking, this stunningly underused public platform now provides a spectacular view to some one hundred private vehicles. We still live in a society in which the mechanics of our economy result in this kind of exploitative use of urban land, and the civic mechanisms must still be found to bring this piece of the city to its full potential as a public space. With relatively minor modifications, it could be the most cogent and positive public platform in the city.

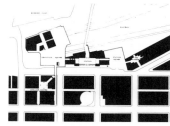

11. A sequence of interconnected interior spaces and public platforms along the northern edge of the downtown peninsula (proposal and drawing by Lance Berelowitz)

12. The putative public space "Station Square" is one of the most stunningly underutilized public platforms in the world

Finally, this sequence is connected to the recently renovated building to the east, The Landing,[14] which has a semi-public atrium carved out of its centre. Currently this space is accessible to Station Square only through double-fronting shops, but it would be simple to facilitate a better connection and thereby intensify Station Square.

As for Station Square itself, it also has a direct relationship with Cordova Street, which passes behind it. It is a true square, in the sense of space carved out of the city, as opposed to an open block surrounded by streets. One can imagine the kind of space this could become when the cars are removed and the handsome buildings embracing it are opened up to the square. A new edge wall, a unified design that combines access, surface treatment, furniture and lighting, and perhaps the relocation of the adjacent War Memorial Statue to form a focal point would result in a rich public domain animated by people, traffic and trains which converge here. Without aping the contrived historicism of adjacent Gastown's beautification, the task here is simply to complete the square. Perhaps here, finally, one could imagine a true Public Geography.

And what of the Natural Tableau? Looking out from Station Square, Vancouver's historic essence is richly revealed. The ever-changing shoreline, the containers of goods that enter the country here, the trainloads of grain just arrived from the prairies are all evident. Beyond is the bustle of the port with its ferries, cranes and tugboats. Across are the North Shore settlements with the silos holding Canada's ransom. And beyond, above the traffic and the commerce of the burgeoning city, floats a majestic panorama of Nature, a fitting backdrop to an active scene, neither dominating nor demeaned, but balanced with the city.

Notes

[1] "Sous les pavés, la plage…" was the anonymous graffiti slogan taken up as the battle cry of protesting students in the Paris riot of May 1968.

[2] Charles-Pierre Baudelaire, *The Flowers of Evil*, Marthiel and Jackson Mathews, eds. (New York: New Directions, rev. ed. 1963); *Les Fleurs du Mal* originally published Paris, 1857.

[3] See Raymond Chandler, *The Collected Works*, 1939–59.

[4] Robson Square, Vancouver, completed 1979, Arthur Erickson, Architects; Landscape Architects: Cornelia Oberlander, Raoul Robillard.

[5] Camillo Sitte, *The Art of Building Cities: City Building According to Artistic Principles* (Vienna, 1889).

[6] Sir Frederick Gibberd, *Town Design* (London: Architectural Press, 1953).

[7] CRAB Park is the acronym of Create a Real Accessible Beach Park, 1986/87, City of Vancouver.

[8] Richard Sennett, *The Fall of Public Man* (New York: Knopf, 1977).

[9] Portal Park, Vancouver, 1987, Thompson, Berwick, Pratt, Architects.

[10] Granville Island Public Market, Vancouver, 1975–88, Hotson & Bakker, Architects.

[11] Rem Koolhaas, *Delirious New York* (New York: Oxford University Press, 1978). On p. 104 Koolhaas coined the phrase "Culture of Congestion" to describe one of the ideals of Manhattanism.

[12] Sinclair Centre Redevelopment, Vancouver, 1986, Richard Henriques, Architect and Toby Russell Buckwell, Architects.

[13] CPR Station Renovation, Vancouver, 1978/79, Hawthorne, Mansfield, Towers, Architects.

[14] The Landing Renovation, Vancouver, 1987, Soren Rasmussen, Architects.

MAKING/BREAKING THE CANADIAN STREET

Trevor Boddy

Implicit in the theme of this conference, "Metropolitan Mutations: The Architecture of Emerging Public Spaces," is a neo-modernist bias toward new forms, innovative combinations and never-before-seen permutations of urban space. I have chosen the essentially conservative and seemingly dull task of writing about Canadian streets and contemporary architectural interventions that help or hinder them. I believe that the street, understood conventionally as a zone defined by two walls of buildings and containing sidewalks, car storage and an active carriageway, is by far the most important type of public open space in Canada. I believe that most metropolitan mutations that remove traffic, use grade-separations, break the street-wall, or filter variety are doomed to failure because they break the logic of the street. Such bold post-war experiments in genetic engineering of the city have failed more often than they have succeeded, resulting in widespread urban sterility.

The street is not just another urban element, a toy from the typological box, but the essence of city-making itself. The making of streets with buildings is so essential to urban experience that all other design interventions pale by comparison. While a comprehensive review of all kinds of public open space is long overdue, we must not forget that streets are the most important zones for movement, orientation and repose; indeed, they are the essential urban room. Squares, gardens and monuments are only high-profile embellishments of an urban order and character set by the network of streets. If a new Canadian urbanism is to be forged, a matrix of ideas and policies that nurture and extend the street must be drafted. The time has passed for mild taxonomies (Eaton Centre catalogues) and dispassionate historical narratives (*As for Me and My City*). We need critical analysis of what has worked and what has not in our cities, criticism that is independent of immediate political, economic and stylistic vagaries.

This paper attempts that surprisingly difficult task. Streets **can** be made and **are** being made well, just as surely as they can be unmade. They are not solely historical artefacts to be preserved or replicated, and their destruction is often foisted by the finest of architects with the very best of intentions. What follows is a series of projects that variously break or make the Canadian street.

BREAKING THE STREET

1. Rideau Street Bus Mall, Ottawa

Ottawa has unfortunately won a reputation over the past three decades as a graveyard of discredited urban design concepts; mistakes are built later here (such as the removal of the downtown rail station and the malling of Sparks Street) with little learned from precedents. The sad story of the Rideau Bus Mall is an urban design disaster of the highest order, even for overfunded and underconsidered Ottawa.

Once the pre-eminent shopping boulevard of Lower Town east of the canal, Rideau Street has been in decline since the 1950s from the usual causes: competitions from suburban malls, bad marketing, aggressive tattiness and federal office relocations. In the late 1970s, a former railway marshalling yard at the point where the street meets the canal was proposed as the site for a regional shopping centre, seen to be the means to promote Rideau's revival. After a number of false starts, a design team including Ottawa's Griffiths, Rankin, Cook and Toronto's Diamond & Myers with Webb, Zerafa, Menkes, Housden was assembled to form the Rideau Centre project, as it became known, and its urban environs. Diamond & Myers proposed glazing the street under a galleria with traffic diverted to adjacent streets and bus traffic rechannelled under the complex. Sadly, this team and scheme were dumped during the ensuing political machinations and Toronto's Crang & Boake built a much less vigorous shopping centre along more typical lines.

With growing political activism in the Sandy Hill and Centretown areas uniting with a left-populist mayor in the person of Marion Dewar, the diversion of traffic from Rideau Street into these surrounding neighbourhoods became increasingly unpalatable. At the same time, the Sankey Partnership were engaged to propose design and traffic management strategies for Rideau Street, specifically asked to address the pressure from the shopping centre owners for a major transit terminus, as well as the desire of the merchants on the street to have the same environmental and visual amenities as inside the adjacent mall.

At first, the Sankey Partnership designed only bus shelters for the bus malled street, serviceable rounded glass and aluminum frames reminiscent of the bus mall street furniture erected in Portland, Oregon, in the 1970s. However, the street continued to decline throughout this period of political decision making, and as the remaining merchants became increasingly nervous, the earlier Diamond & Myers galleria proposal became an *idée fixe* among them. They sought and secured a vestige of this grand scheme in Sankey's final design. Sloping glass was simply added to the already-designed bus shelters to abut the second storeys of the largely Edwardian

1. Diamond & Myers galleria concept for the covering of Ottawa's Rideau Street, a concept that became an *idée fixe* for merchants on the street

buildings along the street. Continuous glass canopies with sliding glass walls were to provide a climate-tempered zone (only radiant heaters, not full air conditioning, were to be provided) along the sidewalks. These would mimic in both environmental and architectural terms the shopping mall idiom of Toronto's Eaton Centre and the adjacent Rideau Centre. While all the planning studies and Sankey himself had insisted that the scheme would fail without a major retail or hotel anchor at the eastern end of the two-block bus mall, these recommendations were ignored. As a result, Rideau Street was simply bus malled and expensively furnished.

2. The Sankey Partnership's design for continuous glazed canopies along Rideau as constructed. Doors close in winter, with interior radiant heaters to temper the climate. The canopies visually "knee-cap" the strip of Edwardian commercial buildings along Rideau, and create an indeterminate urban space, neither true street nor shopping mall

The banning of all traffic except buses from Rideau Street only accelerated its decline. The covered sidewalks emerged as strange urban creatures, neither fish nor fowl. They lack the vitality of a true street, on the one hand, and the comfort and convenience of a shopping arcade, on the other. While none of the adjacent buildings is of the first rank, the rhythm of windows and doors, and the decorative repertoire of voussoir and string courses is crudely violated by Sankey's canopies; the existing elevations are visually knee-capped by the canopies. The architectural code of the canopies themselves suggests a large and pricey bus shelter, rather than a grand urban space, and indeed they have been treated as such by the people of Ottawa. Drug dealers, skateboarders and the inebriated have predictably filled the vacuum of this revisionist urban space as retailing has gone decidedly down market or into bankruptcy. The five-million-dollar urban repair job on Rideau Street has gone dangerously wrong, and the mistake is all the more glaring in comparison to the increasing success of the adjacent Bytown Market, where a historical fabric of streets with traffic and uncovered open space prevailed.

What sets the Rideau Bus Mall apart from other troubled urban mutations in the recent history of Canadian cities is that it will be undone. At the time of writing, Ottawa City Council has voted to tear down the canopies and reintroduce traffic onto the bus mall, in short, to return to a state resembling a conventional street, the first reversal of an urban vasectomy in Canada. Before the Rideau Bus Mall has even been paid for through property assessments, it is being removed. Whether this is a signal event in Canadian urbanism — to be followed now by the dismantling of elevated walkway systems, ill-considered plazas and other crimes against the city — remains to be seen.

2. Portage Place, Winnipeg

A virtual museum of Edwardian architecture, Winnipeg boasts some of the most splendid period streetscapes in the country. Two former Assiniboine Indian trails define the key streets of the city, and their intersection — Portage and Main — is the most famous intersection in the country. Visitors from warmer climes (that is, everywhere but Iqaluit) have been astonished at the street-life that used to exist on Portage and Main at twenty degrees below. I remember standing on the north side of Portage

3. Winnipeg's Main Street near its intersection with Portage at the height of the pre–World War I immigration boom

4. Winnipeg's Portage Avenue, broken by the pedestrian bridges of the Portage development linking Eaton's with the Bay. The architectural detailing and loading of retail uses onto the Portage Place bridges only adds to their rupture of the urban room which is Portage Avenue

in 1982 and watching the native kids chattering in Ojibway as they ran from pinball parlour to fast-food joint in their shirt sleeves, curls of frozen exhaust giving the scene the atmospherics of *Blade Runner*. At the time, the *Winnipeg Free Press*, located just off Portage, was leading a campaign to "do something" about the leakage of inner-city poverty and urban native street-culture onto the city's most important boulevard. "Something" has indeed been done.

In the dubious cause of downtown revitalization, Winnipeg has recently used public funds to break one of the most famous streets in the country. The Winnipeg Core Initiative was sponsored by former Cabinet Minister and University of Winnipeg Urban Affairs Institute Director Lloyd Axworthy as a means of improving the social and physical environment of downtown Winnipeg. While many of the Core Initiative's programs are excellent — most notably the upgrading of the Historic Warehouse district, and a housing renewal and infill-building fund — its showpiece project, Portage Place, shows huge insensitivity to the city's most important street.

Portage Place is a downtown shopping centre on the Eaton Centre model. Land was assembled in the early 1980s along the north side of Portage Avenue, with the two poles of the retail force field located on the south side. This split was seen to require connection across the street. While a tunnel underneath was briefly considered, a bridge above it was chosen as more marketable, and as a result a magnificent wide street has been sliced twice.

The architectural detailing of the Portage Place bridges only adds to their distraction. The bridges are not orthogonal to Portage, but cross at an oblique angle, destroying the implicit room-like quality of the street. Contradictorily, after crossing the street with the minimum angle, the bridges were widened to include tacky retail shops, a soulless, T-shirted mimicry of the Ponte Vecchio in Florence. The mid-street structural support and the precast concrete detailing add to the heavy appearance of the bridges and visually truncate the street.

While the shopping mall has some interesting decorative flourishes along the Portage elevation, it is certainly no replacement for the lively collection of 1900 to 1913 buildings it replaced. Gestures toward the creation of retailing that faces onto Portage as well as the internal mall are too few in number and are subverted by retailers who care only about internal traffic. Pedestrian traffic along the north side of Portage is a fraction of its previous levels, and formerly healthy local businesses outside the hermetic island of Portage Place have begun to fail.

Portage Place has used huge federal subsidies to undermine one of the country's finest streets and to suck retail energy from the rest of downtown Winnipeg. With the finest of architectural and planning advisors and the tightest of scrutiny by three levels of politicians, Portage was broken in the quest to homogenize downtown Winnipeg into a bland and neutered vision of middle-class propriety. Winnipegers overreacted to the video arcades and urban natives who invaded the north side of their prime street in the early 1980s. Of course, the video arcades and natives are still there, but the visuals are much less threatening; they have been contained and filtered by the safe new paradigm of urban life, the shopping centre with its assuring flash and logos, its rhythm of escalators and "sidewalk" sales and its immutable typologies of food fairs and fashion floors. Portage Avenue has been the hapless victim in this misdirected battle of imagery.

3. Museum of Civilization, Quebec City

While elevated walkways, shopping centres and bus malls are new mutations of public urban space that threaten the street, the street can just as surely be broken by the misapplication of historicism. The Museum of Civilization in Quebec City was Moshe Safdie's first major commission in Canada since a variation of his McGill architecture thesis was constructed as Habitat at Expo'67 in Montreal. Designed in association with the well-connected Quebec City firms of Belisle, Brassard, Gallienne, Lavoie with Incesulu Desnoyers Mercure, the museum was to be a major nationalist showpiece for the former Parti Québécois government of René Lévesque. The design served as the test run for the blend of populist-historicism wedded to Kahnian structural expressionism that marks his current work, including the National Gallery of Canada, which was designed shortly thereafter, and Toronto's proposed Ballet-Opera House.

5. Moshe Safdie's Museum of Civilization in Quebec City, the architect's self-styled populism creating an unlikely conflation of Mediterranean village with motifs borrowed from French Canadian domestic and religious architecture

The historicism of the Museum of Civilization is of two types: reference to French Canadian domestic and religious architecture, redone in concrete and granite; and the appropriation of Mediterranean street-and-townscapes born of Safdie's youth in Haifa, Isreal. Inside, Safdie's detailing of the concrete structure makes explicit reference to French Canadian log building, while the roof structure and fenestration is a hugely overscaled variation on 18th- and 19th-century roofs in the area. On the exterior, Safdie's most astonishing device is a spire-like tower, whose similarity to parish churches of the same period is no accident. The employment of an architectural device borrowed from religious tradition for a showpiece building for a Quebec nationalist government can only mean the end of the Quiet Revolution, which in architectural terms was associated with anti-clericism and the most strident adoption of modernism in the country.

Safdie has laminated these devices to a meandering stair that rises, as if through a Mediterranean village, from the portside plaza over the building to the commercial street behind. While this could have worked like the ramped through-route of James Stirling's Staatsgalerie in Stuttgart, bad detailing has defeated much of its original purpose; because the pedestrian route is so close to gallery skylights, the path must be blocked at night for fear of vandals. It also begs the question why a picturesque element is needed in the midst of one of the richest townscapes in North America. As in most of Safdie's recent work, it is the appearance of populism, not populism itself, that is the driving ideology.

The detailing of the east, west and north elevations only accentuates this lack of fit with the Quebec City context. Safdie has imitated 18th-century window forms in Old Quebec, with similar proportions, sills and surrounds, but has enlarged them to ten times the traditional size. These windows satirize rather than harmonize with the surrounding buildings; like the steeple, roof and log detailing in concrete, they are a ham-handed attempt to please and to fit, but their insensitivity at scale and finish does neither. Safdie's Jerusalem work has given him a love of flush-jointed masonry, similarly detailed for both floor and wall. To have detailed masonry this way, on so large and internalized an institution as a museum, only exaggerates the differences between the new building and its older neighbours. The Museum of Civilization demonstrates that the street can be broken by misdirected historicism as it can by the new metropolitan mutations of bus malls, elevated walkway systems and shopping centres.

6. Safdie's pseudo-vernacular pedestrian path over the Museum of Civilization must be blocked at night because of its proximity to skylights and to exhibits

4. Queen's Quay, Harbourfront, Toronto

Seldom does a major city have the opportunity to design a major new street from scratch in one of its most desirable locations. The City of Toronto had that opportunity with Queen's Quay, the spine of the redevelopment of Harbourfront, and missed it, but not for lack of good intentions. While the Byzantine tale of the assembly and planning of Harbourfront cannot be retold here, the importance of Queen's Quay was clear from the late 1970s when the federal government announced the massive redevelopment of these extensive industrial lands by the water. Queen's Quay was to be transformed from a service road of an industrial port into the main street of a new neighbourhood that would provide an engaging mixture of cultural activities along with highly desirable housing. Early design studies by architect Michael Kirkland and others had proposed a neighbourhood street of a distinctly European flavour with continuous arcades and carefully modelled buildings defining a street that would be something between a Grand Boulevard and a Neighbourhood Collector. These proposals were vetted and distorted by traffic and municipal engineers, who have a degree of influence over the appearance of Canadian cities that is virtually unequalled

172

in the Western world. Just one of the many changes insisted on by the traffic engineers was the disfigurement of the new park, Spadina Gardens, to improve traffic flow. The result is an oddly shaped piece of land that George Baird has, nevertheless, managed to turn into a handsome small park.

As has often been said about Harbourfront, and can increasingly be said of all of Toronto, it was a victim of its own success. Its period of greatest expansion coincided with the beginnings of the current great building boom, and pressure for rapid approvals and shortened design time ever mounted. Only the most banal elements of the streetscape — carriageways, sidewalks and general massing of buildings — were used to control the burgeoning development along Queen's Quay. This "default option" in which civic engineering and expedient development generate the look of our streets is endemic to high-growth situations across the country. Because the municipal engineers speak in quantifiable tangibles, because they are insinuated deeply into the civic bureaucracy, and because of an endemic Canadian reverence for both authority and infrastructure, we have allowed even the highest profile of our streets to be shaped by these concerns, and these alone.

While patch jobs in the form of high-standard street furniture and landscaping are now being done, the potential for Queen's Quay was lost. Buildings on the north side of the street ramble irregularly, following their own architectural whims and the internal efficiencies of above-grade parking garages. Even the levels of arcades and podia were not co-ordinated, and the visual confusion is particularly embarrassing

7. Neighbourhood Collector or European Boulevard? Queen's Quay, with its traffic-engineered curves, near a condominium project by Arthur Erickson

considering how much was spent on urban design by the Harbourfront Corporation. The Harbourpoint Towers by developers Huang and Danzky have taken much of the criticism, but they are only the most dismal products of a failed urban design process. What Harbourfront needed to shape the chaos was a seeming contradiction in terms — a fine scale master planner. A senior urban designer with a good eye (they do exist) was needed with the powers to vet the details, arrange the transitions, arm-twist improvements in cladding, poke and cajole excellence out of architect, developer and engineer alike.

MAKING THE STREET

1. Granville Island, Vancouver

The success of the streetscape at Granville Island makes an excellent comparison with Queen's Quay. Both were major federal government initiatives to capture underutilized industrial land for urban uses on downtown waterside locations. Both had mixtures of retail, tourist, restaurant and cultural facilities along with mixed-income housing, and both proceeded through complicated negotiations involving three levels of government. The key difference is that the Vancouver architectural firm of Hotson & Bakker followed through the entire process, from earliest urban design concepts through to exterior renovations and signage changes years after the first phase opened.

The earliest of the second-generation downtown redevelopment schemes (the first generation being the disastrous post-war urban renewal), Granville Island was sponsored by former Cabinet Minister Barney Danson and senior CMHC staffer Ian MacLellen. A natural extension of the medium-density housing redevelopment of the south shore of False Creek, Granville Island was then the site of a tatty harbour-related industrial area underneath the abutments of the Granville bridge. Some of the industrial uses, like a concrete plant and boat manufacturers, were not movable, and it was decided that the industrial character would be maintained, even discretely enhanced. It took considerable effort on the part of architects and planners to maintain even the most decayed of the industrial sheds, especially when retail and restaurant success demanded a visual cleansing of the area. Many of the tin-clad post and beam buildings were maintained as parking buildings or sheltered workshops for artists and arts groups. Today, tastes have caught up with Granville Island, and now there is a problem of new businesses wanting all too eagerly to simulate the decayed industrial vocabulary.

Early on, Hotson & Bakker decided against pedestrianizing the island, feeling that the mixture of industrial, tourist, residential and pedestrian traffic could be managed by proper design. They developed an exquisitely simple system of bollards, rails, light stands, ground pavers and signage that were used in various combinations throughout the island. The system provides visual clues to orientate the public and

174

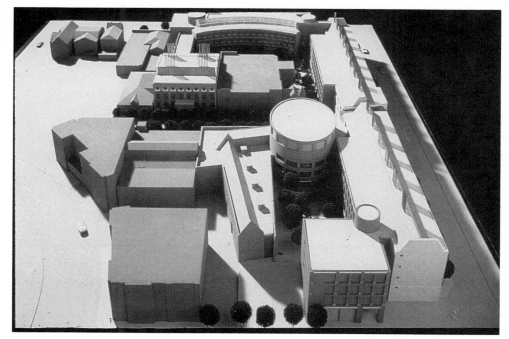

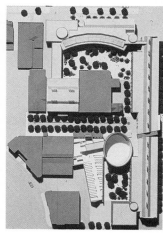

gently separates uses while visually tying the project together. The Hotson & Bakker design philosophy accepted the logic of the street and worked in an incremental and improvisatory way, deferring to its logic and visual clues.

Unlike the episodic binges of urban design studies commissioned by Harbourfront in Toronto, Hotson & Bakker stayed on as consultants after the basic infrastructure was in place and influenced thousands of tiny design decisions made for both private and government-controlled buildings and rights of way. Since the Second World War, both architects and the clients have tended to underemphasize the importance of aesthetic decision making about design; instead this essential craft has been repackaged in pseudo-science, so-so sociology or, more recently, mock-management theories. The ongoing enhancement of the streetscapes at Granville Island by Hotson & Bakker is a tribute to the unique contribution that the judgment of talented architects can bring to the renewal of an urban area.

2. Earth Sciences Building, University of Toronto

Since parting with former partner Barton Myers, Jack Diamond has slowly built Canada's most important architectural practice. Not since the glory days of Erickson's office in the late 1960s and early 1970s has so much expertise and design talent existed within one Canadian architectural firm. The largest project currently in the office is a massive complex for the University of Toronto, near Spadina Circle. The Earth Sciences Building will consolidate the departments of Botany, Forestry and Geology. The building will include offices and support services for nearly one hundred faculty members, a huge variety of teaching and research laboratories, graduate and undergraduate study areas and libraries, not to mention the largest lecture theatre on the campus. The Earth Sciences Building is strongly indicative of a predilection in the firm toward architectural and urban conservation, the careful deference to patterns of the street system and the creation of boldly defined urban "rooms" for public outdoor space.

Diamond and his partner Donald Schmidt fought long and hard to convince university authorities of the advisability of maintaining a group of Edwardian campus buildings on Spadina. The architectural centre of gravity has accordingly been displaced off the major street, withdrawing like a servant before these dowager-bitches in red brick. Closer to the centre of the site, another modest brick building is framed spectacularly by the new construction, its location at a hinge-point making the whole ensemble slyly read more as bit-by-bit elaboration than all-of-one-stroke megastructure. The essentially conservative character of the project masks the design skill that crafted it.

Architecturally, the Earth Sciences Building engages in the formal collision of platonic spatial elements such as drums, cubes and wedges that was already seen in the downtown Toronto YMCA and other projects of the office. While the perimeter displays the quiet conservative urbanism long associated with Diamond, within the block there is a mannered intersection of disparate shapes, the interstices of their overlap turned into foci by making them into arcades, oversized stairs, skylit atria and other indoor public spaces. There is a tension in both plan and section as quiet and generic uses like offices and laboratories are set against formally assertive elements for special uses like theatres and libraries; the zones between them have been made as contemplative spaces of relaxation and pause. That this internal complexity is reconciled with respect for the urban street pattern and existing buildings on the perimeter is a tribute to Diamond's team and a positive sign for a bold new urban architecture.

3. Main Street Program, British Columbia

While the building boom in central Canada has temporarily soured many architects on the heritage movement that they helped found in the 1970s, an excellent pro-street initiative can be found in Heritage Canada's Main Street Program. "The Queen City of the Kootenays" was chosen as one of the first sites for the program, and a decade after it began the program can be considered a clear success. Once a mining boomtown, Nelson has ridden the ebbs and flows of natural resource prices since its founding in the 1880s. The past decade has been particularly difficult, with the closing of several local mills, the termination of David Thompson University and the relocation of many provincial government offices away from a handsome town that dared vote for the wrong party. However, some new Nelsonians have taken advantage of the low costs for land and housing: first, a counter-culture wave from California in the early 1970s and more recently a "post-industrial" group ranging from writers, to software coders, to canasta-playing trailer park retirees. All of these were attracted by the town's combination of urban amenity and spectacular natural beauty. With Winnipeg now belatedly joining the demolition derby that has disfigured all other Western cities, Nelson remains the most unified collection of Edwardian architecture in Western Canada. Ranging from Francis Rattenbury's

10. Rodeo in boomtown: Baker Street in Nelson, British Columbia, c. 1920

11,12. Before and after views of Nelson's Burns Block

176

13. Baker Street today, an island of urbanity in the wilderness

sublime Court House of 1903, to the Burns Block — an exuberant example of what can only be called the Rodeo Style — to a fine neo-classical Catholic Church, Nelson had a distinguished, if decaying, building stock when Heritage Canada arrived.

After some preliminary studies, Heritage Canada hired several designer/co-ordinators to work with local businesses on Baker Street. Without indulging in a "great man" theory of history, I would suggest that the success of the Nelson program is in no small part due to the skill and determination of Robert Inwood and Hans Honegger. To their credit, they worked with, rather than against or on top of, the surprisingly subtle urban ecology of the street. Business upgrading and promotion was balanced with visual beautification, architectural restoration often becoming the means, rather than the ends, of the program. Such popular gestures as planters and benches were balanced with low-key renovation and advertising for Baker Street businesses. Unlike many American Main Street programs, which tend to over-emphasize tourist promotion and small business marketing, the architectural strengths of the street were constantly enhanced. Street furniture was crafted by newly trained locals, rather than bought, and free design services were offered to local merchants and building owners.

14. Post-modernism in lederhosen: nearby Kimberley, British Columbia's ethnic theme parking, with a Bavarian Esso station in the foreground, the Bavarian fire hall behind

While there were some slips into scenographic schmaltz, the design standard is surprisingly high, with a few key early projects demonstrating the renewed vision of the street clearly to all. The authenticity and urbanity of Nelson is striking, especially when compared with neighbouring towns that have indulged in the false ethnic historicism of "theme parking"; Kimberley has gone "Bavarian Revival" to promote its ski hill, while Osoyoos has remade itself "The Spanish Capital of Canada" despite there being absolutely no local historical or architectural connection to the colonial missions and explorers, and to the considerable disgruntlement of a significant local Portuguese-Canadian community. (Spanish and Bavarian were thought to be more marketable by Chamber of Commerce types than Portuguese and German.)

Baker Street is today an island of urban character in the wilderness, a vital symbolic and economic artery. While few other towns have Nelson's architectural treasures, most can learn from its respect for the inherent strengths of the street, both visually and economically. Heritage Canada could have spent its entire budget on a half dozen state-of-the-art historical restorations, but wisely chose instead to renew the street. Whether small town or big city, streets can be renewed, demonstrating how effectively they can continue to serve public culture.

4. Rue Ste-Catherine, Montreal

My last example has not had a name architect, has not been tied to an innovative program, has no singular look, theme or program. It has survived honky-tonk, urban renewal and megastructures. It will also likely survive being sliced by shopping centres and edged by boutiques as the latent vitality of Montreal explodes into built form. Ethnic nostalgia may prompt Mordecai Richler and Peter Rose to promote St-Laurent as the city's greatest street, St-Paul may have the finest ancient buildings, former Mayor Jean Drapeau's efforts to make Sherbrooke Street the Champs-Elysées may have created a discount La Défense, and the windswept but imperious Dorchester may have been renamed in favour of René Lévesque, but I feel that Ste-Catherine has no rival as the heart of Montreal. It is the public zone where all classes, all races, all languages come together in a happy, sometimes frenetic parade. It does not have a single outstanding building along its entire length, yet remains visually fascinating. It is the scene of a good-natured bumper-to-bumper *ballet mécanique* virtually any time of the day or night, even while wider and more splendid boulevards remain empty. No day, certainly no week, is complete for a Montrealer without a walk down some portion of its oversubscribed sidewalks, and most make the same choice as the McGarrigle Sisters: *"Moi je promène à Ste-Catherine."*

This is the street where the hockey teams play, where the buses leave for Toronto, the home of the Fouphone Électriques, the Étoile Des Indes, the Canadian Centre for Architecture, the Théâtre du Nouveau Monde and the largest credit union in the world. Ste-Catherine prospers while Toronto's Yonge Street is in decline, no longer the location of the *corrida*, implicitly bifurcating into sub-zones territorily marked "tourist," "rough trade," "gay," "rock and roll," "upmarket" or "highway out of town," and now treated by Mayor Eggleton as just another traffic path. While Winnipeg's Main Street once knew similar vitality, and Vancouver's Robson Street will know it soon, Ste-Catherine is this country's most overwhelmingly human and most irrepressibly vital street.

Ste-Catherine has remade itself during every generation over nearly three hundred years, the residual strength of its urban genes triumphing over all forms of environmental stress. For Canadians, the street **is** public open space, and the new metropolitan mutations can only be considered more or less healthy curiosities, genetic diversions from these fecund pools of information on city-dwelling. Like many of the finest Canadian virtues, the quality of our streets is often obscured by their conservatism, their incremental evolution from banal beginnings. We have been too slow to recognize the strength of Canadian streets, and our architects have been too willing to import exotic urban creatures. I wrote the following words eight years ago in the *Architectural Review* about Calgary's +15 pedestrian system and I believe in them today: "The street, that ancient but subtle invention, imposes its order, even on those brash young cities who choose to ignore it."

Nan Griffiths

Paradise is a strange land but a familiar presence; few have been there, but many people have an idea of what it is like... a garden at one end of time and a city at the other.

William McClung, *The Architecture of Paradise*

One may wonder what Paradise and Confederation Square in Ottawa have in common, and particularly, what Paradise has to do with the theme of emergent or mutant public space in Canada. The idea of mutation contained in this paper is a simple one; not so much the cataclysmic transformations effected on traditional urban morphologies by elements such as shopping centres and expressways, but the idea that urban space should help us to remain in touch with the cultural particularities that make us different from the Americans and/or any other nation. The paper is therefore about the way that we as Canadians feel about space and the ways in which its formal structuring could express our national and regional essence.

Confederation Square, spatial centre of the national capital, is a symbol of the civilization of Canada as a single country. The paradisal dream, "where immaterial vision and a material structure or system of relationships are brought together,"[1] has been the symbolic inspiration of civilized existence throughout history. The form of public urban space is inevitably a reflection of civilized values and thus related to the paradisal dream.

During the past eight years I have been responsible for the direction of a series of largely academic projects in the City of Ottawa in search of an "architecture of

1. Confederation Square seen from the bridge over the Rideau Canal

Canadian space," both sacred (Crown) and profane (town). Two Canadian squares and a number of linked discoveries of perception centred the search. Confederation Square, omnipresent in Ottawa, mildly boring but mysteriously provocative as the greatest non-square in the world, sets itself in dialogue with Toronto City Hall Square as a great modernist spatial phenomenon.

Further, a personal childhood view of Canadian history as excruciatingly dull, thanks to abysmally uninspiring texts and teachers, was blissfully displaced after reading Susanna Moodie's pioneer accounts of early settlement in a sublime and fearful landscape. The thesis work of a former student[2] in making connections between Canadian literature, painting and architecture opened my eyes to the work of the Group of Seven as a bold penetration of a previously romanticized and distanced landscape; the intersections between these cosmological artistic positions and the literary perceptions of some of our great writers suggested a powerful direction for the discourse on architecture and the city.

Finally, William McClung's book on *The Architecture of Paradise* coalesces the metaphorical associations between identity, place making, the paradisal dream and utopic architecture, and thereby reinforced the essential proposition that principles of space should be particular to place and time.

The simple mutation is offered as a potentially powerful and dialectical alternative to the seemingly popular but falsely manipulative contemporary "market square." In my most optimistic moments, I believe that Canadians are not irrevocably caught in the destiny of shopping centres and +15 systems as the ultimate Garden of Eden, but that there is still something of the freedom-loving spirit of the Western settler whose views of Eden were expressed by the exclamation, "O, the prairie...can you imagine being able to hear silence? I have stood outside alone and listened — absolute quiet prevailed. It filled the air. It must have been like the Garden of Eden, I think."[3]

Confederation Square and the paradisal dream come together as an issue because our grip on civilized existence is slippery, for the many reasons to be touched on in this conference: pluralities and complexities, consumerism, loss of spiritualism, narcissism, the physical disorientation or negative mutations of urban morphologies and social orders.

As we approach what appears to be the threshold of a national wave of spatial development of different kinds, we should remind ourselves of the Aristotelian precept that the real purpose of cities is the material **and** spiritual comfort and happiness of humanity. The inspirational factor of all paradisal and utopian concepts is the eternal quest for happiness and goodness, the search for a holistic and cosmological relationship between society, nature and craft. Notwithstanding the pervasiveness of current mutations, (to subvert Gertrude Stein's poetic rose) a human being is a human being is a human being, and these trends are surely waves of evolution like the other great waves of evolution in the history of continuing civilization.

We should, therefore, consider the ultimate futility of symbolic urban spaces, such as Confederation Square, that do not make some spiritual and cultural connection to our physical and mental environment, that do not assist in the construction of existential identity. Of course, the understanding of the city as a dwelling place of artistic and ideological importance, so fundamental to the history of Western culture, was undermined by the changes in scale, technology, industry and materiality that were initiated in the 18th century, changes ratified and symbolized by the 1747 establishment in Paris of civil engineering as a profession separate from architecture and dedicated to design by scientific calculation.

Since that time, urbanity and the appreciation of genius loci have been eroded by the singular orientation of planner/engineers, the transformation of building into market ventures of massive scale and financial transaction, the persuasiveness of the suburban dream and, of course, doctrinaire modernism. In spite of the pedestrian and citizen's revolutions of the last two decades, the physical development of the Canadian city is still fundamentally directed by the planner, the transportation engineer and the developer; the visually and culturally uneducated. The loss is clearly manifest in the mediocre or downright ugly roadworks and bridges, extremely insensitive urban road accoutrements, such as signage and lighting. "If beauty ceases to be the primary intention of a civilized world, ugliness will be its ineluctable outcome."[4]

The theme of this conference is a summary signal that the issue of positive urban space has begun to touch the public consciousness, in other words, that Canadians are approaching urban maturity and outgrowing the frontier exigencies of survival. There are many signs to indicate that we are ready to receive some greater gratification from the architecture of our public space and buildings. The public ecstasy that greeted the recent opening of the National Gallery in Ottawa is evidence of a universal, deep-seated need to be stirred by the built environment. Perhaps the most interesting aspect of the opening hype was that "everyone" was talking about architecture.

Confederation Square, like the National Gallery, is a spatial monument of national importance, and as such it offers itself as a testing ground in the search for significant and Canadian urban space. With a unique siting at the centre of the capital, the junction of the two Canadas, and on the edge of the wilderness, it is an achingly open, provocatively inarticulate tablet. The obelisk presence of the War Memorial makes it a central reference for the collective Canadian conscience (if only we could hear it). As such it offers a potent setting for the exploration of the Canadian dream and of our political and cultural values, as Northrop Frye contends in *The Bush Garden*: "Identity is local and regional, rooted in the imagination and works of culture," but "there are imaginative forms common to the whole country which bind us together," such as, for example, the simple "seasonal factor of latitude."[5] The Square is a symbol of this unity, of the remarkable act of federation; even its physical character is analogous to the sparsely inhabited landscape.

2/3. This view of the Brigham Family, Hull, c. 1890 (personal collection of author) shows the beginnings of a new paradisal dream specific to the Canadian experience, and indebted to the European romantic tradition as represented by Edouard Manet's "Déjeuner sur l'Herbe" of 1863

To say that it is to architects as the Holy Grail was to Arthur is probably an exaggeration. This most significant of urban spaces has, however, eluded satisfactory definition through generations of "official" as well as speculative projects since the first explicitly City Beautiful plan of Holt/Bennett in 1915.

Thus the site still offers a challenge to those who believe that there are untapped desires in the Canadian urban dream that are not satisfied by the simulated public space of the ubiquitous climate and brain controlling shopping centre. Our 19th-century spatial remnants, such as Dominion Square in Montreal and the Public Gardens in Halifax, are still welcome parts of the urban experience, but they hardly offer a Canadian paradigm for the late 20th century. The open space interventions of the last three decades in most of our cities vacillate between spiritless landscapes of pink interlock paving, concrete planters, nostalgic bench and lamp standards, and the highway landscape of public engineering vigilantly asserting the ascendance of vehicular accommodation as the pre-eminent 20th-century form.

The pink landscape is, of course, preferable to the latter, but is generally non-provocative, without the least metaphoric association or memorability. Few have found a means of moving beyond the early modernist rejection of context to a reinterpretation of its form and meaning in the making of 20th-century space that reflects its particular genius loci.

The problem is not uniquely Canadian, but is common to many countries, even those with well-defined and sustained urban traditions. In Canada, however, we have a conservative view of public presence; until very recently our public spaces, such as the park systems, have been frequented primarily by newly arrived immigrants. The wide open spaces and the promise of a private paradise (cottage, lake and canoe) are too much to resist. This is one of the obvious reasons that we have developed so few imaginative or significant models of public space.

We need to take something from countries whose deeper urban traditions advance more confidently the cause and judgment of imaginative work in our own era. The Parisian "Grand Projects" of François Mitterrand (and others) are indicators of a dynamic and visionary renaissance of art, architecture, spirit and, no surprise, economy. I. M. Pei's startling and elegant glass pyramid renews the historic fabric and composition of the Louvre and recognizes the importance of vitality in continuity. The "people's" park at La Villette, the result of an international competition, is an extraordinary spatial concept. Its complex cinematographic narrative promises paradise for a day; it is a superb combination of imagination, wit, comprehension, architectural control and populist appeal.

The current wave of creative municipal policies was set in motion by the administration and architectural zeal of Oriol Bohigas, appointed head of Barcelona's planning department in 1982, who, "against current city planning practice, gave priority to architecture over engineering."[6] The Spanish projects, which pursued a systematic inhabitation of the leftover spaces of the city and the refurbishment of the

old, have set an example of civic design in the 1980s. Explicitly non-mimetic and free of revisionist escapism into "paradises of the past, they are fragile constructions, without either rhetoric or a false sense of certainty, of the present."[7] The spaces satisfy the prosaic accommodation requirements of the particular place. At the same time "avant-garde" in materials and form, they carry metaphoric messages about the state of the art and society, which may or may not be permanent, but must nonetheless be a morally recordable stage in their evolution.

However, we are not without some examples of spatial invention. One of the most important inspired civic structures of the century is undoubtedly Viljo Revell's competition-winning Toronto City Hall and Square of 1958. A Finnish reading of Canadian landscape and rising urban culture, this is a civic offering of unique architectural brilliance — unequivocally modern, yet an urban ensemble that satisfies traditions of spatial definition, generates ritual and social dynamics and resonates with symbolic imagery. The Square is dominated by the curving elements of City Hall itself; its focal points include the three parts of a triumphal arch, soaring above a people's paradisal pool or winter skating rink. The garden wall is powerful but minimal, a simple band of concrete that contains the spirit and eye, creating space both finite and place-centred, yet permitting a secondary flow between inside and out; focus and expansion all at once.

Revell's powerful composition seems to be a direct transplanting of the spirit of the landscape into an urban form. Lawren Harris's reductive interpretations of this land — vast, open, brooding, abstract forms — are the cosmological force of this architectural space. It is a complete urban statement, an invention that seems totally in tune with the New World and the dynamic open-endedness that was the inspiration of so much of modernist polemic and architectural creativity.

As a manifestation of a search for authenticity in the making of urban space in Canada, it is worth mentioning the modest square opposite Toronto's Ryerson Polytechnical Institute. A corner site, without wall or gate, a faintly druidical cluster of well-proportioned rocks around a pool, also skating rink, it is a somewhat literal miniature wilderness park, but has a distinct urbanity and is explicitly a **Canadian** urban oasis.

We should mourn the shelving of the 1984 Montreal "Fountains" competition, which brought forth a new wave of architectural statements mostly from young architects, which were powerful and memorable because they fused a modernist/futurist spirit with situational imagery and conceptual narrative. Many of the works conveyed

4/5. Viljo Revell's powerful composition of square and City Hall in Toronto (1964) seems to be a direct transplanting of the spirit of the landscape into an urban form; Lawren Harris's reductive interpretation of this land as vast, open, brooding and abstract forms is the cosmological force of this architectural space. Shown here is Harris's "Iceberg, Davis Strait," 1930

a sense of both primal and intervened landscape.[8] We should promote a more widespread and serious interest in the kind of projects produced in the exhibition "Toronto Interotta" of 1986, for example the intriguing architecture of road intersection by McKay, Pearce and Soules.[9]

All these projects present architectural and ideological positions, interpretations, challenges or critiques of Zeitgeist. What is important is the recognition of the necessity for search in the making of architecture and urbanism. Obviously we cannot endow all our emergent spaces with industrial imagery or great rocks and forms from the landscape of the Group of Seven. These projects do suggest, however, that architects are most effective when they engage sites and relevant issues through a cultural framework. The combination of national, cultural and literary searches are what made the works of our great writers, like Northrop Frye and Margaret Atwood, so significant in a world context.

Set in dialectical counter-position to this visionary urbanism of Montreal and Toronto is the Capital City itself, paradisal model for the scattered regions of the country and central reference of the values and matters of conscience that distinguish us from our American neighbours.

Like Washington, Ottawa is the face-in-the-jar by the door, a nostalgic or front parlourish image of a nation of diverse realities. Manfredo Tafuri, in his *Architecture and Utopia*, calls Jefferson's idealized anti-urban utopia the "bad conscience" of America[10] — a city as a monument to the nostalgia for European values, while the rest of the country was destroying these values through its powerful press toward economic and industrial development. The willful image of the people is centred on an axis and given the form of shining white temples in the landscape.

Not so the capital of Northrop Frye's "thrifty little heaps of civilized values,"[11] the sublime landscape that both delighted and terrified Susanna Moodie. The Canadian settler was "inspired by tradition and history and a mild-mannered desire for land and peace."[12] The immigrants' search above the 49th parallel for a New Jerusalem led them to a vast, tangled, dense, terrifying and largely uninhabited landscape — indifferent and silent. In *Pax Britannica*, James Morris explained that, as part of the "Divine Order," which made Britain supreme and Victoria sixty years a Queen, the moral confidence of the Empire allowed the Canadian settler "to respond to the vicissitudes of pioneer life in a stoic [and modest] manner," with practicality, diligence and energy, in both survival and play. Non-Darwinian, the Canadian settlers "rejected the freewheeling individualism to be found in the United States," and the general idealization of the idea of progress.[13]

When these Upper Canadian migrants carved their spaces from the landscape and introduced their own vision of paradise, it was shaped by the moral vision of the British Raj, but without the notions of governorship and patronage. The nostalgic and picturesque communitarian forms of neo-Gothicism suited the spirit of adventure that inspired individuals in the name of the Empire, the community, or the

184

6. The offset junction of the parliamentary axis with the street grid of Ottawa seems an eloquent manifestation of the deep-seated instinct of personal freedom and thematic empiricism inherited from the British part of our founding cultures. Photo c. 1889-95

collection of communities.

If in our homesteading we cut back and subdued the forests, in our symbol of national centre we followed our instincts for the sublimity of the landscape, choosing a "sacramental site" in the Greek founding convention. Our national imagery does not sustain axial conventions of urban order. The offset junction of the parliamentary axis with the street grid of Ottawa seems an eloquent manifestation of the deep-seated instinct of personal freedom and thematic empiricism inherited from the British part of our founding cultures.

The capital city offers a paradigmatic idea, therefore, of the adage "to thine own self be true." Italo Calvino's statement that "every city has an implicit program, something which distinguishes it and gives it meaning" underwrites the message of the unique and unmistakable humanity offered by the capital to the rest of the country.

Apart from the implicit spiritual communitarianism of the neo-Gothic forms, humanity comes from the directional empiricism of its growth, the lack of rhetoric in the development of its form and order, the insistence of landscape in its midst.

Unlike the ad hoc, entrepreneurial and dynamic Toronto, the paternal hand of successions of federal planners has ensured for Ottawa a hierarchical imagery almost as succinct as, say, Florence. The cathedral of God is replaced by the cathedral of democratic power; the market squares lie below in sundry typological form, the palaces of culture are caught in the landscape edge. Its conspicuous spatial systems link wilderness, state, municipality and neighbourhood.

However, notwithstanding the importance of maintaining the integrity of this communitarian sensitivity and unique capital imagery, Ottawa is suffering from a lack of vital, dynamic, 20th-century relevance. The industry-less capital is hovering on the edge of paradisal identity and the surreality of a 19th-century Disneyland of the North. Western drought and the commercial inevitability of MacMillan Bloedel's take of seven-hundred-year-old virgin spruce make no visible ruffle on the city beautiful. And I have a feeling they should.

Finally, returning to the hierarchical spatial centre of the city and the focus of this paper: the elusive Confederation Square and its configural challenge.

Set in the confident persuasiveness of the communitarian, Gothic imagery of its site, the amorphous triangle of the Square is a shock, an apparent anomaly among the predominantly medieval forms and picturesque landscape. Raw and open, a monument to the heroes and heroines of modern wars as its centre of gravity, it crowns the intersection of grid, canal and landscape which is the meeting of the Upper and Lower towns. It lacks most of the traditional characteristics of an urban place. It has little enclosure, its definition is a residue of traffic planning, and its logical points of access are legally inaccessible to pedestrians.

Its position in the traffic and urban morphology, the lack of articulate boundaries and its sloping configuration make this as challenging a site as that facing

7. The bridging of the Rideau Canal eventually led to the formation of Confederation Square

8. Aerial view of Confederation Square, Rideau Canal, Parliament Hill and Wellington Street

185

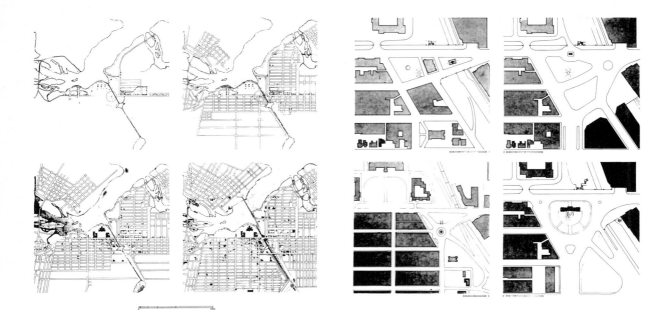

9. Confederation Square evolution in city/regional context, based on: (top left) Map of Upper & Lower Bytown by John Burrows, O.W., 1831; (top right) Map of Ottawa & Vicinity by W. A. Austin & Co., Engineers & Architects, c. 1857; (bottom left) Map of Ottawa & Vicinity by Woodburns Directory, c. 1877; (bottom right) Map of Ottawa & Vicinity by Cauchon & Haycock, Consulting Engineers, c. 1912 (author's project, drawings by M. Glassford)

10. Confederation Square evolution of design proposals, drawings based on: (top left) Plan showing location of proposed National Monument in Conaught Place by Department of Public Works/T. W. Fuller, Architect, c. 1924; (top right) Confederation Place Proposal by N. Cauchon, Architect, c.1928; (bottom left) Confederation Square Area by J. Greber, Architect, c. 1937; (bottom right) Confederation Square by J. Greber, Architect, c. 1938 (author's project, drawings by M. Glassford)

Michelangelo as he approached the reinvention of the Roman Campidoglio in the 16th century. Confederation Square's monument has one day of glory in a year, the November Remembrance Day ceremony. On July 1 it becomes a scene of collective and joyous self-affirmation when the monument is forced to participate in an act of life. For 363 days of the year, the Square fails to exploit the message of the monument or Confederation, and further, is socially uninviting.

The first impulse in trying to transform it into a coherent urban space is a sort of knee-jerk instinct to enclose it and shut out the landscape, if not the climate. As soon as serious enclosure is proposed, however, one begins to appreciate the spiritual openness that the site embodies and the somewhat cautious sense of adventure that it conveys; the echoes of the determined communitarianism of our ancestors.

The Square, like the city, is on the edge of the wilderness. The northwest side of its vast sweep has a direct visual link with the Gatineau Hills in the distance; on the south, the dynamic movement of Colonel By's canal. It is an urban site like no other.

The current proposal of the National Capital Commission (NCC) for Confederation Square treats it as a node in the proposed Ceremonial Route that would link Ottawa with its sister city Hull on the Quebec side of the Ottawa River. Route is, once again, to take precedence over place. In this proposal, presently on hold, Sparks Street is extended to become a continuous plateau (pink, in fact) with the Square. All traffic is rerouted to a two-way system between the Square and the east-lying bank of the canal.

From the modest body of non-official projects, I include the ideas and several drawings of my own and of three young Ottawa architects who participated in an ideas "charrette" in the summer of 1987. I pursued my own abiding interest in the space with a brief but intense project search in 1984. All my deeply felt views were poured into the designs, and I have to say that every idea I had came to the surface and vied for expression; its seems that distillation will have to wait.

All of our projects leave the present circulation of the Square in place, as the dynamic experience of this centre is both pedestrian and vehicular. If the assumption that the obvious points of pedestrian access should be given priority seems like wishful thinking in our road engineer-dominated region, the arguments for

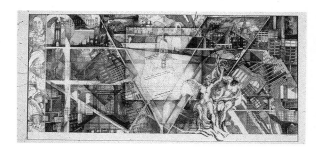

11. "Echoes of the Square," Nan Griffiths, 1984

appropriate coexistence in the ritual centre of the capital should persist and be reinforced. In the project of the NCC mentioned above, they have been obliged to move pedestrians below grade.

The ideas of my young colleagues generally exhibited a fascination with the monument itself and questioned the effectiveness of its forms and setting to convey its meaning to younger generations. A proposal by Steve Pope, for example, challenges the specificity of the monument and proposes to extend its message over the site. A chapel inhabits the subterranean void below the Square's bridging platform; the book that contains the names of Canadian victims to war and is currently housed in the parliamentary Peace Tower is relocated in the chapel. Stripped of its angels and soldiers, the monument has become a headstone ("next time there will be no heroes to walk through the triumphal arch").

A project by Mark Bunting confronts the concepts of memory, time and Confederation. The central geometry of the Square has been maintained, added are urban structures representing permanent dialectical personae for the Square: the Keepers — three columns with internal flames for the survivors of the two world wars and the Korean war, the flames being ignited only with the passing of the last known survivor of the respective conflict; the Watchers — guardian representatives of the ten provinces and two territories; and Security — a transient urban construction by New York architect John Hedjuck in the southern section of the Square, a visiting observer.

My own perception of the Square does not, like those of my young colleagues, include the extension of the monument's energy, but establishes a larger agenda; a hierarchical order, which although preserving an acropolytic centre, invites both social occupation and contemplation of the sense and structuring of nationhood. It is tempting to consider moving the monument elsewhere; back to Major's Hill Park where its siting was once considered, but then, what would take its place as a national "obelisk"?

In my search I used the elements of the Canadian wilderness to signify the reluctant urbanism of the capital city: the journey from sea to sea, the mountains of the West, the plains, the shield, the forests and the lakes. They are used physically to establish the place as a series of theatrical platforms dropping down from Parliament to the canal.

The provinces and two territories are represented by menhirs that contain the names of their war dead. The grid represents the meeting of rural and urban settlement and the circumstances of topography; the superimposed cross axis represents the true north, strong and free. The southern point of the triangle is deflected off the axis of Elgin Street, the only monumental axis in the city, and holds a bronze marker displaying the principal plans for Ottawa, the dead-ended parliamentary axis and a tribute to empiricism. A circular order expresses unity and attempts to diffuse the site's triangularity.

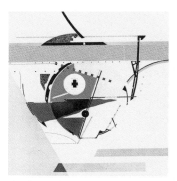

12. "Crown, Town and Canal, Upper and Lower Ottawas," Nan Griffiths, 1984

In urban terms the intention was to give a sense of "being in" without destroying the open sweep by the construction of plateaus and low walls, which would also appear as base "facades" to the monument from Elgin and Rideau streets. In contrast to Greber's proposal to create a dense vegetal and symmetrical backdrop to the monument, density is achieved through the asymmetrical reorientating of the triangular site with the elements of the landscape narrative.

I have, in this paper, attempted to address the importance of setting ideals in the development of significant and contemporary urban space in Canada. The fascinating diversity of potential spatial types being discussed in this conference begs our commitment to the setting of vision and the articulation of essential cultural values within each place or system. Without agendas and contemporary interpretations, the art of place making is reduced to trivial gesture.

I suggest that it is important to open the discourse on this critical aspect of urban design and call on the federal government to stage an open national, or even international, design competition for Confederation Square. It should be more than a "node." The greatest urban spaces of the world were didactic and spoke of ideologies, mythological or aesthetic issues. It is our responsibility as architects to show informed leadership in the shaping of the public realm or we will lose the waiting palette of urban space entirely to gardeners, planners, developers and/or traffic engineers, all of whom, by the nature of their training, are likely to bring forward myopic, single-aspect solutions.

For this we need to be cognizant of urban spatial principles and typologies, be prepared to push boundaries and promote visionary understanding. We need also to take a stand as a profession to bring some balance to the current practice of architectural selection in public projects. Fresh ideas rarely come from closed competitions; it is unimaginable that Toronto City Hall, or La Villette Park in Paris could have emerged from the sterile processes of the invidious Proposal Call, with its emphasis on cost-effectiveness and political manipulation. Compared to Paris and Barcelona, our own founding past and the energy of our present cultural mosaic, the political will of Ottawa is dull and short-sighted.

Notes

[1] William McClung, *The Architecture of Paradise* (Berkeley: University of California Press, 1983), p. 1.

[2] John Edwards, "Architecture in a Sublime Landscape," Carleton University Research Thesis, 1981.

[3] Linda Rasmussen, Lorna Rasmussen, Candace Savage and Anne Wheeler, *A Harvest Yet to Reap* (Toronto: The Women's Press, 1976), p. 32.

[4] Leon Krier "Plan for the Athens-Piraeus Motorway Exchange," *Lotus 31* (Milan, 1981), p. 79.

[5] Northrop Frye, *The Bush Garden* (Toronto: House of Anansi, 1971), p. ii.

[6] Odile Henault, *Section A*, Vol. 3, No. 3 (Montreal, 1985).

[7] Ignasi de Sola Morales, "Civic Art Against the Functional City," *Lotus 39* (Milan, 1986).

[8] Ruth Cawker, "The Forgotten Gesture," *Section A*, Vol. 3, No. 1 (Montreal, 1985).

[9] Graham Owen, "Toronto Interrupted," *Section A*, Vol. 3, No. 1 (Montreal, 1985).

[10] Manfredo Tafuri, *Architecture and Utopia* (Cambridge, Mass: MIT Press, 1976), p. 34.

[11] Frye, p. 138.

[12] Quoted in Edwards.

[13] Quoted in Edwards.

SUBURBAN INTENSIFICATION

Kenneth Greenberg, in collaboration with Robert Maguire

1. Introduction

The physical manifestations of early suburban growth in Canada, while similar to
that of the United States, resulted from different social and economic conditions. In
the second stage of suburban growth, the political and policy environment in Canada
has encouraged the establishment of suburban subcentres as a means of deflecting
growth away from the city centre.

1. "Your World of Tomorrow," New York World's Fair, 1939

The physical form that post-war suburbs initially took was clearly anticipated in
the exhibition the "World of Tomorrow" at the 1939 New York World's Fair. This
highly dispersed, low-density pattern of separated land uses was served by an elaborate road hierarchy. Public spaces, in the historic sense, did not exist in this pattern.

In the second stage of suburban growth, this low-density, homogeneous and
dispersed pattern is being substantially altered at certain points in ways that strongly
suggest urban characteristics: high densities, an intense mix of uses, and increased
pedestrian activity in public spaces connecting several destinations. There is increasing evidence that these suburbs, which many imagined to be permanent, distinct and
non-urban, are actually new cities in the making. In fact, there are many analogies to
be drawn between this second-generation suburbia and the European faubourgs of
the 19th century.

This paper sketches the evolution of two emergent suburban subcentres in
Metropolitan Toronto from the perspective of both policy and physical planning as
well as development. The purpose is to illustrate how different forms of suburban

growth present particular problems and opportunities for the creation of true urban
patterns. The initial reasons for the emergence of suburban subcentres are explored
and reveal the strong role played by public policy in establishing the new suburban
"downtowns." The physical impediments to the development of more urban forms
will be identified along with local initiatives, which illustrate both the transformation
of suburban values and the physical design problems that are encountered when low-
density suburban environments evolve into medium-to-high-density urban environments.

Before examining these current examples, however, it is worthwhile to observe
a concrete example of this phenomenon of "intensification" in the city's recent
history. The intersection of Yonge Street and Eglinton Avenue in the City of Toronto
was surrounded by a low-density fabric of houses until the 1950s when the subway
was introduced. Then, as was the case at a number of similar locations, the subway
exerted a powerful influence, creating a "node," which now has a population of tens
of thousands living and working within walking distance, and an increasingly rich and
varied array of urban functions.

In this example, the first wave of dense urban buildings, which were constructed adjacent to the subway station, were externally awkward and crude. No attempt
was made to relate these buildings to the existing fabric, which was seen as entirely
expendable. No significant new public spaces were created. At a certain point,
however, the intensity and abruptness of this change triggered a reconsideration of
the appropriate density, form and extent of redevelopment. More recently, Yonge and
Eglinton has begun to "fill in" at an intermediate scale and to change in character,
particularly in the way that new and renovated buildings are now relating to the
public sidewalks. With the knowledge that such transformation can occur in relatively short periods of time, we now face the challenge of planning and designing the
new suburban subcentres.

2. The Politics and Planning of Urban Growth in Toronto: Nowhere to Turn but the Suburbs

In order to examine the emerging physical form of suburban subcentres in Metropolitan Toronto it is necessary to begin with a brief overview of the political pressures that began to mount in the late 1960s and early 1970s, and the subsequent
planning policy framework that emerged in the mid-1970s. This historical context

will help us to understand the reasons behind the growth of subcentres as a regional phenomenon. But more important, for our purposes, it will provide us with a policy framework within which to study the physical form of subcentre evolution.

Fight for the 19th-century City

In Toronto, the impetus for suburban subcentre growth was provided by a strong, negative political reaction to what was seen as "overdevelopment" in the central city. As in many North American cities, the 1950s and 1960s in Toronto were characterized by the rapid development of high-rise buildings. Urban renewal was in fashion among the planners and politicians. The low-density Victorian and Edwardian residential neighbourhoods, which remained the predominant urban form in Toronto's central area, were being threatened by the development of high-rise apartment buildings.

The predominantly three-storey, street-related houses, which characterized the inner-city neighbourhoods and had been adapted for commercial uses along the commercial streets, were the target of redevelopment. Having experienced "degentrification" in the post-war period, these previously upper- and middle-income neighbourhoods were considered ready for redevelopment.

The City government aided this seemingly imminent transformation of the central city into a high-density regional service centre through a permissive Official Plan. This Plan was adopted in 1969 and encouraged high-density residential development to replace the earlier Victorian city fabric. Local service functions were ignored in favour of high-density, homogeneous use districts and specialized business centres. As well, the completion of the Metropolitan Expressway system was projected to destroy many existing residential neighbourhoods. The federal government's taxation and housing policies also aided this process of urban renewal through a series of tax incentives that encouraged the development of high-rise apartments and subsidized low-income housing.

Unlike many American cities, however, a significant portion of the middle class, which wielded considerable political power, continued to reside in neighbourhoods adjacent to the commercial centre of the city. A different social structure did not lead to the creation of a ghettoized non-white urban underclass in Canada and attenuated another factor in the American flight to the suburbs.

But, with the implementation of the planning policies of the 1960s the official and moral edifice of urban renewal began to crumble. The high-rises of St. Jamestown and Regent's Park and the numerous apartment towers that began to appear in low-rise neighbourhoods throughout the city enraged those directly affected. A groundswell of public resistance to development and growth began to emerge and by 1972 achieved the stunning defeat of local politicians who were pro-development and the election of a reform City Council that promoted liberal and social democratic values.

The political and social "elites" who continued to live and work in the City supported the reform Council and their policy of neighbourhood conservation, for in some cases it was their own neighbourhoods that stood to be razed by transportation and urban renewal projects. A new Central Area Plan was finally adopted in 1976 following four years of public controversy about the future of the central city. During these years, the public began to understand the consequences of urban redevelopment and to appreciate the architecture and urban fabric of the 19th and early 20th century. Community groups also began to recognize that they could, if organized, change the course of urban planning in Toronto.

A Plan for Deconcentration
The Central Area Plan of 1976 for the City of Toronto not only established local land use and transportation policies for the city centre, but by implication provided a policy framework for a metropolitan urban strategy. Although no overall metropolitan plan existed at the time, the politics of planning in the City of Toronto, along with regional transportation pressures, were the antecedents of a new regional planning policy. The previously held policy of centralized growth was reversed in favour of a multi-centred urban structure supported by a good regional transit system.

The new plan was strongly conservationist and promoted the preservation of inner-city neighbourhoods and historic buildings and the revitalization of traditional shopping streets. The regional function of the city centre was to be limited in order to give priority to the accommodation of local service functions. Mixed-use developments were encouraged both within and surrounding the financial core. But the primary means to preserve the downtown neighbourhoods was the diversion of population growth to suburban subcentres by limiting the development of office space in the central area and refusing to improve the road and highway network that linked the downtown with the periphery.

While it took a number of additional years for the implications of this initiative by the City to be absorbed into the planning framework for the metropolitan region, the political benefits of deconcentration were clear. The strong anti-development groups in the inner-city neighbourhoods were, for the most part, satisfied. But equally important, suburban municipalities, which had until then served as dormitories for Toronto, were offered a commercial tax base for the first time. In the suburbs, local politicians welcomed growth and resident groups were less resistant to new development.

A New Multi-centred Metropolitan Structure
Between 1976 and 1980, the current metropolitan planning policies were refined by the regional planning authority and concomitantly by the local municipalities. It was agreed that there would be two major subcentres — one in North York and one in Scarborough — as well as a number of minor subcentres, all of which would be linked to each other and to the central area by an improved rapid transit system. With the

approval of Metroplan in 1981, the local boroughs, soon to be legally recognized as cities, were required to adopt "development plans" for their subcentres to become:
- multi-functional in land use;
- compact and pedestrian orientated in their internal organization and design;
- intensive in their development relative to surrounding areas;
- focal points of business, government and community activity; and
- transportation hubs for local surface transit.

Ten years after the formulation of this multi-centred regional policy, it is evident that the goal of employment and population deconcentration is indeed being achieved. The Toronto region, with a population of 3.6 million (estimated to grow to 4.7 million by 2011) has been expanding by fifty thousand people per year since 1981. The regional office market, now the eighth largest in North America, has quadrupled since 1966 for a total of 92 million square feet in 1985.[1] This rapid growth has been characterized by a significant shift from the central area to the suburbs. The central area's share of office space has fallen from 76 per cent in 1966 to 55 per cent in 1985. As of the end of 1986, the subcentres accounted for fully 15.3 per cent of the region's office space, a considerable amount given that virtually none had existed twenty years ago. Moreover, the market for subcentre office space was particularly strong, with average vacancy rates in 1985 of only 5 per cent compared with other suburban and central area rates of 9 per cent.

The growth of subcentre office space is likely to continue; indeed, there is currently a boom of construction particularly in downtown North York. The popularity of office locations with rapid transit service continues to increase at the expense of offices served primarily by automobile. Between 1976 and 1980, 54 per cent of new office construction was transit orientated, and this increased to 65 per cent in the period 1981 to 1985.

Although there has been little time to evaluate the success of regional planning policies to divert growth to suburban subcentres, office construction trends over the past ten years suggest that the policy is working. However, despite this success, multi-use urban environments remain to be realized in these subcentres.

Prior to examining two subcentres in Metropolitan Toronto in more detail, it is worth reviewing the essential physical characteristics of suburban built form. It is these basic characteristics of transportation and land use that must be altered if parts of the vast suburban environment are to become truly urban, physically and socially, and if true public spaces are to be created.

4. Transportation planning for a multi-centred region; Scarborough's recent proposal "Network 2011" indicates the new suburban emphasis

3. The Emergence of Suburban Subcentres as Urban Places

We are now in a period of rapid transition in which the parameters that shaped the suburban landscape of the 1950s to the 1970s are being revised. The "first generation of residential and commercial buildings" is being transformed by a second and third generation of buildings that are generally denser, more mixed in use and more urban in form.

The subcentres emerging in the traditional suburban municipalities around the City of Toronto are attracting substantial office employment in addition to their existing base of retail and public sector employment. Along with this increasing diversity of employment, the subcentres are witnessing the construction of high-density residential buildings and hotels, and a broad range of cultural and recreational facilities. This has set the stage for the emergence of truly urban places, that is, places with the richness, variety, amenity, walking environment and intricacy that has until now only been associated with the historic city core.

The greatest challenge in realizing this new potential is finding appropriate ways to fundamentally alter physical environments characterized by high-speed, multi-lane arterial roadways with infrequent crossings, large open parking lots and low buildings dispersed in the landscape. These elements are mutually consistent parts of an auto-orientated pattern that is resistant to change. The form, scale and texture of the suburbs is the product of a particular set of economic conditions, social-psychological preferences and political decisions. The transition to an urban form is not automatic. It will require a consensus on the part of politicians at various levels of government, the market and local residents. This consensus has not yet been fully achieved, as residents remain sceptical of rapid urban growth.

Since it is obviously not possible to jump directly to an urban typology, strategic adjustments have to be made while still producing buildings and spaces that work within the current political and economic environment. At this stage in the evolution of the subcentres, buildings have to address two time frames — a present that is still fundamentally suburban in operation and a future that will be more urban.

Transitional Forms
What then are the characteristics of the new forms? With respect to buildings, there is a change from highly dispersed objects in open spaces (mostly parking lots) to buildings that give form and shape to open spaces, that fill in the voids, albeit in isolated pockets within the overall suburban pattern. With this new emphasis in employing buildings to configure public spaces, there has emerged a renewed interest in an intermediate scale of building, between low-rise and high-rise. It is this middle scale, which is the pervasive building block of cities, that has been missing in suburban settings.

Until recently the most significant impediment to any kind of cohesive grouping of buildings has been the need for vast surface parking lots. But as the value of land increases to the point that it becomes feasible to create structured and below-grade parking, and as the introduction and improvement of public transit service begins to alter the modal split, this is changing. Even where the economics to justify parking structures do not yet exist, the anticipation of this inevitable change some-

194

times leads to the siting of buildings in a manner conducive to further "urbaniza-tion."

The effect of designing and building for the double imperative of present and future conditions sometimes produces buildings that are temporarily awkward, that extend an invitation that is not yet answered. There is a temptation to revert to the isolated project, complete in itself. Clearly there is a tension here, and where a number of landowners are involved, public commitment and leadership are essential in convincing developers that their interests will be served best by fitting into an emerging urban context.

The Change from Roads to Streets
In addition to the siting and design of individual buildings, another set of fundamen-tal changes is occurring with respect to public spaces in the suburban subcentres. Whereas, in the traditional city, the primary social spaces are the streets and squares, which also serve to carry traffic and subdivide land, the suburban pattern has been devised to separate and disperse the intensely interconnected "functions" of the city and to provide a hierarchy of traffic facilities — freeways, arterials, collectors and res-idential crescents — such that private and social activity are as far removed from traffic as possible.

From this premise produces such low densities that there is a need to drive everywhere, resulting in vastly increased traffic volume, ubiquitous parking lots and the absence of sidewalks; uses are so thinly spread along arterial roads that there are no opportunities for people to walk from one use to another. Public life becomes highly privatized in institutional settings, as the "buildings" fail to define spaces suffi-ciently pleasant for outdoor socializing.

Along with a more urban building typology, the subcentres are attempting to revive the urban street, park and square as the foci of public life. The stage for this has been set by the deconcentration policies of the Metroplan and the changes that have followed in the economics of parking, the introduction of public transit and the densification and mixing of uses within walking distance of one another.

The prototypical road pattern can be characterized as a super-grid of arterials at intervals of a mile and a quarter and that contain traffic mazes, few intersections and reverse lot frontages. The new suburban subcentre implies a significant move away from suburban design orthodoxy. Pressure is mounting for new streets to be introduced to create smaller blocks, more public edges, more alternatives for traffic flow, and walkable sidewalks. It has not passed unnoticed that the most significant traffic bottlenecks in the region do not occur in the city centre, where alternative choices of routes exist despite relatively high densities. In suburbia, low densities do not necessarily provide for free-flowing traffic.

The physical transformations that are now occurring with greater or lesser rapidity and effect in a number of suburban subcentres in Metropolitan Toronto are

5. The Town Centre Shopping Complex in Scarborough (foreground) creates the context for further City Centre growth

quite different from one another and reflect the particular circumstances of their histories. A comparison of two of these subcentres, Scarborough City Centre, and Downtown North York, reveals that different starting conditions are having a dramatic effect on the form of emerging urban places.

Scarborough City Centre

The emerging Scarborough City Centre was a farmer's field only twenty years ago. In 1968, three hundred acres of virtually vacant land were designated for "Town Centre Uses" in Scarborough's Official Plan. Unfortunately, the city centre's essential street and block pattern was established by a typical suburban shopping centre, and not by a coherent plan for urban development. The Scarborough Town Centre Shopping Complex was completed in 1979–81 and is surrounded by extensive surface parking lots that are connected to the nearby arterial roadways by a high-volume vehicular access road. It contains over one million square feet of retail space and employs three thousand people. The street and block pattern that is now in place for the City Centre is primarily the result of this initial land use.

Since the mid-1970s, two million square feet of office space has been built in the City Centre, including the Scarborough City Hall, a health and fitness centre and a number of other public buildings. The current City Centre work force is approximately ten thousand people. Another 2.5 million square feet of office space has received zoning approval.

A development plan for the Town Centre was prepared by architect Raymond Moriyama in 1974.[2] It called for a network of multi-level pedestrian routes, a block development grid of 200 feet by 200 feet, low-to-moderate-rise development with maximum heights of ten storeys and an east–west axis of growth. Although adopted and followed in spirit, this plan has largely been ignored in its specifics by subsequent development. The plans for the City Centre have continued to emerge as it has developed, and its success to this point has posed a number of very significant new planning and design challenges, which relate to its initial structure and beginnings.

The Transportation Dilemma

A transportation dilemma results from the location of the Centre. The light rail transit system, completed in 1985, links the City Centre to the subway system, but has thus far failed to offer a truly effective alternative to the automobile. Its slow headways and limited capacity have not attracted sufficient ridership to significantly reduce vehicular trips to the City Centre.

Consequently, traffic and parking plans for new office and residential development continue to be based on typical vehicular trip generation and ownership patterns found in non-transit environments. This requires significant numbers of parking spaces for each new office building along with the design of roads and intersections to accommodate the volume of traffic expected in a non–rapid transit suburban environment. The design of urban buildings with pedestrian scale street relationships is particularly difficult in the City Centre, due to the constraints on below-grade parking garages caused by a high water table.

Although long-range plans do call for the extension of a subway line directly to the City Centre, current efforts to establish an urban form are frequently confounded by parking and automobile access requirements. The growth of the City Centre must be very carefully monitored to ensure that traffic congestion does not produce a call for more stringent parking and transportation planning policies that would further foil the goal of an urban downtown.

The Ring Road Problem
The complex and disorientating geometry of roads within the City Centre has created odd-shaped land parcels, which are very difficult to develop. The streets and blocks inhibit straightforward design solutions with good pedestrian linkages. The grade separated pedestrian network proposed by the Moriyama Plan has never fully materialized, while at the same time the introduction of a more conventional pattern of streets, blocks and sidewalks is rendered difficult by the present road system.

The presence of a twenty-three-acre single-storey shopping centre in the middle of the City Centre continues to impede the creation of a more normalized pattern of streets and pedestrian routes. In effect, the shopping centre and its parking lots sterilize a good portion of the City Centre and will continue to block the full establishment of a modified street grid until some of the lots that surround the shopping centre are developed as part of the City Centre's new urban fabric.

Definition of Public and Private Space
A City Centre that contains a shopping centre is one thing, but a City Centre that, in large part, is still a shopping centre is another. The inherent problems of ownership and control, the definition of "publicness" and the public interest are compounded by the unclear blending of public and private spheres. The shopping centre is a private facility, which until recently has provided the place for public social activity. Although limited in scope, social activity in the Town Centre revolved around the shopping experience, for both teenagers and adults. The limits of acceptable social behaviour were ultimately controlled by a private property owner, in this case one of Canada's largest property developers.

With the development of a new City Hall and its public spaces, this relationship is beginning to change. However, the more genuine public spaces outside the shopping centre have not been sufficiently animated to attract significant public interest at various times of the day. By default, the shopping centre remains the principal locus of social activity.

A City Centre or Suburban Subcentre?
The pattern of land ownership, the presence of an extensive regional shopping centre

that is orientated solely to cars, and the absence of rapid transit until 1985 have produced a subcentre that remains essentially suburban, despite well-intentioned planning policies. The pedestrian environment is poor, with long distances between uses, incomplete at-grade connections and uncomfortable winter routes.[3] The pattern of roads contributes to this unacceptable pedestrian environment by relegating the pedestrian to circuitous routes designed to serve the ingress and egress of vehicles. The elliptical road pattern must be seriously questioned even in terms of its capacity to serve vehicular movement. The pattern of uses remains essentially segregated, with mutually exclusive institutional, office and retail precincts.

The City Centre has only partially realized the goals set for it in Scarborough's Official Plan. The irregularly shaped parcels in much of the City Centre are difficult to access, both by pedestrians and vehicles, and consequently have not developed as quickly as anticipated. In fact, the gravity of the City Centre has shifted farther to the east where vehicular access is more direct and land parcels are more regular and readily developable.

Despite these fundamental difficulties, the City is seeking to ameliorate the suburban form by introducing new uses, particularly a substantial amount of residential accommodation, and requiring new development to address the street through limiting setbacks and creating pedestrian scale street edges. It remains to be seen whether the City will have the political conviction to stringently enforce its new urban design policies, which attempt to reverse the attitudes and design practices of suburban developers, politicians and local residents. If these new urban design policies are realized — and there are now several projects that reflect these changes — then it is conceivable that a concentrated and vital urban form will evolve. However, the current parcelling of land and the road pattern still remain significant impediments to the development of a truly urban subcentre.

Downtown North York

Unlike Scarborough's City Centre, where the centre of development is physically and economically antithetical to an urban environment, North York's new downtown has grown out of a pre-war pattern of rectilinear streets and blocks. The City of North York, until as recently as the late 1970s, had no identifiable centre. Its "main street," Yonge Street, is a broad arterial route that leads north from Toronto and has several towns located along it, but consisted of one- and two-storey commercial buildings, many with parking along the street frontage. The Borough of North York, which became a City in 1984 as well as Scarborough, is primarily composed of low-rise single family dwellings and strip plazas.

The rapid and continued growth of its new downtown has been largely due to the northward extension of Toronto's major north–south subway along Yonge Street. The subway extension, which opened in 1974, twenty-five years after the original subway line was first constructed, linked the Borough with downtown Toronto. At

6. The rapid emergence of Downtown North York

198

the same time, the new policy of deconcentration, which was emerging within the City and Metropolitan governments of Toronto, was officially recognized by a new Masterplan for North York Downtown.

The speed at which growth has occurred since 1975, although welcomed by the majority of municipal politicians, especially the popular mayor, has given rise to concerns by many residents who have witnessed the transformation of their quiet suburban enclave into a busy and expanding commercial, retail and residential centre. Prior to 1975, there were only 1,000 dwelling units in multiple-unit buildings and 447,000 square feet of office space in the twenty-four-block area now defined as the downtown. By the end of 1987, there were 4,300 new residential units and 4.57 million square feet of additional office space built and under construction. Another 1.5 million square feet of office space has been approved, with a number of significant mixed-use projects in the planning stage.

The current planning and design challenges facing Downtown North York are somewhat different from those facing Scarborough City Centre.

Definition of the "Downtown"
Not contained within a superblock, but growing in relation to a major street and subway, there has been no clear consensus as to just how big Downtown North York will be or what shape it will take. Its extremely rapid growth has thus far been directed by individual landowners, which has fuelled speculation and fears about uncontrollable growth. A realistic long-term look at the potential and the desirable boundaries for growth is urgently needed.

The presently abrupt and unstable "cliffs" that occur where new high-rise buildings tower over two-storey bungalows are a physical manifestation of this problem and suggest the urgent need to define transition zones in terms of land uses, densities and building heights to allow for stable long-term boundaries between the new downtown and the residential areas on its periphery.

The Role and Design of Streets
Attempts have been made, without much success, to apply suburban design principles *ex post facto* to the streets of Downtown North York, that is, to introduce a free-flow ring road, which has the geometry and limited access of suburban arterials, and to rely on the superblock formula. This approach has to be reconsidered. The "downtown" already has a great deal of pedestrian activity and will have more. There is a need to intensify the "grid" of streets and temper the present highway characteristics of Yonge Street itself as part of a comprehensive plan for a downtown environment that will work for pedestrian as well as vehicular traffic.

To this end, a pedestrian route study for the downtown was undertaken in 1986 for North York. Initial inclinations to internalize the routes mid-block, where they would be removed from the street traffic, were largely resisted in favour of improving the pedestrian environment on Yonge Street itself. The report, which was adopted,

7. Radical juxtapositions of scale and type are occurring along Yonge Street, which is a traditional retail strip

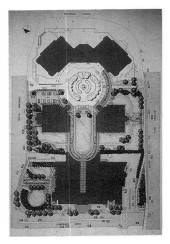

8,9,10,11. The Consilium, a project by Prudential Insurance and Royal Trust, is organized to create new city blocks and to introduce more urban building forms into the suburban context of the Scarborough City Centre (Bregman & Hamann, Architects, with Janos Szabo, Design Architect; urban design by Berridge, Lewinberg, Greenberg)

calls for significant improvements to the existing Yonge Street streetscape to enhance a "main street" pedestrian environment.

4. Conclusion

In a recent book entitled *Bourgeois Utopias: The Rise and Fall of Suburbia*,[4] American historian Robert Fishman describes the end of suburbia as peripheral residential areas related to a downtown core, and its replacement in the United States by the "techno-burb" or nebulous, decentralized, highway-related zone in which all land uses are dispersed over vast distances outside of the traditional city and unrelated to it. To the extent that this is an accurate description of what is happening in the United States, it is not necessarily reflective of what is occurring outside Canadian cities, which have always had a very different history from their American counterparts.

In the municipalities surrounding Toronto, two of which have been discussed above, a strong pattern of new city centre building is evident. Like the "techno-burbs" observed by Fishman, they involve a significant broadening of the land-use base in suburbia and a greater degree of self-sufficiency, but unlike the techno-burb, there appears to be a purposeful attempt to create diversity, intensity, transit access, a pedestrian environment and cultural amenity in a concentrated urban form that is increasingly city-like.

The attempt to create urban places in the suburban subcentres is related to the largely positive attitudes that Canadians have toward their cities. The established cities, especially the larger ones, are seen as places to emulate, not to flee. The plan for deconcentrating growth in the Toronto area was a deliberate response to potential overdevelopment in the central area, not ceaseless migration from the city centre. It is not surprising, therefore, that the current generation of suburban growth in the Toronto area is seeking to re-create the urbanity of the central city, which itself continues to attract much of the development interest and public activity.

The physical transition that this implies, particularly for centres shaped largely by a heavy reliance on automobiles and forms of development scaled to its use, is a very challenging one. There are, nonetheless, a number of examples of suburban "city centres" or "downtowns" that aspire to an urbanity that may now exist in nascent form. The decisions and policies that are now being formulated and applied are particularly important as they will shape the next significant stage of growth in the suburbs. This new physical form will endure well into the 21st century. If properly crafted, it has the potential of nurturing a richer public and social life in the vast 20th-century suburban communities that surround our 19th-century cities.

Notes
[1] City of Toronto, Planning and Development Department,"Quinquennial Review, Overview Report," 1986.
[2] Scarborough Planning Board, "Scarborough Town Centre Land Use Study," prepared by Raymond Moriyama, Architects and Planners, Toronto, 1974.
[3] Madis Pihlak, "Urban Design of the Pedestrian Realm within a Suburban City Centre: Scarborough (Metropolitan Toronto)," Department of Planning, Arizona State University, Tempe, Arizona, 1987.
[4] Robert Fishman, *Bourgeois Utopias: The Rise and Fall of Suburbia* (New York: Basic Books, 1987).

PIAZZA CANADIAN TIRE: Emerging Urban Space in the Suburbs

Tom Emodi

> The city is both a physical utility for collective living and a symbol of those collective purposes and unanimities that arise under such favoring circumstances.
>
> Lewis Mumford, *The Culture of Cities*[1]

Introduction

The outstanding fact of recent city building in Western cultures is the post-war suburb. This urban form is still by far the predominant way that we build our towns.

But architects, as a group, have developed a condescending attitude to contemporary suburbs; we have rejected and ignored "suburbia" as it was being built by the hectare without us. Even when we have designed for the suburbs, we have tended to view them as an inferior cultural form. We have laughed at the suburban lifestyle and image, as we saw ourselves best qualified to work on the built expression of urban life. Given the predominance of the suburbs, this attitude by architects can only lead to a degeneration of that expression, and indeed, of that life.

The propositions in this paper are based on the belief that we cannot afford to ignore the potential of the suburbs. Since the suburban parts of our cities represent by far the greatest portion of our urban investment, we have to make them work for a richer variety of activities, without losing their suburban essence. Since the suburbs are predominant, they express our culture and we have to learn to understand them and work to enhance them.

1. Photograph entitled "Patterns of Congestion" from *The Culture of Cities*, by Lewis Mumford, first published in 1938. Today we regard this tighter suburban fabric as more desirable than the loose pattern of later suburbs

History

Early versions of the post-war suburb resembled the tightly knit patterns of the city before the car: rectilinear grids and small lots. Later versions, inspired by Howard's garden city concepts embodied by Stein and others at Radburn, were based on curved roads, culs-de-sac and increasing lot sizes.[2] All used the single family house on the single family lot as the basic unit of city building. Mumford has called early suburbs "patterns of congestion" because of their tightness. The suburbs and the modern movement in architecture were both born of social hopes for increased amenity (space, light and air) and an optimism about technology. During the 20th century, suburban fabric evolved into a looser, less dense pattern with little clear geometry. The community and civic centres, originally proposed at Radburn and other experimental new towns, gradually disappeared, to be replaced by shopping malls. Today the majority of Canadians live in post-1945 suburbs and carry out many (if not most) of their commercial and leisure activities in shopping malls.

It seems important to know that suburbs have always aroused negative feelings. In general terms, suburbs have existed since "inside the town" has been distinguished from "outside." In 1386 Chaucer wrote of the "suburbes of a toun … lurkynge in hernes and lanes blynde." Because suburbs are by definition new and at the edge, they are essentially problematic. They represent a discernibly different pattern of life, which conflicts with the established pattern. In the quality of newness there is something to be admired; in the quality of being at the edge there is something to be feared.

Although we have given the name "suburb" to the new parts at the urban edge throughout the history of Western cities, the physical form of these parts has varied greatly. For example, in 14th-century London "immediately outside the walls the

2. Cartoon from *Life* magazine of 1907, shows the rush to the suburbs, and indicates the private nature of urban space behind fences. The issue of public space in the suburbs has long been recognized

clusters of buildings by the gates were beginning to take on the appearance of separate villages"[3]; in the 16th century London's great increase in population was housed in expanding suburbs, many of which were poor and squalid "with alleys of small tenements and cottages."[4] The extensive suburban development of London in the 18th century is well known, and according to Summerson, roadside development extending out from the main gates was "the most obvious and natural form of expansion for a town" — this form "goes back in principle to the middle ages."[5] The extension of London soon evolved into the form of streets around squares. "The London square became simply an element in the economics of estate development. The square, with its railed **private** garden, was the magnet with which to draw wealthy buyers."[6] Other cities used different forms for their extension, but urban growth made the suburban fringe inevitable. Nineteenth-century suburbs, based on mechanical or electrical rail transport, and 20th-century suburbs, based on the car, are parts of a continuity of this growth.

Arguments

Critics of the suburbs say that there is no collective life "out there." This is clearly not so. Whole streets of households come to know each other; all kinds of meetings and conversations take place around gardening, car washing, snow clearing, street playing, walking to school, visiting each other's houses, and so on. The block party is a suburban phenomenon. Having lived in apartment houses, rowhouses and detached suburban houses, my experience is that within this range of dwellings human interaction that occurs in daily life is not necessarily reduced in the suburban setting. However, it is true that the contemporary suburb does not easily lend itself to a rich collective life.

There are three main kinds of public activity in the contemporary suburb: the public activity related to the residential street, the activity related to public institutions such as the schoolyard, and that which is related to the commercial centre, which is predominantly the shopping mall with its parking lot. While these activities are not **essentially** different from previous times, their **distribution** is different. The public places in which they occur are separated from each other, whereas in other urban forms they overlap and merge. Town square, market and dwellings often occupy the same place in the historic city; we must find ways of allowing this multivalence to emerge again.

Critics of the suburbs cite the socio-economic homogeneity of the population as an impediment to diverse spontaneous human contact. This homogeneity is not necessarily introduced by the urban form of detached buildings. In the history of cities, homogeneity of various parts is a commonplace occurrence. The development of cities generally consists of discernibly different areas of housing, the differences being predominantly based on wealth. For example, in Boston this has been well documented by Warner.[7]

In 18th- and 19th-century London it was not uncommon for ordinary working people to walk four miles to work, a journey of about three-quarters of an hour. At the end of the 19th century the population of the County of London was four and a half million, but less than thirty thousand lived in the City of London. The great majority of workers returned to the suburbs at night, using the railway. Again, the journey was probably about three-quarters of an hour.[8] In Boston, the dominant way of life at the turn of the century was suburban, with the streetcar being the major means of transportation, and the journey was about the same length of time.[9] The contemporary city, with its automobile suburbs, has substituted space for time. In most cities commuting time has not increased significantly although distance has.

The variety on downtown Main Street has been replaced by the enclosed shopping mall to which we have to drive. Small corner stores within walking distance of houses have been replaced by supermarkets (often within the enclosed malls) to which we also have to drive. The cultural and physical pattern of commerce has fundamentally changed; it is less connected than before to civic life.

The first enclosed shopping mall, with so-called "anchor stores" at each end of a two-storey covered "street," was Southdale at Edina, Minnesota. Its designer, Victor Gruen, "conceived of the large shopping mall as an antidote to suburban sprawl. He saw it as a centralizing influence, an organizing principle, as well as an adaptable mechanism for creating community centers where there were none."[10] Gruen had seen the mall as a development of the 19th-century arcades and gallerias of Europe.

The obvious and basic difference between arcades and malls is that arcades usually connect parts of the city to each other, whereas malls do not. However, many successful 19th-century arcades were parallel to the street. More than the orientation of the arcade, the key factor seems to have been the proximity to residential civic activity.

The automobile suburb has created the discontinuous city in which the voids are as large as, or larger than, the solids. We have created a fabric in which infill and densification are difficult because the voids and the potential new solids do not easily match in size. As well, we have to find appropriate mixtures of activity and they are often outside the existing zoning controls.

The infill of urban voids is not essentially a **new** kind of condition or problem. A city develops loosely at first, followed by successive growth through infill, redevelopment and densification. If necessary, the first layer of growth is demolished to make way for the next. If we see the contemporary suburb as the first (rather than the last) layer of city development, then our attitude to the suburbs can be markedly different. And, as we have seen, there are more than enough voids, albeit difficult ones, to allow the next layer of growth to occur without having to demolish much of the first.

This study accepts that the suburb has emerged as a problematic urban form.

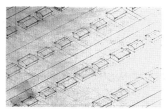

3. An abstracted view of Fairview, Nova Scotia, a typical North American grid suburb of the 1950s and 1960s. The evenness of void and solid has grown apparent, as has the lack of enclosure of the street. The bungalows are one of two sizes and often have "blind" ends, suggesting that the side yards have considerable potential in developing the next layer of growth (Tom Emodi)

4. The next layer of growth using the side yards of existing lots. Although the pattern is much more dense, it preserves essential qualities of suburban fabric (access on all sides to light and air; privacy). The new buildings accept a mixture of uses and define the public space in stronger terms (Tom Emodi)

5. Southdale Center, Edina, Minnesota, U.S.A., 1956, by Victor Gruen, Associates, Architects. The first shopping mall that used the formula of "anchor stores" connected by enclosed "streets" lined with smaller shops on two levels. This totally internalized building type with its surround of car parking has fundamentally influenced the shape of our cities for thirty years. This suburban form is resistant to growth and change, yet provides significant potential in most cities

While in many ways they are not essentially different from previous urban forms, there are some crucial distinctions. The key issues are **density** and **variety** of activity. The following preliminary study establishes that it is physically possible for a denser and more varied form to emerge through infill, which would be sensitive to those qualities that make the contemporary suburb attractive to such a significant portion of the population. The political will, public policies and mechanisms necessary to implement these propositions are major issues that must follow.

Propositions — The Next Residential Layer

Because it provides a ripe opportunity for redevelopment, this section will focus on the 1950s residential suburb. In comparison with previous suburban patterns, that of the 1950s included larger lot sizes and setbacks leading to lower densities, fewer zones of transition between public and private zones, and fewer kinds of use (single-use zoning controls).

Each of these qualities has been to some extent detrimental to suburban life. The low densities have led to fewer community activities and services than before; the unarticulated public space has led to characterless streets that are uncomfortable for walking; the single-use zoning has led to homogeneity and to unadaptable house forms tightly fitted to a nuclear family lifestyle.

Two related sets of propositions will provide a new and positive direction for the next layer of growth in residential suburban streets:

1. Propositions for Private Lots
1.1 encourage infill buildings between houses wherever possible;
1.2 decrease the minimum setbacks at the fronts of all lots;
1.3 encourage compatible mixed uses;
1.4 encourage craftsmanship and detailed treatment on the public faces of houses.

2. Propositions for Public Spaces
2.1 reassert the importance of streets, especially the landscape aspects (continuous sidewalks, planting, lighting, enhancement of views);
2.2 stress the importance of all other public places such as school grounds, playgrounds, and parks;
2.3 encourage the development of neglected "semi-public" spaces into fully fledged public places, for example strip-mall parking lots and church grounds.

Of course, different approaches are needed for the grid suburbs of the 1940s to 1960s than for the curved road and cul-de-sac suburbs of the 1960s to 1980s. These two patterns are based on quite different ambitions about how to make residential neighbourhoods. For reasons that are explained below, this paper will deal only with the 1950s grid suburb.

A more detailed exploration of these propositions will be aided by the example of Fairview, a suburb in Halifax, Nova Scotia, which has relatively clear boundaries and a series of small developments, spanning the period from 1920 to today, that show different approaches. This study will concentrate on the 1950s part of Fairview.

Fairview includes a typical 1950s subdivision, which is a grid pattern of streets with residential lots that measure 70 feet by 110 feet. The roadways are 32 feet wide. The city owns 20 feet on one side and 15 feet on the other side of the street, but (with the exception of two streets) has not provided sidewalks on these easements. The easements are landscaped, mainly with lawn, as if they belonged to the private land. The houses are set back a further 30 feet from the easement line. They are typical bungalows with a basement set about 5 feet into the ground, a main floor, and a shallow gable roof running parallel to the street. The ridges of the roofs are about 18 feet from the ground, and the eaves are about 13 feet. The houses are almost 130 feet from each other across the street. There are minimal porches and other articulations on the fronts of the houses.

The plans of the houses are almost always rectangles, ranging from 24 feet by 36 feet to 30 feet by 40 feet, and set 10 feet from one side of the lot. This provides space between the houses from between 20 to 40 feet. The plan is typically divided into a "living" side and a "sleeping" side. Quite often the houses have no windows onto the side yard, especially on the bedroom side.

The slightly abstracted axonometric view of this section of Fairview provides us with the pattern of hundreds of typical 1950s Canadian suburbs. These suburbs are now one generation old. They are experiencing rapid turnover of population as retired people move out and new, generally younger, families move in. These suburbs provide opportunity for innovative experiments for an additional and enriching layer of urban growth. This opportunity is not yet as strong in suburbs that are younger, and for that reason this paper focuses on the 1950s suburb. The rest of this section describes how a richer layer might be achieved.

In providing the next layer of growth we need to adopt a strategy that addresses the problems, but also preserves the desirable qualites of suburban life. We should re-examine earlier urban patterns for positive aspects that might be regained. In preserving desirable suburban qualities we should stress that families prefer the suburbs because of the freedom, privacy and control afforded by the single family lot, and the tangible benefits of access to light, air and the outdoors.

First and foremost, keeping these qualities means keeping the pattern of ownership. The single family lot should remain the basic unit. However, the size of the lots may be modified, and the design of the site and the buildings should allow for variety of use and density in a way that the existing pattern does not. By decreasing the side yards to a minimum, we can gain a new lot between existing houses. Since most houses have blank end walls, at least on one side, we can insert a narrow building on this new lot without affecting the access of light too much. The new inserted buildings should be taller, and they should be set forward on the lot as far as possible to give a better sense of enclosure to the street. To examine the extreme case, the pro-

6. Galleria Mazzini, Genoa, Italy, 1875. Gruen based the internalized mall on the galleria of Europe, believing that the form would act as the civic and cultural centre of the newly evolving post-war automobile suburb. Malls have not developed in this way, to date, but still have the potential to do so

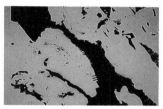

7. Map of Halifax-Dartmouth, Nova Scotia, showing in black the suburban land devoted to single-use retail activity (not including downtown shopping and car parking areas). In a metropolitan area of 250,000 people, this area, used essentially for retail parking, amounts to about three square miles (Tom Emodi)

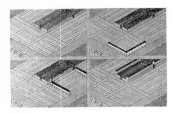

8. Sketches for potential densification of suburban shopping malls. Top left shows the typical condition; top right depicts thin buildings providing residential edges to undefined street-carpark conditions; bottom left suggests thin insert buildings of retail and residential activity, minimally disrupting the car parking yet defining and giving scale to the urban spaces created; bottom right indicates the potential for developing roof scapes with residential activities (Tom Emodi)

posal shown here sets the buildings to the front edge of the lot, so that car parking is incorporated within the building, not in front of it. The buildings should be designed such that the option exists to include small professional offices and shops at the ground level, with residential use toward the back and at the second floor. The existing houses should be encouraged to extend forward, providing a zone where the materials, detail and craftsmanship should be subject to public guidelines.

These ideas can be compared with those that others have made for the densification of existing suburbs. The most notable of these is Dolores Hayden's scheme, which would utilize existing back-yards for communal uses.[11] This would change the existing pattern of ownership and life so much that the suburbs would no longer be recognizable — and this is part of Hayden's aim. However, I would argue that it is not desirable to transform the suburbs so fundamentally, for the suburb contains and sustains qualities that are basic to our contemporary culture.

The inserted buildings maintain four aspects, providing access to light and air for existing and new buildings alike. Differences between front and back are also maintained so that important suburban qualities of privacy remain. The private, single family lot remains for the existing houses as well as the new, but the possibility of compatible work-related uses is created through increased density and closer relationships with the street.

The new private buildings should define the street better as well as places of transition between the public and private domains. This is where public responsibility in developing better suburban environments becomes important. With the increased density and variety of uses, the life of the street will be intensified. The provision of sidewalks on all streets is a municipal responsibility and will be both necessary and possible as the density increases. The provision of public landscaping, for example, avenues of trees, will help to define the public realm and to make it a continuous and coherent part of the fabric. The focal points of the public landscape (for example, school grounds and sports grounds) should be given special consideration to define edges, offer vistas and provide focuses for activity. In addition, tangible encouragement in the form of municipal tax incentives should be given for the definition and enhancement of semi-public spaces that act as public space in the suburbs, such as church yards and strip-mall parking lots.

While such ambitions may seem difficult in a contemporary municipal context, it seems clear that those urban places, which we now cherish, were most often created with this kind of public investment. The residential suburbs, which represent so much of our cities today, deserve no less.

Propositions — The Next Commercial Layer
Contemporary shopping centres and malls make an urban pattern that has similar characteristics to the residential one; larger lot sizes and setbacks create a loose grain. Human activity is restricted to commerce of particular kinds. Gruen's vision of insti-

206

tutional activity is sometimes incorporated, but not often and only in minor ways. Perhaps a branch library or an electoral office is located in the mall, but other civic activities rarely are.

The typical parking area around a mall is a major interruption in the fabric. It is large, unloved, unarticulated, unlandscaped and has almost nothing facing onto it; not even the shops in the mall face it. Adjacent housing usually has its sides or back to it. This problem requires bold steps.

A set of propositions will provide a new and positive direction for the next layer of growth for malls:

1. Reconceive the Parking Lots and Buildings as Sites for Mixed-use Development
1.1 carefully design places of transition between residential and other activities;
1.2 include residential and civic/institutional activities in the new development;
1.3 carefully size and clearly shape spaces for car parking, so that they emphasize their possible use as civic spaces;
1.4 "insert" buildings to make street edges at the periphery of the block and give shape to the internal parking areas;
1.5 add mixed-use components to the roofs of malls where other factors prevent adding to the parking lots.

The large parking lot of the mall is one of the least friendly urban spaces our culture has created. The space lacks definition, scale and order. Since malls are commercially based, the majority of the elements that might be introduced to provide definition, scale and order will have to earn their keep.

In the past few years, the second generation of development of shopping malls has begun. In most cases this has meant expansion and renovation of the mall; office space or an entertainment component such as cinemas have been added. In very few cases is a civic element, such as a library or public art gallery, included. In essence, the mall has remained commercial in the broad sense and still closes "after hours."

Experiments in some places, for example in Mississauga, are underway to urbanize the parking areas with the use of street grids and additional buildings. Some malls (Winnipeg has several) occur underneath apartment buildings. These developments illustrate the direction being proposed here. However, there has been little concerted effort yet to study systematically the potential of the thousands of shopping malls throughout Canada. This paper is a beginning in that respect.

The propositions here emphasize the inclusion of residential components, such as apartments, hotels, and senior citizens' homes. These components can pay their way and will generate the permanent activity essential to integrate existing malls into the city.

The edges and corners of parking lots can be defined by the insertion of buildings that address the existing streets as well as the parking areas. If necessary, the buildings can be designed to accommodate cars underneath so that the parking for

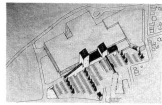

9. Development of mixed-use buildings at an existing mall (West End Mall, Halifax, Nova Scotia). Preliminary design studies in repairing 20th-century urban space with a system of 20th-century elements. By eliminating sixteen car spaces, a theatre, a senior citizens' home, an eight-storey apartment building and a wall of studio/artisan apartments can be developed. As this mall is a major bus interchange (the bus stops are at grade under the proposed new building), the proposed uses are entirely appropriate. A pavilion for the bus terminal office and coffee shop, as well as landscape elements, further define the urban space of the carpark, which can be used for civic activities. At right, a summer skateboarding ramp and winter skating area (Tom Emodi)

207

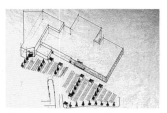

10. Another preliminary design study for the West End Mall in Halifax. Twenty-four car spaces are replaced by a series of pavilions that provide opportunity for residential and retail activity; landscape elements suggest paths of connection, helping to give definition and scale to the urban space of the carpark (Tom Emodi)

the mall is not diminished initially.

Where parking lots are large and undifferentiated, similar buildings can be inserted to divide the area into properly scaled courtyards. Again the landscaping would have to be thoroughly redesigned, including planting, lighting, ground textures and so on. Access and circulation to the mall and the visibility of main entrances would be enhanced by the careful siting, proportioning and design of such buildings.

Mall buildings themselves are often low and provide large expanses of roof, which can also be developed. This is obviously a more difficult and disruptive process than the previous suggestions, but where the parking lot is limited and the location is suitable, the potential of the roof as a site is rich. Access through the mall into the residential and civic components is an opportunity for varied activity throughout the whole day.

The illustrations suggest in general terms how thin insert buildings might be used to provide definition, scale and order to otherwise amorphous areas. Detailed development of these ideas in specific situations will be the next step in evolving strategies for the integration of existing shopping malls into a more varied suburban life.

Conclusions

These propositions, when developed further through design studies, will provide the direction for repairing and improving the large sections of cities that we have made in the past forty years. It is vital that we change our attitude from disrespect and disregard to respect, repair and improvement.

Both the residential and commercial fabric of suburbia have potential that is generally not recognized. For many cultural and ecological reasons, it is now time to consolidate the urban growth of the last forty years. Working with hope and optimism for the suburbs, we can create better private and public realms within the urban fabric that we have. This paper has demonstrated some of this potential. Along this path, we can accommodate more people in ways that make the city a better physical utility for collective living, and a richer symbol of our collective purposes.

Notes
[1] Lewis Mumford, *The Culture of Cities* (New York: Harcourt Brace, 1970), p. 5.
[2] Ebenezer Howard, *Garden Cities of Tomorrow* (London: Faber & Faber, 1944); Clarence S. Stein, *Towards New Towns for America* (Cambridge, Mass.: MIT Press, 1978).
[3] Christopher Hibbert, *London: The Biography of a City* (Harmondsworth: Penguin Books, 1980), p. 30.
[4] Hibbert, p. 39.
[5] John Summerson, *The Architecture of the Eighteenth Century* (London: Penguin Books, 1986) p. 275.
[6] John Summerson, *Georgian London* (Harmondsworth: Penguin Books, 1978), p. 163.
[7] Sam B. Warner, Jr., *Streetcar Suburbs* (Cambridge, Mass.: MIT Press, 1962).
[8] Hibbert.
[9] Warner.
[10] William Severini Kowinski, *The Malling of America* (New York: William Morrow, 1985), p. 120; James Ross McKeever, et al., *Shopping Center Development Handbook* (Washington: The Urban Land Institute, 1977).
[11] Dolores Hayden, *Redesigning the American Dream* (New York: W. W. Norton, 1984), p. 188.

DIGESTING THE INDIGESTIBLES: The Urban Expressway

J. Michael Kirkland

1. Rendering of "Lakeshore Expressway, Humber River Interchange" by Margison, Babcock and Associates (Metropolitan Toronto: Proposed Lakeshore Expressway Functional Report, July 1954, plate 1)

As the road deflects to avoid hitting Palace Pier, the red Corvette that converged at Mississauga appears again to my right. Two women with dark sunglasses smile, coiffured and set for a night in the city; chewing gum. The Cobra detector on the dash goes as crazy as a missile lock-on when the cars leap the hump at the Seaway Inn. Tat-tat-tat, tat-tat-tat, it's K-Band, fast cars swerve down to 100K, until we see the trap has caught the bullet bike which disappeared at the Credit River. Unlike the Teutonic machinery that conducts its elegant march down University Avenue each morning, the Gardiner Expressway has a wilder quality about it — Harleys, 16-Wheelers, Pick-ups, Cadillacs and Trans Ams; it anticipates Road Warrior.

The sun hits my eyes in the rear-view mirror as we bend past the Ex. A beautiful pink iridescent mist envelops Toronto at twilight; glittering objects appear to exchange positions as we bend and drift at 140. The gold reflection of the Royal Bank competes with the orange sun in the mirror; cars slide down ramps at Spadina, York and Yonge. The Corvette has disappeared.

Detlef Mertins, with his penchant for polite naughtiness, has suggested I speak to the question of the expressway as public space; in particular, the Gardiner Expressway in Toronto. This topic might be better reserved for someone who has a more catholic view of the virtues of the metropolitan city, say Donald McKay; but that would be too obvious.

The Gardiner Expressway had its origin in 1943 as Superhighway A. Construction commenced on its western extremity in 1955 and was completed in 1964. It is approximately seven miles long and is elevated in its central section varying in height between 35 and 70 feet. The Gardiner, in its short life span in Toronto, has been the source of an almost continuous crisis of misfit with the physique of the city. Reform-faction politicians have called for its removal or burial, architects have offered unsolicited proposals, the Ontario Association of Architects has even conducted a design "charrette," and a professional urban design study is currently underway by du Toit, Allsopp, Hillier with Steven Fong of Toronto.

The question is, what do we make of the Gardiner and other elevated urban expressways? Does it provide a kind of urban life, however mutant, that is to be regarded with the deference afforded archetypal elements of the historical city, i.e.,

2. Frederick G. Gardiner, the father of Metro Toronto, strolling down an unfinished portion of the Gardiner Expressway, 1960 (photo Kryn Taconis). He served aggressively as Chairman of Metro Council from its inception in 1953 until 1962. The expressway was only one of many projects that he spearheaded in the boom years of the 1950s; like some of his sayings ("Toronto has shrunk at the core and burst at the seams," "You'll never leave footprints in the sands of time if you sit in your cabana on the beach," "A mathematical phenomenon exists in our suburbs — multiplication by subdivision") it serves to remind us of the aggressive and pioneering spirit of that time

3. The expressway, photographed in 1966, snaked its way between the railway lands and the industrial harbour along the central waterfront

4.&5. While the elevated urban expressway has the superficial appearance of a colonnade, as an urban type it is actually a viaduct

street, court and square?

In the American psyche, mobility is most closely associated with the notion of freedom. Indeed, it could be said that migration for advantage is at the root of the national identity. Perhaps the greatest threat to national security in recent memory was not the tumult of the Vietnam War or the civil rights movement, but rather the frightening psychosis of the 1974 gasoline crisis. It was as if the country was engaged in a gigantic version of musical chairs and at a most unfortunate moment the music stopped. The loss of the possibility of escape requires acceptance of one's condition of habitation, one's locus, with or without genius. Americans maintain that utopia is something you go and find. Never mind that I live in Newark, Manhattan is thirteen miles away. Never mind that I live in Cleveland, I can drive to the Grand Canyon this summer. In that sense, **mobility** is the opium of the masses in America, the vicarious pleasure of possibility that along with television (the purveyor of what you need to know) and youth (what you should be) completes the alchemy of the good life. All dressed up but no place to go.

In a master stroke in 1960, the Pentagon and Highway Lobby devised a joint venture to produce a national highway defence network. The highway construction program that ensued produced one of the most extraordinary physical systems ever undertaken. This system allowed a citizen in peace time to drive from anywhere in the United States to Disneyland in two days and for the Pentagon in war to move missile launchers great distances at speed. Although this system produced accessibility, it did not, of course, produce any place to go. This means that Boston and San Francisco are full of cars from Ohio.

The American Expressway had its genesis in the German **autobahn**, which in turn, the Italians remind us as they do about French cuisine, was modelled on Mussolini's **autostrada**: an exclusive right-of-way without pedestrians or even intersections, unaffected by terrain and custom. It is a pure system that allows man to soar at the limit of his machine and imagination. If a piazza can be seen as a social condenser, the highway might be seen as an escape shoot — the discourse is between you and the medium, just as skiers negotiate moguls and windsurfers play the wind. Not to claim that there is no communication among fellow travellers, but that discourse which does occur is of a preverbal life form: the shared pleasure of escaping the radar trap; the exhilaration of the narrowly avoided accident; the admiration of an exotic body; the Freudian, if jocular associations with headlamps, bumpers and tail pipes; the primal dislike of being overtaken from behind. This is the culture of the caribou and the sabre-toothed tiger.

Some have suggested that the highway system is by virtue of its extraordinary reality the most important physical construct of the 20th century. It follows that such objects must possess certain pathos, even a brutal sort of beauty. The objects (we are told) are simply not yet digested by urban culture; they remain a gang of ill-mannered teenagers. They are designed by engineers (say no more) and have not yet

210

received the pedigreed attention that would present them in their best form. Robert Venturi in the 1972 publication *Learning from Las Vegas* suggested that the paraphernalia of the highway, e.g., street lights and signs, might be compared to the lexicon of traditional cities. To make such a comparison would, he admitted, require an appreciation of the inverted and ephemeral values of a strip commercial vernacular. To say the least, Venturi's prognosis of an incipient new architectural form remains unrealized. We must take his word for it that it is almost all right; our eyes tell us otherwise.

The expressway falls within the lexicon of devices produced by the Modern Project: Zoning, the Super-Block, the Housing Tower, the Freed Ground Plane, Pedestrian Bridges and the Express Motorway. The project produces the familiar paradigm, the city as machine, with each subsystem optimized in efficiency. Pedestrians are separated from cars and buildings, buildings are separated from each other, so that they might breathe and take sun, and cars are separated from pedestrian interference and from each other so that they might go as fast as possible. Everyone must go very fast, in the city which made neuroses possible. The composite plan produced the Hook new town and plan and was partially realized at Milton Keynes. Today elevated urban expressways are, of course, in disrepute almost everywhere.

The expressway is one subsystem of the urban type, **street**. Although the street is concerned with the problem of getting you from place to place as a pedestrian or in a vehicle, it is also concerned with providing a system of address and appearance for buildings and people: a public space for shopping, rituals and parades, and a civil service and security network. The Romans produced extensive networks of what they called highways. These systems were in the countryside, and when they came downtown, they became streets, much as Highway No. 2, the predecessor of the Queen Elizabeth Way/Gardiner Expressway tag team, does in southern Ontario.

If a street is a synthetic, integrated urban type, the expressway, a subset of the idea of street, must be seen as a utility that, like hydro transmission corridors, is difficult to digest precisely because its singularity of purpose resists the dialectic that produced historical types.

This delamination of the historical street was very much the intention of the Modern Movement forefathers. As stated by Le Corbusier in a speech of October 18, 1929, in Paris:

> We must kill the street. We shall truly enter into modern town-planning only after
> we have accepted this determination; (the historical) impenetrable web of streets,
> passages, houserows, courts, avenues or boulevards, adjoined by pedestrians, walks,
> traffic lanes full of cars…(must go).

The expressway, then, was seen as a sanitized transport system (as opposed to the street), and a revolutionary device for dismantling the historical city. That it does not possess the quality of *civitas* is not a surprise, since avoiding *civitas* is at the root

6. Only in odd cases of circumstantial multi-valence, such as the Brooklyn Esplanade Park on the East River in New York, have the city and the expressway found it possible to coexist.

211

of its existence.

In an attempted détente with traffic engineers, one suspects, much of the recent speculation as to what to do about the Gardiner falls into one of two categories: 1. camouflage and 2. reinterpretation.

These tactics are addressed to a wide array of complaints that have been visited upon the Gardiner, including:

1. elevation (blocking view)
2. width (problematic crossing)
3. geometry (antithetical to city grid)
4. noise and air pollution
5. kinetic hostility (to adjacent developments)
6. physical design (object quality)

In addition to these formidable if conventional expressway difficulties, the Gardiner is largely superimposed over another arterial road (Lakeshore Boulevard), is juxtaposed to the railway lands, and is in the process of falling down. And its undisciplined exit ramps produce blockage between the city and its waterfront over a substantial length of its central section.

In 1986, two Toronto architectural firms, Ferguson & Ferguson and Paul Reuber, members of the City's task force for the Gardiner/Lakeshore Corridor, conducted analysis and made proposals for the Gardiner.

The latter conducted a survey of urban expressway precedents, citing familiar and obscure examples of how one might integrate the Gardiner into the urban conditions of downtown Toronto. The spectre of linear cities and megastructures is very much alive in this work. Perhaps the most striking thing about the survey is the dearth of convincing solutions. After fifty years, we have generated a handful of odd experiments. And we must ask, were the Gardiner to be fully incased by building, could its alleged virtue as described here by Sigfried Giedion in *Space, Time and Architecture* survive?

> Full realization is given to the driver and freedom to the machine. Riding up and down the long sweeping grades produces an exhilarating dual feeling, one of being connected to the soil and yet hovering just above it, a feeling which is like nothing else so much as sliding on skis through untouched snow down the slides of high mountains.[1]

Only in odd cases of circumstantial multi-valence, usually entailing topography, has the city and the expressway found it possible to coexist. The Brooklyn Esplanade Park and the Carl Schurz Park on the East River in New York are among the often-cited examples.

More subtle and perhaps more possible are the Ferguson & Ferguson proposals, which suggest a reinterpretation of the Gardiner in terms of its typological allusions. This strategy entails classification of segments of the Gardiner as Colonnade,

Gate and Ramp, modifying the appearance of the highway so that it looks more like its purported type, and by reconfiguring its more indigestible ramps (which, in any event, are not described by any known historical type).

While the economy of this attitude is both artistically and financially of interest, it proceeds from a most unfortunate misappropriation of language. A gate is not a hyperstyle hall much less an elevated highway. The report shows an example of the transformation of a segment of the Gardiner into a gate; setting aside the fact that the gate looks more like the sail of a catamaran than a gate, the "Gate" is totally independent of the highway, and this raises the question as to whether the highway contributes anything at all. Is the gate merely camouflage for the highway?

Continuing in this quarrelsome tone, can one seriously consider the Gardiner to be a Colonnade? In a word, no. It has the superficial appearance of a colonnade, but does not allow processions along its long axis except by car on Lakeshore Boulevard, in some sections. In fact, as a **type**, it must be seen to be a **viaduct**, which the *Oxford Dictionary* defines as "an elevated structure consisting of a series of arches or spans, by means of which a railway or road is carried over a valley, road, river, etc."

The allegorical use of language by architects should, to borrow a Canadian aphorism, be put in the penalty box for misconduct. A street in the air is not a street; it is probably a corridor or viaduct. We have been the mid-wife in the distortion of architectural language to render our own "inventions" as well as commercial marketing concerns more palatable. It is easy to see why "street in the air" is an easier sell than "apartment corridor with tricycles" or "limited access high-speed motorway." But have we fooled ourselves?

The du Toit team, whose work follows the earlier studies and is now nearing completion, proceeds from a more convincing point of departure. They interpret the Gardiner as comprised of a series of sections with varying conditions, in each of which the relationship of the Gardiner to the city might be made more compatible. In the western section a conventional block plan is proposed and amendments to the Lakeshore and Queen's Quay Boulevard suggested to allow the normalization of the ground plane.

In the central section — the railway lands now being redeveloped — the ideas of extending the city to the waterfront and normalizing the ground plane are taken as a given. Personally, I would have preferred to maintain the railway lands as a garden of indigestible objects in a city obsessed by small-scale city fabric: the exceptional place like the space around the Roman Colosseum. Already contained within the space defined by the Front Street embankment and the picket fence of the Gardiner is the railway round house, a convertible colosseum, miscellaneous industrial fragments and, of course, the greatest indigestible object of all, the CN Tower. Perhaps this should be the home for Safdie's impending Opera House. If only the Gardiner were actually a wall! But Torontonians are also obsessed with the idea that the railway lands are blocking their access to the lake. Like millions of earnest lemmings,

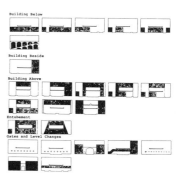

10. Alternative approaches to building along the Gardiner Expressway, Paul Reuber, Architect, "Urbanizing the Gardiner," 1986

11. Gate proposal by Ferguson & Ferguson, Architects, "Guiding the Gardiner," 1986

12/13. Proposals for civic improvements at underpasses by du Toit, Allsopp, Hillier, with Steven Fong, 1988

14. The Gardiner Expressway, 1987

Torontonians are not content to follow the orthogonal grid to the water, they wish to be able to jump in the lake everywhere, all the time.

The du Toit scheme accommodates them only at streets. In this section, crossing Lakeshore Boulevard and passing underneath the Gardiner are viewed as pivotal issues. The proposals renovate the existing threshold points, which are currently unsavoury and dangerous, with treatments of the undercroft of the expressway, sidewalks and lighting thereby creating a finer-scaled and more civilized intersection. In the eastern section, beyond the Don Valley, the Gardiner is proposed to be removed, which raises the obvious question why not remove it altogether? For when one adds the noise, pollution and vibration to the imagery of this structure, the indigestible reality of the Gardiner Expressway becomes clear again, and even the most sensitive attempts at beautification seem insignificant.

The reconciliation of utilitarian viaducts to the fabric and image of the city is an ancient problem. Early medieval maps of Rome that show the presence of viaducts reveal the failure of the Romans to find ways of occupying or integrating these structures in the city. Stefano du Perac's drawing of ancient Rome (1574) shows them running as an expressway might in the less built-up areas, and coexisting uncomfortably with the city in denser zones. The aesthetic possibilities of viaducts were evidently so minimal to Vitruvius that he offers little advice in his sixth book as to what to do with aqueducts except "when it has reached the city, build a reservoir." Aqueducts and viaducts become poignant icons when their utility recedes into memory or rumour, just as Stonehenge is probably more interesting as a monument to prehistoric religion and astronomy than it may have been as an instrument in use.

The Gardiner viaduct stands as a monument to the positivistic determination of the Modern Project. It is now quaint, almost ridiculous. It has the appearance of a by-pass route, but now only delivers people into the centre of the city; an on-grade boulevard would do just fine for traffic. The Gardiner Expressway should be removed, of course, for all of the now obvious reasons and as confirmation of the enduring nature of the city and human culture. Architecture and the city have a nature of their own and it is resistant to cataclysmic change. They might be seen as a stable datum against which more ephemeral things are registered.

Like the demolition of the Pruitt-Igo Housing Project twenty years ago, the demolition of the Gardiner will signal yet another defeat for the Modern Project. A small section of it should be kept as a monument to its time and its simplistic faith in technical progress. After stripping the Gardiner of its overwhelming utilitarian meaning, we may learn to cherish it as a memento of our collective childhood.

Notes
[1] Sigfried Giedion, ed., *Space, Time and Architecture*, 5th ed. rev. (Charles Eliot Norton Lecture Series, 1938–39) (Cambridge, Mass.: Harvard University Press).

GARDEN AND PARK: THE CCA PUBLIC SPACES[1]

Phyllis Lambert

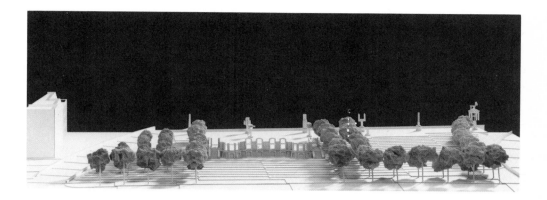

Garden and Park

Robert Smithson, in his article "Frederick Law Olmsted and the Dialectical Landscape," commented on the creation of art and public space in a mutating world:

> The site of Central Park was the result of "urban blight" — trees were cut down by the early settlers without any thought of the future. Such a site could be reclaimed by direct earth-moving without fear of upsetting the ecology. My own experience is that the best sites for "earth art" are sites that have been disrupted by industry, reckless urbanization, or nature's own devastation.[2]

The site of the Centre Canadien d'Architecture (CCA) in Montréal can be described in similar terms, for the land on which the building and landscapes of the CCA were to be created had been derelict, laid waste by highway construction three decades ago.

The new landscapes of the CCA have several roles to fulfil. They must delight, as well as heal the scars of traffic engineering. It is also appropriate that the new park and gardens relate to the ecological and built history of the site and the city, and that they comment on urban landscape, a subject that is sorely neglected in Montréal today.

The principal elements of the CCA landscape are Parc Baile at the entrance, two court gardens and the CCA Garden to the south of boulevard René-Lévesque. They have been designed by landscape architect Diana Gerrard, Peter Rose, the architect of the building, Melvin Charney, the designer of the CCA Garden, and myself, consulting architect and client.

The new building houses the CCA's collection of architectural documents, public galleries, theatre and study centre, and is built around the Shaughnessy House, a historic monument of 1874, to which it is connected; together they occupy one-third of the three-acre block on which they are situated. The remaining two acres of land have been landscaped to form Parc Baile — a large entry square or forecourt to the building — as well as two small courtyards — the Visitor's Court and the

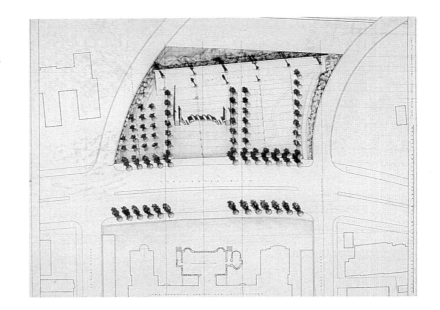

1. Melvin Charney's "Plan of the Canadian Centre for Architecture Garden, Montréal" (coloured pencil and ink on vellum paper, 90.5 x 121.5 cm, July 1987) shows the sloping field flanked by orchards in which is set "The Arcades," a re-representation of the Shaughnessy House of 1874 across the street. The allegorical columns and belvedere form the southerly edge of the Garden and overlook the Lower City and the St. Lawrence River beyond

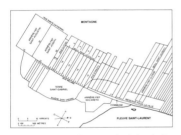

2. Farm concessions on the island of Montréal, 1663 (adapted from Marcel Trudel, *Montréal, la formation d'une société 1642–1663*, Montréal: Fides, 1976). Research by Alan Stewart. Cartography by Daniel Thibeault

3. The original pastoral character of the site is shown in Charles Dawson Shanly's "Château des Messieurs de Saint-Sulpice," September 29, 1847 (graphite on paper, 23.4 x 30.2 cm)

Scholar's Court — which are shaped by the outline of the building on its southern side.

The structure of this landscape is extended to the south, across boulevard René-Lévesque, by a one-and-one-half-acre sculpture garden. It continues the CCA's domain to the edge of the escarpment, where the land drops sharply to the railway and highway below. Entry and exit ramps to the highway bind the east and west edges of both the garden and the city block which holds the building. Situated as it is at a major access point to downtown Montréal, the garden heralds entry to the city. Both garden and park are public places operated to the standards of the Montréal Parks Department, but designed and maintained by the CCA.

History of Site

The history of the city and the site are important to both the design of the CCA building and its garden and park. The essential urban form and architecture of Montréal were constructs of the 17th-century French mind. Three powerful aspects of the mentality of its founders still mark the city: seigneurial governance, a rational geometric order imposed on the land to structure settlement and a carefully prescribed manner of building.

By rights ceded to the Sulpician Order under a medieval French system of feudal prerogatives established in France, the Gentlemen of the Seminary of Saint-Sulpice became the seigneurs of the island of Montréal in 1663. As landlords of the island, the Sulpicians had the obligation to settle the land, which they organized through land grants. The concessions granted by the Sulpicians on the island of Montréal were an orderly series of long, narrow strips of land starting at the Saint-Laurent, running inland northwards and perpendicular to the river. The concessions were modular, either two arpents wide by fifteen arpents in length, the equivalent of 384 feet by a half mile in length, or one arpent by thirty. As settlement advanced, these modules were extended northward. The long north–south streets of modern-day Montréal, which run between river and Mount Royal, were laid out along or

216

within the cadastral lines of these 17th-century concessions. Streets running east and west were essentially circumstantial, following geomorphological features.

Among colonial cities it is unusual for an original pattern of settlement to give such strong detail of structure to such an extensive area. The 17th-century cadastral system was so deeply imbedded in the 19th-century city that it directed its development and future growth into the 20th century.

The CCA stands at the edge of the great Sulpician mountain domain, which parallels the old city in historic importance. Here, the first stone fortification had been built by 1694, which was the culmination of efforts to establish a mission to Christianize the Huron and Algonquin populations; two of its stone towers remain three blocks north of the CCA site. (The stone walls of the Fort de la Montagne significantly predate the use of stone to replace the wooden stake walls that surrounded the city. The stone fortifications of the city were begun in 1717 and completed in 1737.) By the 1690s it was already changing from fortified mission to villa, becoming a *maison de plaisance* in keeping with the tastes of Vachon de Belmont, the aristocratic Sulpician who built the fort, and with those of the Gentlemen of Saint-Sulpice at their elegant manor house and gardens at Issy-les-Moulineaux, in France.

The orginal pastoral character of the area is known from iconographic and textual sources. Drawings and descriptions of the 17th and 18th centuries show vineyards, orchards and gardens, as well as dovecotes, vast breeding grounds for fowl, and pasturage. It was referred to as a *paradis terrestre*.[3]

Quite properly for his time at the end of the 18th century, Isaac Weld emphasized the picturesque in his description of the area:

> The base of this mountain is surrounded with neat country houses and gardens,
> and partial improvements have been made about one-third of the way up; the
> remainder is entirely covered with lofty trees. On that side towards the river is a
> large old monastery, with extensive enclosures walled in, round which the garden
> has been cleared for some distance. This open part is covered with a rich verdure;
> and the woods encircling it, instead of being over-run with brushwood, are quite
> clear at bottom, so that you may here roam about at pleasure for miles together,
> shaded by the lofty trees from the rays of the sun.
>
> The view from hence is grand beyond description. A prodigious expanse of
> country is laid open to the eye, with the noble river St. Lawrence winding through
> it, which may be traced from the remotest part of the horizon. The river comes
> from the right, and flows smoothly on, after passing down the tremendous rapids
> above the town, where it is hurried over huge rocks and with a noise that is heard
> even up the mountain. On the left below you appears the town of Montreal, with
> its churches, monasteries, glittering spires and the shipping under its old walls.[4]

The traditions of the *maison de plaisance* of the Sulpicians were continued with

Pinsoneault, circa 1907

4. "Shaughnessy House block and quarter, c. 1907." A. R. Pinsoneault, *Atlas of the Island and City of Montreal*

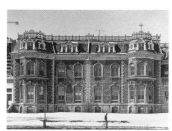

5. Phyllis Lambert and Richard Paré, *Shaughnessy House, 1923 Dorchester Boulevard west, Montréal*, W. T. Thomas Architect (gelatin silver print, 17.5 x 22.5 cm, 1973)

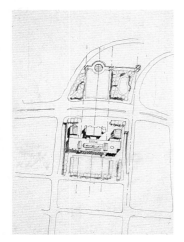

6. Peter Rose, *Diagrammatic Study of Final Design Parti CCA: Relationships* 1985 (pencil on vellum)

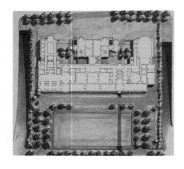

7. Jill Alexander, Office of Peter Rose, Architect, *Site Plan with Public Park, CCA, Montréal,* 1988 (coloured pencil on mylar photocopy reduction)

the building of private villas and mansions surrounded by their gardens and similarly by the vast conventual complexes of the Grey Nuns and the Congrégation de Nôtre-Dame as well as the grand Séminaire and the Collège de Montréal, built on the Sulpician mountain domain in the middle of the 19th century.

In contrast, another Sulpician domain, known as Terre Saint-Gabriel, on the plain below what is now boulevard René-Lévesque, was used for pasturage and then factories and warehouses. Construction of the Lachine Canal in the 1820s and its improvement in the 1840s supported the development "below the hill" of industry and working-class housing. This sharp contrast between land uses on the upside and downside domains is still evident in the CCA sites, north and south of the boulevard, and is reflected in the CCA Garden.

Design

In developing the design of the CCA building and its gardens, Peter Rose and I were intent on embodying and signifying the cadastral division as it has ordered the urban structure of Montréal. This land division is marked in the Shaughnessy House — a double house where each side is a mirror image of the other — by the pronounced coigning at the centre-line of the building that marked the original cadastral division between the two properties. This line is expressed in the structure and the architectural articulation of the new CCA building and in elements of landscape in both park and garden. Similarly, the cadastral lines, which defined the former property divisions immediately to the east and west of the Shaughnessy House, are signified by the centre-lines of the entrance court and the library court of the new building. Beyond, to the north and south, they are the primary lines of organization for the CCA gardens and park.

Peter Rose laid out the form of the landscape, the relationship of trees to open spaces. For me, it was also essential that the CCA landscape express a fundamental relationship between nature and the city. Diana Gerrard, of Gerrard and Mackars, Landscape Architects, was asked to design a landscape based on the ecology of the area. Historically, there are three coexisting plant associations: first, the indigenous climax forest as it had developed before European contact; second, the plants introduced by the European settlers; and third, the cultivars (species genetically altered to produce particular characteristics, for example, pollution resistance). A study was made to identify the plants of these three eras.

The microclimate of the site was then mapped to show the effects of wind, sun and shade and the environmental stresses of a contemporary northern city. These included the sensitivity of plants to salt used for melting snow and ice, and to air pollutants. Trees and plants of the three periods were located according to these stresses within the overall intentions of the design. This resulted in the formulation of ecological types — forest, edge, meadow, orchard — each reflecting a particular and

218

specific structure of individual plants — the indigenous, the introduced and the cultivars.

Ecologically, a maple-beech forest community is natural to the climatic zone of Montréal, and an elm-ash-oak climax forest is more specific to the Dorchester Plateau on which the CCA is located. These are reflected in the new landscape of Park and Garden. Introduced Norway Maples (*Acer platanoides*) are used by the city today as street trees because they are resistant to salt, drought and heat, soil compaction and pollutants; they will border the east–west boulevard René-Lévesque, continuing the city's scheme of planting. The north–south direction will be differentiated by rows of salt resistant cultivars, Green Ash (*Fraxinus pennsylvanica*), edging the highway ramps. The botanical community will be able to study the performance of the native Sugar Maple (*Acer saccharum*) in the city and the effectiveness of controlling the acidity content of the soil in combating the effects of acid rain. Similarly, the performance of the native American Elm (*Ulmus americana*), which is now reappearing spontaneously and disease-free in the forest, will be monitored.

In a preliminary report, Diana Gerrard described the site as "re-representing its own biological history in a shortened and idealized manner," an approach she termed "regionalist," a broadening of the realm of landscape architecture "into discourse with other areas of design theory involved in the same (architectural) investigations."[5]

The CCA Garden metaphorically re-represents the CCA. This garden, designed by Melvin Charney, resumes the design issues engaged by the building of the CCA and, in so doing, deeply embeds the ideas they represent. Charney was awarded the commission for the garden sculpture through a competition for the integration of art and architecture that was established by the Ministère des Affaires Culturels, Québec.[6] The CCA had proposed that the locus of the competition be the garden across from the Shaughnessy House, on the south side of the boulevard, because of its visibility and public nature. The sculptors chosen to compete were qualified by their interest in site-specific art. The competition offered the opportunity to involve the whole site, a possibility understood by Charney.

Like the building, the garden is both non-sited and sited in design. The taxis or disposition of formal elements, whole/part relationships, issues of light and procession apply to gardens as well as to buildings. In the fine tradition of European 18th-century narrative gardens, the CCA Garden is composed of sections: the orchard, the field, the Shaughnessy House re-represented as a "folly," and a series of allegorical columns. In these columns the industrial chimneys of the industrial sector of the city below the escarpment become column and obelisk in homage to Alberti's dictum that "gardens should not be wanting of columns and obelisks"[7]; the twin towers of a church below are represented by the archaic symbol of bulls' horns; a grain elevator is transformed to a temple; the traditional Montréal house becomes Le Corbusier's Domino House. Together, they provide a history engaging architecture and its meaning.

8. Gerrard and Mackars, "Environmental Stresses," *Preliminary Landscape Report: CCA,* 1987, p. 27

9. Gerrard and Mackars, "Planting Concept," *Preliminary Landscape Report: CCA,* 1987, p. 26

10. Melvin Charney, "The Situation of the CCA Garden in the City: the two intersecting sets of organizational axis in relation to the previous state of the site," July 1987 (coloured pencil and ink on vellum paper, 90.5 x 118 cm)

219

11. Melvin Charney, "Model of CCA Garden, Montréal," October 1987 (gelatin silver print)

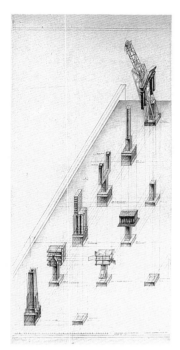

12. Melvin Charney, "Allegorical columns on the Esplanade of the CCA Garden, Montréal," September 1987 (coloured pencil and ink on vellum paper, 190 x 91.2 cm)

The garden is profoundly sited in the history of site and city. Orchard, fields and esplanades overlook the vast stretch of river and city; it is the picturesque Sulpician domain of Isaac Weld. The ancient dialectic of the *paradis terrestre* and the industrial city "below the hill" give the allegorical columns another level of meaning. The nine-foot-high column bases may be seen as workers' houses weighed down by church and factory. The historic and the modern site, Sulpician domain and highway, are conflated in the westernmost column. In the tipped plane of the total garden, cadastral divisions are made manifest in half-emerging lines of stone markers. Finally, Charney's arcadian reflection of the Shaughnessy House, "The Arcades," along with the allegorical columns beyond it, propound their discourse on architecture and the city. Together they symbolize the CCA as a centre for conserving and interpreting the documents of architecture, emblems of the humanist tradition.

As we worked, the identification of these elements strengthened our appreciation of the principles of urban and architectural design, the most important of which is the principle of starting with an analysis of what exists and building on the clues offered by the city, clues that history — when understood — provides.

Notes

[1] This article is drawn from my contribution "Design Imperatives," Chapter 2 of the forthcoming publication *Canadian Centre for Architecture, Building and Landscape*, Phyllis Lambert and Larry Richards, editors (CCA and MIT Press).

[2] Nancy Holt, ed., *The Writings of Robert Smithson, Essays with Illustrations* (New York: New York University Press, 1979), p. 124.

[3] The term *paradis terrestre* was used by Soeur Sainte-Ursule in her "Mémoires," I:30, Archives de la Congrégation de Nôtre-Dame de Montréal, cited by Robert Lahaise, *Les édifices conventuels de vieux Montréal* (Montréal, 1980), p. 292.

[4] Isaac Weld, *Travels Through the States of North America and the Provinces of Upper and Lower Canada during the Years 1795, 1796, and 1797*, 4th ed. (London, 1800), pp. 225–26.

[5] Gerrard and Mackars, "Preliminary Landscape Report: CCA," Toronto: February 3, 1988, p. 10.

[6] The winning entry announced September 21, 1987, was chosen by a six-member jury composed of Phyllis Lambert, Timothy Porteous, CCA; Peter Rose, architect of the CCA; Jean-Claude Leblond, Editor, *Vie des Arts*; Louise Déry, Director, Rimouski Museum; and Ghislain Papillon, Representative, Département des services aux artistes, Ministère des Affaires Culturels.

[7] From *De re aedificatoria*, cited by Melvin Charney in "A Garden for the Canadian Centre for Architecture," Chapter 4, *Canadian Centre for Architecture, Building and Landscape* (forthcoming).

A CHANGING PUBLIC LANDSCAPE

Frank Palermo

Every man takes the limits of his own field of vision as the limits of the world.

Schopenhauer, 1851

There is clear evidence that the public landscape of our cities is changing. Enclosed shopping malls serve as meeting places, allow for casual encounters and, for many, reflect a way of life. Internal walkways, winter gardens and elevated bridges provide connection, continuity and comfort in a Canadian context. These are new types of public/private spaces. Some critics see the emerging landscape as deviant, corrupt, destructive and unacceptable. They argue that all of our efforts should reinforce traditional, historically rooted kinds of public places: streets, squares and parks. Architects and planners, by and large, now see these newer developments as anomalous, idiosyncratic, impure and unworthy of much serious or positive concern. This paper argues that architects need to take a much more active role in formulating a broader and richer repertoire of public places to address the forces and motives behind the creation of these mutations.

It seems appropriate that city forms should change in response to contemporary conditions in a North American context, much as they have adapted to the specific conditions of other settings and other times. Cold winters, hot and humid summers, the profusion of cars, the demands of mass-marketing consumerism, the search for individual expression and other cultural indices all suggest adding a measure of comfort, convenience and intensity to the downtown public environment. However, emerging forms that respond to these conditions raise new questions about the nature of public life in quasi-public places and about the standard of design and amenity that should be demanded.

The Impact of Culture, Cars and Climate

Historically, the distinction between public and private places has been very clear. As the basic components of the public landscape, streets, squares and parks were well defined and easily understood.[1] Streets nourished and sustained daily life. They provided the setting for the play of children, the meeting of friends, the search for bargains as well as the passage of people and vehicles. Squares celebrated special places in the city. Within this context, public spaces and the buildings around them were inseparable. Purposeful, open-air, spatial figures were composed by flanking buildings that served as backdrops. In a sense, the "street" included the buildings located on it. While certain constant relationships may be discerned in the public spaces of the Western tradition, new types and variations have been developed throughout its history and have often given a particular city or district its distinctive character, for instance, the magnificently arcaded city of Bologna, the urban rooms of Baroque Rome, or the sweeping terraces of Georgian London. The notion of the building edge serving a public function is clearly articulated, as well, in Ledoux's design for Chaux where the street was reduced to a path within a natural landscape, the collective and social aspects of the street taking the form of a portico instead. The portico served as a public room and a transition between outside and inside.

> A majestic building is dedicated to wisdom; multiplied porticos surround it. Children play there under cover, young people stroll through them, the old meditate beneath them. There a school is opened where man is taught his duties before being instructed in his rights.[2]

Depending on one's perspective, then, one may now argue that elevated walkways, shopping arcades and indoor gardens are similarly positive additions to the repertoire of public places or that they are negative mutations that are destructive of the basic typology. Regardless of one's view, it is clear that public places in North American cities need to be reconsidered. At a general level, the character of the culture, the pervasive influence of the automobile and the dominant effects of the climate have altered traditional notions and demand new insights.

Current culture puts considerable emphasis on the value of the individual, privacy, freedom of choice, comfort, speed and technology. These characteristics imply that most buildings vie for attention rather than simply serve as backdrop for street and square. The street is now more a neutral link, a two-dimensional surface that does not impinge on adjacent buildings.[3]

1. The arcade of the Hudson's Bay Store in downtown Calgary

Nineteenth-century technological advances made possible large enclosed spaces in addition to, or as substitutes for, streets. The Galerie d'Orléans was built in 1830 as a greenhouse for shops and culture, the Galleria Vittorio Emmanuele in 1877 as a covered street in Milan and a century later Toronto's Eaton Centre as a mecca for fashionable consumerism.

Technological, economic and political forces have also served to dramatically alter the scale of the street itself. The three-dimensional quality of the street is confounded by rows of office towers that are more presences on the sky-scape than on the streetscape.

Cars have substantially redefined the pattern of settlement as well as the very nature of the street. Suburban development has flourished. Home and work are

222

2. Aerial view of downtown Calgary

endistanced. Streets have become roads filled with cars. The car gives easy access to the suburban mall which provides ample parking, choice, comfort and formidable competition to Main Street.

Urban renewal programs in the 1960s illustrate the dramatic difficulties encountered by city centres. Victor Gruen, the Swiss-American pioneer and proponent of regional shopping centres, promoted the mall as "more than just a place where one may shop — it shall be related in their minds with all activities of cultural enrichment and relaxation."[4] While entertainment, recreation and shopping flourished in suburban malls, drastic measures were implemented in response to the reduced sales and declining residential population in the city centre. To compete with the suburbs, so-called "slums" were cleared, traffic removed from some key streets, trees planted, sidewalks widened, shopping malls built following suburban prototypes and pedestrian walkway systems were added.

The street and the activities in and along it promoted its role as a social condenser and as a locus of common interests. Similarly, the best-known streets and the city centre came to symbolize the collective interests and values of the surrounding community. Today, these public spaces have often been reduced to automobile rights-of-way. Satisfaction of the demands of private transportation and the management of traffic have usurped the principal role of the urban street — that of promoting an open setting for communications and exchange — and transferred this function to building interiors.[5]

3. In many cities in Canada it is frequently too cold, too hot, or too windy to be outside

Climate also argues against the traditional street. Most North American cities are not conducive to year-round outdoor activity. Crowded streets, sidewalk cafés, plazas resplendent with fountains, concert performances and pigeons waiting to be fed provide powerful images of public life in urban places. Unfortunately, such ideal conditions are not always attainable. In many cities, it is frequently too hot, too cold, or too windy to be outside. Sitting in an outdoor café is not always pleasant. Snow, rain and wind can make outdoor performances uncomfortable, if not impossible. Frequently, conditions are so extreme as to render walking down the street a decidedly unpleasant experience. Is it any wonder that more and more of the "public" life is seeking refuge indoors?

Climate, cars and culture have contributed to the emergence of enclosed malls, walkways and indoor gardens. The city square has been transformed and adapted to become an indoor garden. The street has been reinterpreted in the form of the suburban shopping mall, the downtown retail arcade and elevated or underground walkway systems.

Selective Observations

Individually or even collectively as architects and planners, we may not like the fact that such mutant forms are being built, or particularly admire how they are done, or

223

4. The climate-controlled interior mall of the Halifax Shopping Centre

5. The multi-level interior atrium of Complexe Desjardins in Montreal

6. Elevated walkway in Halifax, leading to the Xerox Building

7. Elevated walkway bridge in Halifax, leading to the Xerox Building

willingly admit to frequenting such places; however, examples of indoor "public" places are found in most (if not all) cities and any casual observer would have to conclude that this emerging landscape is the setting for a multitude of public activities.

A few examples will suffice to illustrate the basic qualities of emerging "public" places as well as to highlight some of the fundamental difficulties.

The Halifax Shopping Centre on the outskirts of Halifax has few, if any, remarkable qualities. It is surrounded by a sea of cars. Shops are organized along the usual two-storey enclosed mall with a major store at each end. The interior street is independent of the rest of the world, artificially lit and of uninspiring proportions and detailing. While the professional may condemn the artificiality of this consumerist world and the perversion of "sidewalk sales" without sidewalks, innocents find life in this indoor environment. On any given day, downtown streets may be empty but the mall parking lot is full. Inside there are shoppers casually looking for bargains. Teenagers spend Saturdays cruising the mall. A few regulars find a special place to meet for their daily dose of gossip, lottery tickets are sold, fashion shows are staged and high-school bands perform. These are all time-honoured traditions of public places. Of course, when the shops close, the mall doors are locked.

Scotia Square and the elevated walkways that connect it to the waterfront, other commercial complexes and the convention centre are the downtown response to the Halifax Shopping Centre. In the worst tradition of urban renewal schemes, Scotia Square turns its back to the rest of the city. It is hermetically sealed and incorruptible by the vagaries of location, climate or history. True to its suburban pedigree, parking is provided on site, although it is concentrated in a multi-level garage demanding astute navigational skills. A department store and chain boutiques line malls focused on a central two-storey skylit atrium. The atrium is connected to an elevated walkway system that straightforwardly crosses a street, passes through a floor of hotel shops, becomes a thin glazed corridor extending some 250 feet over a profusion of redundant roadways to finally connect a series of waterfront offices, parking garage and hotel in a rather circuitous way.

This interior environment consists of an atrium, shopping malls and elevated walkways that have few, if any, positive or memorable physical qualities. In fact, the overall effect is dreary, if not dreadful. There is no drama and little colour in the central atrium. The place has none of the civic dimensions found in Complexe Desjardins in Montreal, which allows the underground walkways to blossom into a grand interior square. But despite its paltry physical presence, Scotia Square shares with Complexe Desjardins a true measure of civic life. Here the elderly regularly pass the day,[6] parents push carriages past shop windows, business executives stop for hurried chats, old friends meet for lunch, loners find a quiet place to read the paper by the fountain and an audience watches the ever-changing stage set.

The walkways themselves can only be described as uninspired. The bridges are utilitarian links rather than public places. They are thin pieces of wire along which

8,9. Episodes in the elevated walkway system — the +15 — in downtown Calgary

electricity might travel but never stops to illuminate. Both the imagery and function are mechanical. When the walkways pass through buildings they are even less self-assured, and are compressed, contorted and constrained to the point of completely losing themselves, and their users.

Clearly, the success of these places cannot easily be attributed to resonant physical attributes. The extraordinary fact is that despite the poor physical quality, the confusing nature of the connections and the lack of easy access, the number of people using the walkway system on a warm summer day is virtually equal to the number using nearby sidewalks on grade.[7] In the winter or during the rain, the preference is complete.

The +15 System, Calgary, Alberta, consists of an extensive network of walkways and bridges 15 feet above the ground. It was conceived in the late 1960s as an integrated pedestrian system consisting of open bridges, mid-block decks and open spaces. In time, the emphasis has shifted to climate-controlled environments providing relief from inclement weather as well as separation from car traffic. The system has been developed as public, but built by private enterprise with incentives provided by the City's bonus system. In that system, property owners are rewarded with extra density if they contribute toward public improvements. Public walkways connect parking garages, office lobbies, shopping concourses, hotels and apartment buildings. Some developments, like the Petro-Canada and the Nova Corporation buildings, provide generous indoor public gardens. The City of Calgary itself funded and operates the Devonian Gardens, a three-and-a-half-acre indoor park complete with landscaped terraces, fountains, wading pool and children's playground. The garden sits atop two floors of retail in the Toronto Dominion Centre and has two office towers perched above it.

The +15 system is warm, convenient and occasionally, if only by accident, provides some exciting views of the city or the mountains beyond. The walkways are generally well used year-round, their utilitarian service function can hardly be disputed. The gardens provide quiet refuge for contemplation and a treat for children.

The vision of a well-connected multi-layered city has its own traditions stretching from Leonardo da Vinci to the Italian futurist Antonio Sant'Elia, the brutalist urbanism of Peter and Alison Smithson in the 1950s, and the 1960s megastructures of Shadrach Woods. In Calgary, the system has been built incrementally and adapted to fit individual building conditions. As a result, it is often circuitous and maze-like, inconvenient and disorientating. It is also uncompromisingly bland. Places of entry are well camouflaged and the impact on adjacent streets is often devastating.

Cultivating Change

Despite the fact that much public life now occurs in indoor walkways, malls and gardens, most architects strenuously uphold the virtues of traditional urban forms and the moral fortitude provided by suffering heat, rain and blizzards. Their case is stated quite bluntly by William Whyte:

> The street is being put almost everywhere except at street level. It is being buried in subterranean corridors; it is being elevated on platforms or put in glass tubes. Finally it is being obliterated altogether as it is enveloped by mega-structures hermetically sealed against the city.[8]

But as Robert Gutman has pointed out:

> Like most romantic ideologies, the nostalgia for the community life of the old bye-law streets and tenements ignores what was bad about the past. The industrial street had genuine hazards, which had given rise to the new town policy, suburban resettlement, the Ville Radieuse, and Broadacre City in the first place. Nostalgia has also produced a myth about the universal appeal of street life, which is not confirmed by what we know of the social structure and life-style of different classes in the Victorian and pre–World War I cities....
>
> There is considerable evidence that the bourgeoisie of Victorian England did not like their urban streets so much either. Most of their social life was carried out away from the street....
>
> To mention the romanticism connected with the new admiration for street life is not to denigrate the current concern for reviving it but to put the issue in perspective. Romantic nostalgia is dangerous because it draws our attention away from the fundamental social changes that account for the real difficulties we encounter in dealing with the urban street.[9]

The changing nature of the public environment, then, raises many questions, but also provides considerable opportunities. There is no doubt that much of the criticism of interior public spaces is well deserved. A broader and richer language of public places has yet to emerge. Indeed, basic questions regarding the distinction between public and private still remain. "Public" is defined by *Webster's* as "of or pertaining to the people...belonging to the community at large, open to common general use and enjoyment." The need to be truly public raises legal issues about ownership, access, control, hours of operation and the range of permissible activities in indoor public places. It also presents design challenges that must be addressed through research, experimentation and criticism. This involves an architectural agenda that goes beyond the concerns of an individual client or building to deal with collective issues of the form and image of the city.

226

The traditional public places in cities need to be reconsidered due to a series of fundamental changes evident in the structure of cities and the values of its inhabitants. Such reconsideration can glean some insights and direction from the quasi-public internal environments that have emerged during the past few decades. The street needs to be seen as more than a public right-of-way functioning within a neutral grid. If streets were designed with passion and intensity, they would awaken civic pride, mediate between public and private interests, encourage idleness and provide a colourful and comfortable panorama for daily life.

10. Proposal for Sparks Street Mall Competition, 1986, by Frank Palermo and Ted Cavanagh

At the same time, the public landscape can be extended to include new types of public places, although this will require changes in both the legal and architectural language of the "public." All public places, whether traditional or new, outdoor or indoor, should meet the following essential criteria:

(a) They should be identifiable as part of a continuous public space system.

(b) Their design should be sufficiently developed to control the grain, scale and pattern of adjacent buildings.

(c) They should be naturally lit and respond to orientation and changing climatic conditions.

More specifically, criticism that is commonly directed at emerging public places can in fact be restated as issues for general architectural investigation. There are three major areas of concern:

1. **Memorable Configuration**. The monotonous and uninspired quality of indoor walkways and bridges demands the same energy and care normally devoted to designing a public place in a civic building. Bridges and walkways can then emerge as places in their own right. Purely utilitarian passageways can assume a multiplicity of functions and meanings as public rooms. These are the qualities that make the Ponte Vecchio in Florence a memorable experience.[10]

2. **Civic Orientation**. Urban renewal schemes in Halifax, as elsewhere, turn their backs to the surrounding streets. In these circumstances, internal malls have tenuous connections with the outdoors. If such complexes are to serve as public places, then the relationship between inside and outside needs to be improved. In exploring this issue, architects might consider the elegance of the Spanish Stairs in Rome or the jewel-like transparency of Paxton's Crystal Palace. Designs can be fashioned for internal public places to contribute to the street environment rather than detracting from it. Comfortable and exciting indoor and outdoor public environments can then coexist.

3. **Collective Connections**. The city normally provides clues about where we are. It offers familiar views, a glimpse of notable landmarks, perceived changes in topography or vegetation or quality of light. Indoor public systems could, with effort, be

transformed from confusing corridors to an urban architecture distinguished by special places, new views of the city, different spaces for collective gathering, play and civic celebration. Intersections could assume added significance, the progression through the system could be filled with many discoveries, and detailed design could reflect a concern for daily and seasonal cycles.

Obviously this is a challenging and contentious agenda. Some will argue that it is anti-urban or even anti-democratic. The cautious will steer toward the more travelled route. A few may find inspiration in Theodore Roethke's words:

> And when I walked, my feet seemed deep in sand.
> I moved like some heat-weary animal.
> I went, not looking back. I was afraid.
>
> The way grew steeper between stony walls,
> Then lost itself down through a rocky gorge.
> A donkey path led to a small plateau.
> Below, the bright sea was, the level waves,
> And all the winds came toward me. I was glad.[11]

The time is ripe to cultivate a richer and more varied public landscape than is provided by either traditional public spaces or the recently emerged interior world of malls and walkways. New possibilities can emerge, but only with the active intervention of architects. Change will not happen immediately, easily or by decree. Its rhythm is more likely to be determined by applying ingenuity, vision and historical perspective to the design of each pedestrian bridge. The test is in the specific artefacts rather than global pronouncements.

Notes
[1] Rob Krier, *Urban Spaces* (New York: Rizzoli, 1978).
[2] C. N. Ledoux, *L'Architecture considérée sous le rapport de l'art, des moeurs, et de la législation*, Vol. 1 (Paris, 1804).
[3] Joseph Rykwert, "The Street: The Use of Its History," in Stanford Anderson, ed., *On Streets* (Cambridge, Mass.: MIT Press, 1986), p. 23.
[4] H. Gillette, Jr., "The Evolution of the Planned Shopping Centre," *JAPA*, Vol. 51, No. 4, 1985.
[5] V. Caliandro, "Street Form and Use: A Survey of Principal American Street Environments," in Anderson, ed., p. 151.
[6] P. Sijpkes, D. Brown and M. MacLean, "Elderly People in Montreal's Indoor City," *Plan Canada*, June 1983, p. 14.
[7] Development and Planning Department, City of Halifax, "Downtown Pedestrian Study," March 1988.
[8] W. Whyte, "The Humblest Street—Can It Survive?" *Historic Preservation*, Vol. 32, No. 2, 1982, pp. 34–41.
[9] R. Gutman, "The Street Generation," in Anderson, ed., pp. 255–56.
[10] Colin Rowe, "I Stood in Venice on the Bridge of Sighs," *Design Quarterly 129: Skyways* (Minneapolis, 1985), p. 8.
[11] T. Roethke, "I Waited," *The Far Field* (New York: Doubleday/Anchor Books, 1971), p. 91.

PUBLIC SPACE ON PRIVATE SITES

Gerald L. Forseth

Rockefeller Center in New York, begun in 1929 and opened in 1933, remains one of the most remarkable urban projects of this century. Not only was it the culmination of the first period of high-rise development in America and the final work of New York's most enterprising skyscraper architect, Raymond Hood, but it made the radical shift from development focused on the single building on its own lot/block to development that subsumed several city blocks and created significant public spaces, outdoor pedestrian courtyards and interior spaces at grade, below grade, at low roof level and at high roof level. For many years the most exhilarating observation deck in Manhattan was the narrow ship-like platform at the top of the RCA Building, and the much-admired roof gardens have recently been re-created and are once again available for public pleasure. Rockefeller Center remains the pre-eminent example of dense high-rise development that creates finely scaled and amenable urban spaces within its site.

In contrast, the high-rise urban evironments of this century in Canada are a miserable lot. As our cities have grown and decentralized, the emphasis has been on the provision of infrastructure, utilities and roads, with little or no development of intelligent and amenable urban space that would promote involvement with the city beyond our private homes and workplaces. There have been too few architects, planners, citizens and politicians who have understood the importance of public space to the full growth of an urban community. The cost of creating public space has generally been considered too high for the public purse to bear. And where efforts have been made, the results are usually poor. Our successes have been few and somewhat insignificant. For example, in my hometown of Calgary, the City had the foresight recently to create a new urban space opposite the new City Hall, in the heart of downtown; but the design and development of this space is disorganized, incomprehensible as a whole, disorientating and unrewarding. And the costs of acquiring the land, demolishing the existing buildings, reservicing the site and constructing the plaza were very high; without Olympic funds it probably would not have been undertaken.

On the other hand, in the same city there is a tiny triangular infill plaza built in 1987 on Kensington Road in trendy Hillhurst/Sunnyside district. The site was taken from a former road, developed with a modest budget to pay for pavers and furniture, has a few interesting low-density buildings facing it, is very popular and considered to be aesthetically pleasing. This public space became necessary because congestion on the narrow sidewalks was spilling over and pedestrians were stopping traffic. It is not a "major" public space, but it is successful in many ways.

In our young and growing country, development has emphasized the basic provision of buildings, renting or selling them, and maximizing the financial return on our land. The contribution that new buildings can make to the quality of urban space and urban experience has been of much less concern. Indeed, the most serious and dramatic urban problem of the past several decades has been the erosion of tradition-

1. Rockefeller Center, New York (Raymond Hood, Architect, 1933) is an exemplary case of public spaces created within a private development on the ground level and also on the low roof gardens. It combines North American densities with European traditions of urban space

2. This "View of the Centre, Calgary, Alberta" of 1914 by landscape architect Thomas Mawson for Princes' Island, Bow River and the central area of Calgary was a grand vision of the city and its public spaces in the tradition of the Beaux-Arts and the City Beautiful Movement. While Calgary does have fine traditions of public spaces, these were largely put aside during the building boom of the 1970s and 1980s as new ideas of traffic separation, high-density and private public space came to the fore ("Calgary, A Preliminary Scheme for Controlling the Economic Growth of the City," Thomas H. Mawson & Son)

3. The emerging petroleum-financed central core of Calgary, Alberta, shows a fascination with tall buildings superimposed on the residue of a small-scale urban fabric

4. The Esso Plaza at Fifth Avenue and Second Street is an open space with a skating rink/reflecting pool that was created on private land by a private corporation. Completed in 1981, with Bregman & Hamann, Architects, it is a clear expression of the municipal bonus system through which developers can gain extra density by providing public amenities. In this case, the plaza suffers in competition with the elevated pedestrian movement system, the +15, which was also promoted under the bonus system. With all of the retail and restaurant activity lifted onto the second floor, the building's edges on the plaza are blank and lifeless. The project also demonstrates that while the bonus system may be able to extract some public benefits from developers, it cannot generate high-quality design

al streets, squares and markets where public life took place, by the form of new developments — isolated buildings cut off from one another by traffic, parking lots and aimless, unused open space.

In response to this situation, some of our brightest planning minds have promoted new concepts to recharge the demand for public space in our fast-paced, high-density downtown cores. These concepts involve mixed-use development with retail at grade; setting back private and public buildings from property lines to permit increased hard and soft landscaping and an occasional outdoor restaurant; and increasing density to help pay for the assumed high costs to develop quality public space. The most prevalent technique that has emerged over the past two decades has been the creation of incentives within the municipal planning framework to encourage private development to create on-site amenities, services and spaces for the public. New kinds of public spaces have emerged as a result of such private industry/municipal authority partnerships, spaces that are often internal to the development, glassed over and climatically controlled, multi-storey and visually "pleasant." In the Canadian climate, the interior atrium has become a popular building type, creating a weather-protected oasis that keeps the building buzzing like a beehive in all seasons.

Whether encouraged by public authorities or not, these kinds of spaces are **private** public spaces. While they are generally accessible to the public most of the time, they are different from public spaces by virtue of their location on private land, and inside private buildings. The atrium type of building, for instance, has been severely criticized for turning its back on the city's streets and becoming a space for a privileged portion of society, accessible only within specific working hours, and heavily monitored by security guards.

This paper will discuss private public space as one aspect of the public domain in the contemporary city and review the system of incentives that has been used to create it, through examples in Calgary.

Traditionally, public squares, markets and streets have offered citizens many things: universal accessibility, shared experiences — both ordinary and extraordinary — in common spaces, a sense that public life expands and enriches our personal and private lives, a sense of safety and security through the subtle monitoring of activity, and a sense of civic pride through the thoughtful design of spaces to achieve coherence, clarity, unity, timelessness and beauty. Now, in our highly commercial world, in addition to these characteristics, private public spaces also offer benefits for private interests: an improved working environment to keep staff loyal and proud of their company, and improved economic return through both the increase in building densities that incentives provide and the increase in rents that a more desirable building provides. It is in this combination of public and private qualities that opportunities, as well as confusions, now abound.

In a Western city of the New World, like Calgary, new ideas do not necessarily scare its movers and shakers, and traditions are often discarded, never to be seen again. During the last two decades an enthusiasm for new building, dense downtown development and innovations in vehicular/pedestrian segregation seized the imagination of planners and developers of Calgary and served to displace the city's traditions of public space. It may be a surprise to many, but central Calgary had a grand urban plan prepared by the famous landscape architect Thomas Mawson in 1914 in which he envisioned an arcaded, white, Beaux-Arts style city on the Bow River. It is considered impossible to recognize any of the Mawson plan in today's central core; however, the terracotta-faced structures of the Hudson's Bay Company (1911, 1929) and the Burns Meat Company (1910) — the former with a continuous arcade and the latter with a glass canopy over the sidewalk — embody the spirit that Mawson pursued in his Calgary Plan of white buildings having continuous weather protection at the sidewalk.

Then, as now, public space has traditionally been associated in Calgary with the appreciation of nature along the riverbank, on the secluded island and in the nearby Banff National Park. And in the city itself there was a tradition of public space created by private donation, as in the case of Central Park and its library built by the Carnegie Foundation in 1911, or the spendid sidewalk arcade of the Hudson's Bay Company store, which recalls the ideas of the Mawson plan. Even in less exalted forms, the streets and sidewalks of Calgary were vital public spaces filled with people whose public lives were made more enjoyable by awnings, gas and electric lighting, attention to detail in brick and stone, large signage on buildings, and the mixture of horses, cars and transit vehicles. There was real and engaging congestion on the sidewalks!

But, like other cities in North America, the face of Calgary has been radically changed through the introduction of two powerful 20th-century ideas: first, the idea of the tall building, which has become the favoured mode of development on prime downtown lands; and second, the idea of zoning controls advocated by CIAM in the Athens Charter of 1933 to bring order to the urban jungle by separating uses into different parts of the city.

While many factors, both technological and real estate, converged at the turn of the century to generate the skyscraper as a new building type, it is the ever-increasing cost of land that continues to drive the development of tall buildings. Not so long ago, a density of 7x the site area was considered reasonable; in most cities today, developers are promoting densities of 15x to 20x coverage. And the system of incentives in municipal planning controls, in Calgary known as the "bonus system," offers a ready device to justify these higher densities on the basis of contributions made in the development toward the public good. The bonus system in Calgary was formulated in the mid-1970s and has gone substantially unchanged since; it represents the values and visions of those who drafted it. Some might say these values and visions need to be criticized or at least redefined. Indeed, most projects have been

5. A typical interior atrium in a downtown Calgary office complex, the Toronto Dominion Square of 1977, J. H. Cook, Architects, and Skidmore, Owings & Merrill, Architects. These multi-storey spaces with escalators and stairs serve to connect the ground floor with the elevated pedestrian network on the second-floor level. In the case of this building there is also an interior garden at the fourth-floor level. See Exhibition Section for photographs of this Calgary site

6. Park Centre (unbuilt project of 1982) by Kohn, Pederson, Fox, Architects, and CK Architectural Group

7. General view of the Nova Building in Calgary. This project opened in 1982. Its client, Nova Corporation, and architect J. H. Cook with L. F. Valentine in charge, used the bonus system to maximize the development potential of the site, but implemented public amenities such as a winter garden, art gallery and auditorium with exceptional architectural skill and with ongoing commitment for funding and management of these public facilities

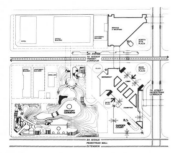

8. Ground floor plan of the Nova Building, Calgary

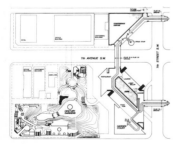

9. +15 floor plan of the Nova Building, Calgary

poorly planned to achieve any real public benefit.

Under the current bonus system all development in the downtown business district must include the items of Bonus Group A, which include at-grade pedestrian space to enlarge the sidewalk along the length of the block and at the corner; open space at grade (say 5 per cent of net site area); and the inclusion of an elevated network of routes and bridges for pedestrian movement (the +15 system). Altogether, these items would permit a density of 7x coverage, which would yield a building of about thirty storeys. If, in addition, a sufficient number of items from Bonus Group B are provided, the density could be increased to 15x coverage to construct a building of fifty-five to sixty storeys. Such items include an at-grade plaza up to 20 per cent of the site area; an open outdoor space at the +15 level, particularly if arcaded; an indoor park at grade directly accessible from public outdoor space; +15 bridges over streets to link with other buildings; and escalators rather than stairs to the +15 system. An additional 3x coverage can be achieved by providing on-site sculpture, retaining heritage features, transferring density from another site, and protecting sunlight in public spaces.

In Calgary, with its "sophisticated" bonus system, there are also Group C items that can be utilized after 15x coverage has been reached, and to a limit of 20x coverage. This yields a building of about eighty-five to ninety storeys. Group C items are principally density transfer from Heritage Buildings and monetary contributions toward off-site public improvements in other sections of the downtown area.

Calgary's bonus system, through which the City has encouraged the provision of public amenity on private lands in exchange for increased density, has been heavily criticized for the following reasons. Many of the so-called public amenities that have been encouraged have questionable public benefit in real terms. The creation of an extensive, interior and elevated pedestrian landscape has had a disastrous consequence for the streets of the city; people and activities have been drawn inside, while new buildings create blank walls and service entrances on the street. Special public facilities, such as an auditorium, may be constructed by private developers but then never used. And finally, the increased density, which generates increased private profit, demands increased municipal infrastructure, utilities and services, which place a heavy financial burden on the public purse.

Despite all this, there are a few positive projects that have been generated under this system, and I would like to cite two examples. The first is an unbuilt project called Park Centre, developed by Cadillac Fairview and designed in 1982 by Kohn/Pederson/Fox and the CK Architectural Group. Park Centre encompassed an entire central block and was to have 2.6 million square feet of space. Briefly, this project used the bonus system to its maximum and the result appeared promising at the ground level. A mixed-use project, it was to include two floors of retail, two office towers and a hotel tower. It included an outdoor urban plaza with porticos, screens, waterfall and monuments, a wind-protected public space of 35,000 square feet that

was to include elements familiar to people who have enjoyed the great historic public spaces of Europe. At least 10 per cent of the full block was allocated to an arcaded walkway on the edges of the building and encircling the plaza. And even the elevated pedestrian bridges were to be lined with shops to increase their function and frequency of use. While the bonus system promoted these provisions, the office towers, at fifty storeys each, are extremely tall relative to the 15-storey, 400-room luxury hotel. Nevertheless, had the economy in Western Canada not declined in 1983, this project would have made one of the few positive contributions to the public space of the central city.

My second example is the Nova Building built in 1982 at the east edge of the Century Gardens in the western end of the central core. It is a built project that embodies the best of the bonus system and the desire of the owner, Nova Corporation, and the architect, J. H. Cook, Architects and Planners (Frederick L. Valentine, project architect) of Calgary, to contribute meaningful public space within their own private site.

First, the project is polite and courteous. It fits a tall building on a small and sensitive site, but provides real benefits to the public within its lower floor space and at grade. By rotating the tower off the usual north/south alignment of the streets, it maximized the amount of sun that would fall on the adjacent Century Gardens. As well, the owners purchased a relief site across the avenue for a low-density component of the building, including the auditorium, cafeteria and loading docks. The main building site includes a handsome and lushly planted winter garden for year-round public pleasure. This multi-storey space also serves as a main entrance and for easy orientation to the +15 pedestrian system, which is of course also included. The space provides colour and animation, not in an artificial or superficial way, but through the use of real concepts that serve real public needs to which the architecture has responded sensitively. Most of the space in the winter garden is used as a civic gallery, showing contemporary visual art to the largest possible audience. For many it has become a building to be visited time and again to take in the latest guest-curated exhibition, just as they would regularly visit the Glenbow Museum near the Olympic Plaza.

Even though there are powerful vested interests at work in the Nova project and the value of the site has been maximized through this development, the building has become an integral part of the life of the community. Citizen conflict was avoided early by ensuring that the neighbouring park would continue to receive adequate sunlight through innovative design. The destructive quality of on-site delivery needs

12. The Nova Building's greenhouse is operated year-round as a gallery of contemporary art. Terminating the +15 system within the building has given activity back to the main street level (photo D. Curran)

was avoided by providing this particular function on an adjacent site, even though this additional site was expensive to purchase. The winter garden is a relaxed and beautiful environment, a straightforward extension of both the street and the outdoor park, and is enjoyed in all seasons; it extends the city's repertoire of public space types in the tradition of public floral conservatories from 19th-century Europe. And finally, the provision of public spaces and facilities for specific community needs, which were identified by the corporation and aided by the bonus system, has provided the citizens of Calgary with new opportunities for public functions. The building includes a 270-seat auditorium and several meeting rooms that are available to the general public and are fully equipped and maintained. It includes a food fair that is unlike the usual suburban variety, in that it promotes the ongoing use of the park on sunny, warm days and the winter garden on days of poor weather. Flower stalls and other retail spaces are allowed to be operated by non-profit service clubs, a concept that combines community service with added colour and animation. One of the finest restaurants in the city is set in a second greenhouse. And most importantly, Nova Corporation's ongoing commitment to the visual arts program in the public areas has created one of the best galleries in town. This exhibition space has become a vital part of the current art gallery space of the city. The corporation seeks adventurous, curated shows having high public appeal. The costs associated with its year-round program (co-ordination, signage, posters, set-up and dismantling) are borne by them.

This project contributes to our public lives because there was an ongoing commitment to the community after the construction of the building. Private public spaces must enhance the quality of public life. All too often, however, developers and their architects still pay lip service to the use of bonus-system public space and simply produce superficial "public amenities." The integrated series of public spaces and activities in the base of the Nova Building demonstrate the possibilities for meaningful urban space constructed within the private realm. The "private" nature of this public space means that a more difficult task is at hand than if the space were on public lands and publicly funded. The success of private public space requires enlightened sponsorship by private industry and their own routine viewing and reviewing to ensure an active level of public use. It is nevertheless an absolutely necessary component of the "private" public space equation that corporations/owners take on this continuing role as part of their agreements with the City and its citizens, especially when receiving immense monetary benefits from increased density.

13. Sculpture installation in the Nova Building during the XV Olympic Winter Games in Calgary in 1988 (photo D. Curran)

234

LOGISTICS AND FRICTION: Political Science of the Metropolitan Frontier

Donald McKay

Twelve months ago, at the conclusion of another paper, I presented a brief hypothesis for reading the contemporary city. In this presentation I want to examine that reading of the city in order to establish a general framework for identifying the opportunities for emerging public spaces.

Briefly, the hypothesis is that we operate today with several simultaneous concepts of urbanity, and while each is flawed by its fixity, the fluid domain of contradictions among these ideas presents a realm of experiment and invention where we can continue to develop as individuals, and perhaps as a community.

In order to pursue this hypothesis I am addressing a discourse established by Max Weber in his 1905 study *The City*.[1] From *fin de siècle* Germany to Chicago between the wars, the discipline of urban studies varies significantly, yet it retains certain key characteristics that influence our attitudes toward urbanism today:

1. By combining the disciplines of history, sociology, anthropology and political science, Weber and his successors develop a proto-structuralist paradigm of the city, one which permits discussion of general patterns as well as particular relationships.

2. As it develops in the Chicago School, the city becomes understood as a social laboratory, a place from which **questions** of existence and society would emerge, rather than an ideal which could **explain** social phenomena.

3. The city is understood as a domain where direct communication between citizens is no longer dominant, where constitutionally individuals express their personal interests through collective representations.

4. The city is comprised of an "urban culture" in which operations of the various systems at the basis of society (economic, political, civic and social) are divided, but interact ecologically, in a way like the various roles of individual lives in an urban community.

5. In order to understand the interrelation of the various systems, functions and roles of urban culture, it is studied at the moments of disorder. The patterns of deviance may define the order of the city.

The moment of disorder illuminates the organization of contemporary urbanity. It is an event, a friction in the logistics of the city. I would like to discuss this friction according to a threefold reading of the city, a reading that is imbedded in the discipline of urban studies. These interpretations may be called the Official City, the Shadow City and the Metropolis.

1. **The Official City** is the city of light, the historic city, the Capital. It is the realm of representation, of stability and of identity. It is the repository of the myth of Genesis. Here are the instruments of rhetoric and political theatre. The Official City has boundaries and a threefold centre representing its spiritual source, its commercial condition and the secular basis of its authority. Its constituency is the burgher, the bourgeois, the propertied citizen, the long-term resident of a permanent community.

2. **The Shadow City** is the city of darkness, the ghetto, the black market, the underworld. It exists in the shadow of the Official City and is its counter-form; in dark times this city of Vice grows to overwhelm the city of Virtue. The Shadow City tends to represent itself in time rather than in space; in place of physical boundary and centre, the Shadow City is contained and identified by its only social authority, the policeman. The constituency of this city is the stranger, one who has come yesterday, perhaps to leave tomorrow.

3. **The Metropolis** is the city as network. Created by state governments in order to broadcast the benefits and security of the Official City throughout the countryside, it can now exist alone. Relentless in the pursuit of its own development, extension and subdivision, the Metropolis promises the opportunity to communicate even as it radically circumscribes the form of that communication. The Metropolis knows no boundary; if it could dissolve its material being it would, leaving behind only the self-regulation of its own ethereal networks. There is no constituency to the Metropolis; its inhabitants operate in isolation, stubbornly resisting representation in favour of solitude in great numbers. They are a population in a state of permanent transition; yet they are no longer strangers, for there is no city wall to define their foreignness.

Michel Foucault[2] describes four major types of technologies "related to specific techniques that human beings use to understand themselves…each a matrix of practical reason":

> (1) technologies of production, which permit us to produce, transform, or manipulate things; (2) technologies of sign systems, which permit us to use signs, meanings, symbols, or signification; (3) technologies of power, which determine the conduct of individuals and submit them to certain ends or domination, an objectivizing of the subject; (4) technologies of the self, which permit individuals to effect by their own means or with the help of others a certain number of operations on their own bodies and souls, thoughts, conduct, and way of being, so as to transform themselves in order to attain a certain state of happiness, purity, wisdom, perfection or immortality.

At least recently, the architectural discourse has been interested in addressing only the first two of these technologies: production and sign systems. Technologies of power and of the self have been, except in a few instances, absent. In a discussion of emerging public space these two technologies must become dominant if we are not to speak only of the **simulation** of public space or the **approximation** of public life. In order to discuss the emergence of new public spaces it will be necessary to discuss the nature of power and self in the contemporary city. This paper is restricted primarily to the technology of power, and specifically to military and paramilitary techniques of regulation. When I began this sketch of the regulation of urbanity I was not intent upon relating my thesis to a more historic discourse of the city. I am making that excursion behind hostile lines now in order to put a fresh reading of urbanity in context.

This fourth reading, **the Metropolitan Frontier,** exists in the common contradictions between the three paradigms of classic urban studies. It emerges as opportunities occur to avoid the logistics of the Official City, the Shadow City and the Metropolis. It is a domain of disorder, in that it exists outside the conventions of order for each of the other three. It is the laboratory of the city anticipated by those urban scholars who optimistically value the by-products of urban civilization.

LOGISTICS: Regulation of the City

The logistics of urbanity are complex, largely because they depend on a compound reading of urbanity — a reading which is traditionally threefold.[3] The simultaneity of these readings is with us since at least the 1950s, when the first critics of the metropolitan expansion of New York City begin to argue for the preservation and reconstruction of the historic city, or at least for a city based on its model.[4]

Previously the three readings of the city are interpreted (1) as separate stages in a historic process of development, by urban scholars such as Max Weber or Georg Simmel; or (2) according to Oswald Spengler, as moments in a cycle of growth and decline; or (3) as an organic event in a process of rational but not entirely predictable development, a position developed in the writings of Chicago School theorists such as Robert Park, Louis Wirth and Robert Redfield. After the Second World War, and in several ways perhaps because of it, these different concepts of urbanity come to be seen instead as coexistent, as conscious choices. In his book *The City in History*, Lewis Mumford spells out the alternatives:

> When we finally reach our own age, we shall find that urban society has come to a
> parting of the ways. Here, with a heightened consciousness of our past and a
> clearer insight into decisions made long ago, which often still control us, we shall
> be able to face the immediate decision that now confronts man and will, one way
> or another, ultimately transform him: namely, whether he shall devote himself to
> the development of his own deepest humanity, or whether he shall surrender

1. Plan of the fortified town of Aigues-Mortes, founded in 1246

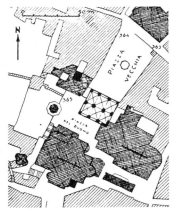

2. Plan of the historic town centre of Bergamo, showing the main civic square and the cathedral square. The north side of the Piazza Vecchia is continuous with the chief market street

himself to the now almost automatic forces he himself has set in motion and yield place to his dehumanized alter ego, "Post-historic Man." That second choice will bring with it a progressive loss of feeling, emotion, creative audacity, and finally consciousness.[5]

The first of these concepts — the one which has evolved as the Official City — is a very material one, preoccupied with permanence and with representation. In *The Idea of a Town*, Joseph Rykwert[6] links the city indissolubly to the myth of Genesis, to the story of its foundation. The Official City is the repository of this myth. The Official City has boundaries, natural or man-made — it is the settlement protected by battlements or the shore of the lake or the river's bank; it is on the hill overlooking the plain below. And if the city has precise boundaries, it also has a clearly defined centre, established by the market square, the cathedral, and the town hall with its clock tower and civic square for assembling the garrison. The function of the Official City is twofold. It is a source and instrument of mercantile wealth, and it is the secure centre of power.

The stranger is only admitted within the fortification by day, to trade; he and his tribe are banished beyond the walls at dusk. The watch patrols the streets by night, and can do so with confidence for it knows every face of the city and can bear witness against the wrongdoer and the disorderly. The enemy is beyond the wall.

The role of the fortification with its promise of security is key in this situation. Security is the paramount drive of the historic city. Throughout the world the first and predominant public service is defence, the first civil organization is the garrison or the watch.[7] Before Charles VIII invades Italy at the end of the 15th century, wars are protracted and relatively bloodless; the methods followed in besieging towns are slow and uncertain; and artillery is managed with such a lack of skill that it causes little damage. The ruler of a state remained secure within his walls.

Even in 1494 when Charles VIII of France conquers the fortified cities of northern Italy with a siege army of eighteen thousand and forty pieces of modern artillery, the city is slow to change. The ruler is reluctant to surrender the fortification, the emblem of security.

> By the operation of that perennial tension between the offensive and the defensive from which…strategy and innovation spring, the challenge of firepower was soon answered by improvements in military architecture that diminished, if they did not nullify, the advantages gained by the new siege guns. The defensive system that came to be known as the *trace italienne* involved the building of geometrically designed fortifications with angled bastions set at intervals to catch the enemy's infantry in enfilading fire, and moats to keep his artillery at a distance, and casements and ravelins to protect the moats.[8]

The cost of this security is enormous, based as it is on the vast scale of the forti-

238

fications and the armies raised to defend and assault them. By the mid-1600s each of the states of Europe maintains an army ten times the size of Charles VIII's invasion force. At the dawn of the Enlightenment, France, Russia and the Cromwellian Republic of England devote between 75 and 90 per cent of their total revenues to war and the maintenance of the military establishment.

3. Siege of Montauban, 1621, as represented by Merian (1646)

The history of cities might freeze here, with fortifications threatening to envelop and smother the towns within, if the nations of Europe do not take their militarism abroad to China and Indo-China, the Pacific, India, Africa, North and South America. There the soldiers of half a dozen modern armies and the merchants of great trading companies establish the settlements and networks necessary to provide the goods and wealth for an economic, technical and social revolution in Europe. The Shadow City that historian Carl Schorske calls the city of Vice grows up out of the prosperity of the Official City, out of its technical development, and out of the growth of the city beyond its fortified walls.

The Official City, the city of Virtue, maintains control of the stranger: he is supervised by the entire community and banished by dark. The stranger is suburban — literally beyond the wall. The Shadow City emerges with the literal or virtual dissolution of the wall: the stranger is within.[9] The stranger takes many forms: the foreign national; the country man; the social, sexual, political, economic or cultural deviant; the disorderly; the insane; the criminal. As a character he is the focus of much of the enduring literature of the last century; Dickens, Engels, Hugo, Baudelaire each portray the constituents of the Shadow City.

The stranger does not exist spatially within the Official City for a significant time after his arrival. Weber, in describing the community of the city, cites several conditions for official urbanity: fortifications, market, law and court, social forms of association related to the culture of the city (for instance, craft guilds, religious alliances, and so on) and partial autonomy — an elected administration. Weber points out that it is the burghers who elect: male citizens, propertied, differentially taxed, and accounted for in records. The stranger is not a citizen, not propertied, not taxed, except perhaps by class or by head tax (this tax by type is, for instance, typical of those imposed on Jews in medieval Europe). Most significantly, the stranger is not accounted for in records — to be recorded is to be a citizen of the Official City, with all the privilege, security and authority of citizenship.

4. Paris: the stranger, in this case a Gypsy family photographed by Atget (1912)

The presence of this city of strangers is not recognized by the great planners and architects of the Enlightenment; the strangers do not yet have spatial presence. The urban ideal of the new planners — Ledoux, Durand, Percier and Fontaine in France; Schinkel and Weinbrenner in Germany; John Nash in England; Thomas Jefferson in the United States — is almost universally small in scale. The vast horde of strangers which will flood the cities of Europe and America after 1750 is invisible.

The Shadow City emerges as a paradigm in the last half of the 18th and the first half of the 19th century, with the recognition of this new class within urbanity:

5,6. London: living in the shadow of the 19th-century Metropolis, as represented in engravings by Doré (1872)

7. Los Angeles: control of the Shadow City, from a *Time* magazine article on the emergence of a gang culture in the ghettos of southern California (1988)

the class of strangers. This class is brought into being with the creation of the modern police force, which defines it as a group and prepares the first census of its population.

The modern police force itself arises from a number of sources — constabulary and marshals, the watch, thief catchers, sheriffs, militias, men-at-arms, the *posse comitatus* — but inevitably these sources are traced back in turn to two great foundations: the army of occupation and the industry of crime. The army of occupation has always demanded the force of police in order to maintain civilian order. Karl von Clausewitz, the Prussian philosopher of war, explains why in his chapter on "Lines of Communication": the police are the permanent civil force left along the lines of communication by an invading army, charged with the day-to-day pacification of the native populace, protecting the line of supply and retreat.

From the Norman Statutes[10] that establish the institutions of constable and watch, to Sir Robert Peel's riotously uniformed Irish Police founded in 1818, there exists the strategic need to create a force of occupation which, although paramilitary in nature, is nevertheless civil in its orientation. In Ireland, Peel creates a new kind of bureaucracy, operating in a social domain midway between the foreign military force and the people to be controlled. It is the paramilitary nature of the modern police developed by Peel which goes so far to develop the class of strangers. In *Police in Urban America*, Eric Monkkonen argues that the symbolic significance of the uniform — created in order to make an open show of the force of order — makes "the dangerous class" an inevitability.[11] By taking the position that crime could be prevented or deterred, the champions of the police anticipate a class of potential offenders; emphasis is redirected from the act to the actor — the "dangerous class" emerges.

But if this class is brought to light with the open show of authority, it is created a generation earlier with the explicit co-operation of authority. The creation of the underworld — the organization of the unruly, the disorderly, the foreign and the frankly criminal into a proper constituency for the Shadow City — is an act carried out under the sign of authority, at the behest of police magistrates, gens d'armes, chief constables…and it is done in the name of order.

In the great cities of Europe and America actual crime, most significantly theft, increases as prosperity swells the city and existing formal and casual social controls collapse in the face of the rapidly growing populations. A new profession emerges. The detective — part police spy, part thief catcher, part bounty hunter — takes a different form from city to city depending on the circumstances. In Paris he is the police spy; in London, the thief catcher; in America he is the constable or marshal who has forsaken his court-appointed duties in order to pursue rewards for the return of stolen goods. In an era before the propertied citizen is protected by insurance, the detective is an important go-between. His contribution to the establishment of the class of the underworld is threefold. First, he inevitably keeps records of known criminals and their society. Second, he often participates in the organization of crime

8,9. Paris: the barricade as transitory fortification — the political riot as institution — 1848 and 1968

10. Jerusalem, the West Bank: continuous riot as national expression (1988)

rings, either as *agent provocateur* or as manager of an inherently disorderly class, inspiring it with the ethic of the growing class of burghers it preys on. Finally, he is seen as the only containment for, and representative of, the growing class of strangers.

But if the police and their agents are responsible for the effective creation, enumeration and subsequent control of the "dangerous class," they are helpless in the face of its political manifestation, the rioting mob. The riot, always present as gratuitous interruption in the temporal order of the city, develops as a political instrument in London in the 1760s. Whig politicians intent on humiliating the Crown raise and control mobs for street riots and lootings. The urban demonstrations in New York and Boston, which help spark the War of Independence, are directly inspired by the political riots in London. By 1780, established interests in London abandon the practice after a particularly disastrous riot, but not before the British and American demonstrations inspire the political tradition of street riot in Paris, where it comes to be identified permanently with the overthrow of the official order, in France and throughout the world. The political expression of the Shadow City is the creation of the Official City. Once created it develops a logistics of its own: the rioting mob becomes the "revolutionary army." The Official City has shed its fortifications; the enemy is within the walls and from time to time the enemy within enjoys great success.

The third reading of urbanity — the great city, the Metropolis — springs out of the tension between the Official City and the Shadow City. The Metropolis is a new kind of urbanity, not simply a larger city, for metropolitan ideology is not a necessary prerequisite of the larger city. For instance, it is not necessary for Paris to reform its structure into a metropolitan one in order to continue to grow. Speaking of Paris in the years immediately before Haussmann, Howard Saalman[12] writes:

> Regardless of whether one considers mid-nineteenth century lower class housing in Paris adequate or inadequate…the lower classes were in one way or another served by the existing city of 1850. Masses of them lived, worked, played and died within the old city which had been their habitat for centuries. If there was anything wrong with the old city, it was that there was not enough of it for the sky-rocketing population. But to a degree that problem was solving itself in the way it always had; the latest comers simply had to take their place at the burgeoning periphery. By the late 1850's, in fact, the mass of newcomers had spread out beyond the eighteenth-century limits, settling in and around the outlying villages included within the new ring of fortifications put up by the July Monarchy in the 1840's. Freshly off the farm with its drudgery and declining income, the new arrivals saw in the city not a prison of industrial slavery but the promise of a rising standard of living. The crowded conditions, sordid smells, rampant epidemics, high prices, lack of adequate public transport, physical insecurity, and sheer filth of

241

the city posed only limited terrors to a group which had left little to regret behind them.

The proto-metropolis of Haussmann and Napoleon III is the project of the national government of *nouveau riche*, the newly created burghers, who on the one hand need to suppress the Shadow City for their own comfort and security, and on the other need to extend the benefits of the Official City in order to be fully included in its culture. The Metropolis (no matter what its form or method) is pre-eminently the infinite extension of **urban culture**, the diffusion of the values, attitudes and behaviours of the Official City, often in the absence of any historically pre-existent city. In its ultimate form it is the nationalization of urbanity: urbanity becomes the responsibility of the state.

Several key innovations are made in order to develop the Metropolis:

1. In London, John Nash initiates at least four in his 1820s development of Regent's Park and Street:

 i. he demonstrates that the future city can take any form, even that of the country;

 ii. he invents the metropolitan expressway, proving that it is not location proper but speed of travel to and from that location that is significant — time supplants space;

 iii. he relates public improvement and urban slum clearance for the first time;

 iv. and perhaps most importantly he successfully proves that deficit financing is possible if the cost of the debt is offset by the profits realized by the improvements.

2. In Paris, Baron Haussmann expands Nash's initiatives into a fully operating city system. And in 1889, Eiffel builds the tower that establishes the vast prospect of the city, which creates a new representation of it as a network viewed from the air.

3. Peel makes his contribution to the Metropolis when he invents the metropolitan police, thus preserving order in time as well as space.

4. In the Crystal Palace of 1851, Paxton initiates an attitude to building that makes it possible to regard architecture as a logical system of ordinance, able to take any shape, accommodate any function, occupy any space.

5. Morse and, later, Bell and Marconi disembody information.

6. In America, John Roebling and his son Washington establish the pre-eminence of the national infrastructure, transcending previously ordained city boundaries and structures with the completion of the Brooklyn Bridge in 1883; not only does the largest bridge in the world join the two largest cities in America into one conurban sprawl, but it also completes the sea-to-sea rail link in America, an act presided over by the president of the United States.

In fact, each of these acts serves a head of state, or is closely supervised by one.

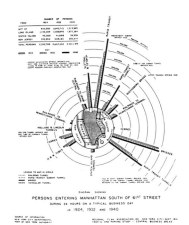

11. Manhattan: the Metropolis as network (1941)

242

The significance of metropolitanism is national. For above and beyond the technical developments of the Metropolis, there is the often unspoken acknowledgment that its planning invokes the supreme material and moral authority of the state, the power to make war. The planning of the Metropolis embodies the strategies of modern warfare with its need for:

1. a potentially infinite, replicable spatial network of communication;
2. a commensurate organization of time;
3. the means to endlessly expand and subdivide this spatial/temporal network;
4. the agency to keep this evolving network clear of obstruction and in working order.

Above all else, this "strategy" must be regarded as the rational expression of rational values, capable of absorbing apparently conflicting concerns into its process of endless expansion. It is best to imagine the Metropolis as the endless preparation for a war that has no front and will never come!

If the emphasis on the relationship between the Metropolis and the field of war seems, at first, gratuitous, reflect upon the typical city of Weber with its fortifications, or the ideal city plans of the Renaissance based as they are upon the geometry of artillery-repelling walls; recall the fortified walls of all the great cities of Europe, some of which endure into the 20th century; remember the first significance of Manhattan's Wall Street. In Viollet-le-Duc's *Dictionnaire Raisonné* of Architecture almost one book of its ten volumes is dedicated to fortifications and the machines of war; less than one page is devoted to the problem of the facade. War has always been one with the city.

If the technology of modern warfare in the 19th century makes the fortification redundant, and if the prosperity of the 19th-century city brings the enemy within the walls, then the idea of the city nevertheless remains imbedded within the structure of the field of war and the psychology of the military state.

Karl von Clausewitz codifies the philosophy of modern warfare in his nine volumes *On War* written between 1815 and 1830.[13] He defines war as "an act of violence intended to compel the enemy to fulfill our will." Of its three key characteristics, one is important here: war is subordinate to the instruments of politics; the means is subordinate to the end. At the outset, von Clausewitz establishes that conditional nature of war: it is always developing, never in and of itself complete, for its ultimate objective is inevitably also its total eclipse. The preparation for war is the preparation for peace.

Further, war develops across space, it takes time, and it involves policy. In his chapter "The Character of Modern Warfare," von Clausewitz sketches the nature of modern war. Realizing that, because of modern military science, the field of war is broadened over a potentially infinite space, he describes a new strategic policy for the nation at war. The army becomes a fluid national construct rather than a fixed entity related to a fixed point. Modern warfare is no longer dependent upon the city or the fortification; the city has lost pre-eminent practical and emblematic significance. The city fortress is still of some value in the modern field of war, but its role is no longer central. Since it can be easily overcome by modern siege guns, the city cannot be defended; the invading army must be met by "force…equal to the enemy in the open field."[14]

The role of the city in warfare is replaced by the concept of the base and the lines of communication. The base is a threefold formation composed of the resources of the country adjacent to the army, the depots of stores along the lines of advance and retreat and the **province** from which these stores come. Von Clausewitz makes it clear that, while these three things are spatially separate, their mutual relationship will always be overlapping and imprecise, due in part to the particular character of each of the components, and in part to the relationship between the base and the army they serve, that is, to the lines of communication. Von Clausewitz establishes the concept that makes the army one with its logistical infrastructure. The foundation is laid here for the hierarchical system of roads that is the basis of every national survey.[15] These surveys are unnecessary before the collapse of the city-fortress as the basis of national defence; after that collapse, they are the primary instrument of national defence.

The battlefield no longer has a "rear" of reserves[16]; it is a continuous "front" organized for the rapid deployment of forces, and the entire field of battle (which may be national or even continental) must be activated, with all forces operating continually to their own purpose — engagement in the field. The battlefield — the nation — becomes effectively "centreless" in war, and war becomes a condition continuously prepared for. The nation is understood simultaneously as base, network of communication, standing army and field of battle. The historic city is a minor component of this field, virtually redundant in the practice of modern warfare, which is based, not on the stability of the fortress, but on the mobility of the modern army. The Metropolis is a radical reinterpretation of traditional urbanity constructed upon the framework made to accommodate the fluid nature of modern warfare.

These three readings — the Official City, the Shadow City and the Metropolis — present a logistical evolution of urbanity,[17] one that ultimately leaves the historic city in a redundant position in relation to the state's power to make war.[18]

FRICTION: The Metropolitan Frontier

Perhaps the logistical redundancy of the Official City would not matter if the Metropolis were not invented to take its place. The culture of cities might have taken a different course, except that the rational and urgent network of the Metropolis found itself interrupted by the City. For if the Official City represents itself in space and the Shadow City exists in time, the Metropolis is present in those instruments intended to dominate space in the perpetual drive to eradicate time. The static space

12. The open field of modern warfare: nuclear devastation as it is imagined during the 1960s on "The Twilight Zone"

of the Official City and the irregular schedule of the Shadow City both affront the rational fluidity of the Metropolis.

Nevertheless, it is unlikely that the Metropolis will go unchanged.

Already, the Official City has begun to transform itself within the network of the Metropolis, re-representing itself as a commodity, transforming the transient inhabitants of the Metropolis into tourists intent on consumption and on the enhancement of their status. The Official City now reverses the significance of the stranger, developing a fresh constituency in order to ensure its survival. The irony is, of course, that the traditional constituent of the Official City — the permanent resident — comes to feel a stranger in his own home as the cost of goods and services inflates and as the very authenticity of the day-to-day environment becomes strained.

Just as the Official City has transformed itself to accommodate the modern structure of the Metropolis, so other urban cultures will emerge, and from time to time form their own systems of space. This thesis can be demonstrated in actual episodes, but for the moment it will be developed theoretically.

The following **theory of the Metropolitan Frontier** is intended to describe the dynamics of the relationships between the contradictory interpretations of the city. It is a thesis of disorder that depends in turn upon several already-developed concepts found in the philosophy of war, in ecological theory, and in the discourse of socio-linguistics: from the philosophy of war (1) von Clausewitz's venerable concept of **friction** and (2) the emerging theory of **contradictory strategies**; from ecology (3) the concept of **gliding evolution**; and from socio-linguistics (4) the concept of **pidgin and creole languages**.

1. The concept of **friction** is central to von Clausewitz's philosophy of war.[19] Friction is the phenomenon that distinguishes theory from practice:

13. The Official City as Commodity: urbanity as it is imagined in 1988 in "Mary Worth"

> The military machine, the Army and all belonging to it, is in fact simple, and appears on this account easy to manage. But let us reflect that no part of it is in one piece, that it is composed entirely of individuals, each of which keeps up its own friction in all directions. Theoretically all sounds very well....But it is not so in reality, and all that is exaggerated and false in such a conception manifests itself at once in War....
>
> This enormous friction, which is not concentrated, as in mechanics, at a few points, is therefore everywhere brought into contact with chance, and thus incidents take place upon which it was impossible to calculate, their chief origin being chance. As an instance of one such chance take the weather. Here the fog prevents the enemy from being discovered in time, a battery from firing at the right moment, a report from reaching the General....
>
> Activity in War is movement in resistant medium. Just as a man immersed in water is unable to perform with ease and regularity the most natural and simplest movement, that of walking, so in War, with ordinary powers, one cannot keep even the line of mediocrity.

14. Friction: urbanity as it is portrayed by the editors of the *Toronto Star* in a series of 1988 articles on traffic congestion in Metropolitan Toronto, a series that championed the transformation of city streets into metropolitan arteries

Elimination of friction is the pre-eminent goal of Metropolitan management. The lines of communication must remain unobstructed, but as von Clausewitz points out, this friction arises everywhere and always. As a result, the channels of communication become very limited, able to accommodate only particular forms of communication. This limitation is maintained in the form of the infrastructure, and in its regulation. When one imagines trying to stop by the side of an expressway to enjoy the view, the dual roles of form and regulation become clear.

Within the contemporary Metropolis this pervasive friction is a product of the fairly straightforward urge of all of its citizens to go about their daily tasks, their recreations, and their associations, in a manner and at a pace that suits them at the time. We do not recognize the degree to which the Metropolitan revolution has succeeded in suppressing this instinct until we observe the anomalies.[20]

2. The theory of **contradictory strategies** is the creation of Edward Luttwak,[21] who makes the disquieting observation that "strategy is pervaded by a paradoxical logic of its own, standing against the ordinary linear logic by which we live in all other spheres of life." In brief, Luttwak points out that any strategy pursued for too long will reverse its effect.[22] In order to resolve this paradoxic dilemma, Luttwak points out that contradictory strategies will tend to cover a nation in war more effectively than a coherent, tightly co-ordinated one. He also points out that, especially for democratically elected governments, this is a difficult policy to pursue.

On the other hand, this is a policy that can develop naturally in the structure of a historically evolving Metropolis, a structure that almost inevitably has imbedded within its fabric pre-existent cities, towns, boroughs and villages. The interests of the Metropolis, with its logistical organization and strategic structure, are often at odds with the pre-existent city governments, which have more stable spatial preoccupations.[23]

3. The concept of **gliding evolution** is outlined in Erich Jantsch's text *The Self-Organizing Universe*.[24] It provides explanation in a theoretical way for the paradox of reversing strategies. Beginning with the observation that, in evolutionary terms, time and history do not have a hierarchical structure, he observes that,

> this implies that it is (not) whole structural platforms, whole civilizations, societal systems, art and life styles which must jump to a new structure. A pluralism emerges in which many dynamic structures penetrate each other at the same level. In such a pluralism, there is no longer the familiar evolution in big step functions. Change, increasing in an absolute measure, occurs not only vertically, in historical time, but also horizontally, in a multitude of simultaneous processes, none of which necessarily has to assume destructive dimensions. The reality of the human world becomes dissolved into many realities, its evolution into a multitude of horizontally linked evolutions.

Simply put, von Clausewitz's "friction" may be reinterpreted not as interference with a structure or system, but as the emergence of entirely new systems, some of which may develop the complexity necessary to achieve autonomy. The strategic response to friction of this sort inevitably guarantees that the form of that strategy will be changed by the institutionalization of the response. The consistent strategy, the structure, has transformed.

4. **Pidgin and creole languages** are examples of emergent structures of language that follow this pattern. A pidgin language is a language not native to any group, and emerges when two or more linguistic cultures exist in the social dominion of another. "When three or more languages are involved and one is dominant, the speakers of the two or more that are inferior appear to play a critical role in the development of a pidgin. They must not only speak to those who are in the dominant position, but they must also speak to each other."[25] Pidgins are the languages of strangers, simplified and uncodified, sophisticated enough to deal with trade and labour (usually), but insufficient to cope with broader cultural activity.

A creole is a vernacular language, the native tongue of a particular group. Historically, a creole probably evolves from a pidgin, but "because it is a native language and must perform a wide range of communicative and expressive functions, it has an extensive vocabulary and complex grammatical system comparable to that of a so-called normal language."[26] The autonomy of the structure is guaranteed by its complexity.

The pidgin or creole is a metaphor for the Metropolitan Frontier. Dominated by the regulating structure of the Metropolis, this pidgin urbanity emerges out of the interference, the need for communication among the different paradigms of urbanity — the Official City, the Shadow City and the Metropolis.

Where there is simply an opposition between two institutions, for instance the governments of City and Metropolis, there is only a struggle for power. Torontonians see this in the spring of 1988 when the development ambitions of the mayor of Toronto, Arthur Eggleton, finally culminate — through a chain-reaction of Metropolitan regulations — in the proposal to turn the main street of the city, Yonge Street, into a one-way thoroughfare. The symbolic significance of the transformation is not lost on citizens and aldermen alike: the Official City is to lose one of its key representations — the space of the market. Given the fair representation of the Shadow City on the seamier sections of Yonge Street, it is interesting to speculate on the **actual** outcome of such a change, but at this point it is worth noting only that the procedure has degenerated, as could be expected, into a drawn out and sophisticated squabble — change versus no change.

On the other hand, where the three readings of urbanity are concurrently in effect, new conditions are arising, which reflect the creole nature of the Metropolitan Frontier. Before concluding, I would like to touch on one briefly: the emergence of an autonomous urban structure beneath downtown Toronto.

Toronto's Underground City has been called a pedestrian network, a concourse

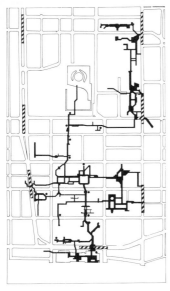

15. Toronto, the Underground City: a plan showing the main public paths (solid lines), the subway platforms (hatched), and the chief entrances

system, the underground malls. Only recently have government publications begun to call it a city, and that has been a daring metaphor. Nevertheless, although it is primitive, the underground has become complex enough to earn the autonomy of city-hood. As described in a consultants' study recently:

> Toronto's underground pedestrian walkway system is a network of shopping arcades connected by tunnels between the complexes or "blocks" which make up this underground city. Altogether there are well over 5 km of these arcades and tunnels and new ones currently under construction will add substantially to this figure.
>
> The system interconnects some thirty office towers, twenty or so parking garages, three hotels and about a thousand retail shops (no one really knows exactly how many there are), two major department stores, five subway stations and a railway/transit terminal.
>
> There are well over a hundred and twenty-five grade level access points of one type or another, major, less major and quite small. In addition, there are some thirty-odd below grade connections between the complexes....
>
> Five TTC subway stations feed passengers into the pedestrian system and also absorb other passengers from it. Just three stops to the north there is another, smaller, underground city at Bloor Street, a subway fare away.[27]

The Underground City still operates in a pidgin condition, simplified yet complex enough to be effective. It has emerged as a distinct paradigm in relation to the three interpretations of urbanity, a construct which has borrowed readily from the Metropolis, the Official City and the Shadow City without becoming subservient to any of them.

From the Metropolis, it has adopted the idea of the centreless field of action, and with it the sense of continuous connection and expansion. It is unlikely that the Underground City would have emerged at all except for the insinuation of the Metropolitan structure of the subway into the downtown district. Although there were several underground installations throughout the centre of Toronto, including public tunnels between different Eaton's department store buildings, and between the Royal York Hotel and Union Station, histories of Toronto underground usually begin with the subway installation in 1954. The quantum jump in activity below grade dates from that time.

In one very fundamental way the Underground City departs from the Metropolis. In an internal Planning Department memo this distinction is observed, but misunderstood:

> One major failing of the system is to develop an understandable network. Like a medieval town, the plans are organic and are seldom built around vistas or land-marks. Although charming, they are seldom comprehensible. The system as a

16. Toronto, the Underground City: a cross section through the Eaton Centre showing the various levels of pedestrian activity and the connection between the underground realm and the subway network, shown in the right-hand portion of the section

248

whole has a curious circuit board like logic. Each block has its own internal and comprehensible configuration which is then joined or "wired" by tunnel to the next block. Each unit is comprehensible but the system is not.[28]

The unknown author of that memorandum misses the significance of the observation. True, the underground does not have the system of representation of the Official City; also true, the underground is not organized in the hierarchical fashion of the Metropolis. Nevertheless, the system is comprehensible, if only according to a different paradigm. The Metropolis is classically arborial — its analogue is the tree with a trunk or stem and branches, leaves and roots. There is a clear differentiation in the parts, and a good deal of communication function between them. The Underground City is rhizomic — analogous to a system of shoots which share the characteristics of stem **and** roots, complete at any point, centreless, non-hierarchical. This becomes very clear when it is pointed out that, of the entire network of walks, less than 3 per cent is purely connecting tunnel.

Insofar as the system is not Metropolitan, it is also not of the Shadow City, yet like the Shadow City it exists outside of both the system of Metropolitan regulation and the tradition of representation at work in the Official City. The Underground City was built with virtually no regulation other than that imposed by the limits of property lines and by the building code. No zoning or planning policies govern it. In fact, although the growth of the system was fostered in the late 1960s, in 1974 the Official Plan of the City was rewritten in order to discourage further growth of the underground and redress the balance in favour of street-related retail activity. Nevertheless, the balance has continued to favour subsurface retail. It could be clearly said that the Underground City only emerged because extra profit could be made in this unregulated realm. Now this realm has such authority that the developers of new projects in the financial district build into the system even if they are not constructing additional subsurface retail space.

And like the Shadow City, the underground is now to be identified as a distinct realm, not by policemen, but by a system of uniform signage.

Finally, it is clear that the underground is not simply a component of the Official City. The system does not acknowledge the realm of representation. On the other hand, it does acknowledge something that is being lost in the city above: the culture of the marketplace. Jan Morris, British travel writer, describes the underground in a 1984 magazine article:

> Among the innumerable conveniences of Toronto, which is an extremely convenient city, one of the most attractive is the system of tunnels which lies beneath the downtown streets, and which, with its wonderful bright-lit sequences of stores, cafés, malls and intersections, is almost a second city in itself. I loved to think of all the warmth and life down there, the passing crowds, the coffee smells, the Muzak, the clink of cups, when the streets above were half-empty in the rain, or scoured

by cold winds; and one of my great pleasures was to wander aimless through those comfortable labyrinths, lulled from one Golden Oldie to the next, surfacing now and then to find myself on an unknown street corner far from home, or all unexpectedly in the lobby of some tremendous bank.

But after a time I came to think of them as escape tunnels. It was not just that they were warm and dry; they have an intimacy to them, a brush of human empathy, absent from the greater city above our heads. Might it be, I wondered, that down there a new kind of Torontonian was evolving after all, brought to life by the glare of lights, stripped of inhibition by the press of the crowds, and even perhaps induced to burst into song, or dance a few steps down the escalator, by the beat of the canned music?

"What d'you think?" I asked a friend. "Are they changing the character of Toronto?"

"You must be joking," he replied. "You couldn't do that in a sesquicentury."[29]

A CONCLUSION...Of Sorts

In *Technologies of the Self*, Michel Foucault explains that, in the culture of the classic Greeks "'to be concerned with oneself' was...one of the main principles of cities, one of the main rules for social and personal conduct, and for the art of life." Now, at the outset of this conference, George Baird spent a moment discussing another concept of classic Greek civilization — the **polis**, which comes into being when two or more citizens come together to discuss. Almost from George Baird's remarks on, however, the discussion of public life has ceased, and in its place came a discussion which was not about public space, but rather the space of representation. I hope that we can leave this conference beginning to think of public life and its relation to the self.

Underground Toronto does not yet, and moreover may never, constitute a proper public space. And, as it was expounded here, the theory of the Metropolitan Frontier is too brief to be a useful theory and too "lumpy" to be an elegant metaphor. Perhaps it should be regarded as the metaphor that got carried away with itself. Nevertheless, in time it may develop into a useful paradigm in theory **and** in practice. For if this conference demonstrates nothing else, it acknowledges that, even in the time of the cellular telephone and the home entertainment centre, as citizens we remain eager for a public life, and as architects we believe we can contribute to one. And if we are to do more than prepare pallid simulations of historic public spaces, then we will have to develop the tools to create ones appropriate to the lives we live.

17. The Metropolis as communication network: RICOH fax (1988)

Notes

[1] Max Weber, *The City*, trans. Don Mastindale and Gertrude Nenwirth (London: Collier Macmillan, 1958).

[2] Michel Foucault, "Technologies of the Self," in *Technologies of the Self*, L. Martin, H. Gutman, P. H. Hutton, eds. (Boston: University of Massachusetts Press, 1988), p. 18.

[3] "Speaking in the broadest cultural terms, the historian Carl Schorske has identified three major areas of urban self-perception since the eighteenth century: the Enlightenment city of Virtue, the Victorian city of Vice, the Modern

city 'beyond good and evil.' In essence, these stages correspond to the metaphors already outlined — a New Jerusalem indicating the perfectability of man; a Babylon punishing him for his dedication to mammon; and a Babel, or decentered city, that seems to thrive on loss of connection and lack of reference to the values of the past, what Schorske calls a city of 'permanent transience.'" William Sharpe and Leonard Wallock, eds., *Visions of the Modern City* (Baltimore: Johns Hopkins University Press, 1987), p. 7.

[4] "If we would lay a new foundation for urban life, we must understand the historic nature of the city, and distinguish between its original functions, those that have emerged from it, and those that may still be called forth. Without a long running start in history, we shall not have the momentum needed, in our own consciousness, to take a sufficiently bold leap into the future; for a large part of our present plans, not least many that pride themselves on being 'advanced' or 'progressive,' are dreary mechanical caricatures of the urban and regional forms that are now potentially within our grasp." Lewis Mumford, *The City in History* (New York: Harcourt, Brace, and World, 1961), p. 3.

[5] Mumford, p. 7.

[6] Joseph Rykwert, *The Idea of A Town* (Princeton: Princeton University Press, 1976).

[7] "The Statute of Winchester (1285) codified the watch and the hue and cry. The constable, subservient to the justice of the peace, arrested those who broke the 'king's peace,' raised the hue and cry, and arrested persons responsible for the 'common nuisances of the ward,' which could range from bakers cheating on the weight of bread to the whole community neglecting to provide for the poor. Although the position of constable was compensated by fees assigned by the court or justice of the peace, the night watch began as an uncompensated, voluntary position. In its thirteenth-century originals, the uncompensated night watch was a method of community self-protection, a responsibility of all adult males....The two legal obligations of the *posse comitatus*, theoretically composed of all males over the age of fifteen in the country as called up by the sheriff, and of the hue and cry, the shout of the victim of a crime or a constable, which legally bound all males hearing it to pursue the offender until caught, formalized community law enforcement." Eric H. Monkkonen, *Police in Urban America, 1869–1920* (Cambridge: Cambridge University Press, 1981), p. 32.

[8] Gordon Craig, "The Art of War," *New York Review of Books* (April 28, 1988).

[9] "If wandering is the liberation from every given point in space, and thus the conceptional opposite to fixation at such a point, the sociological form of the 'stranger' presents the unity, as it were, of these two characteristics. This phenomenon too, however, reveals that spatial relations are only the condition, on the one hand, and the symbol, on the other, of human relations. The stranger is thus being discussed here, not in the sense often touched upon in the past, as the wanderer who comes today and goes tomorrow, but rather as the person who comes today and stays tomorrow. He is, so to speak, the *potential* wanderer: although he has not moved on, he has not quite overcome the freedom of coming and going. He is fixed within a particular spatial group, or within a group whose boundaries are similar to spatial boundaries. But his position in this group is determined, essentially, by the fact that he has not belonged to it from the beginning, that he imports qualities into it, which do not and cannot stem from the group itself." Georg Simmel, "The Stranger," quoted in Kurt H. Wolff, trans. and ed., *The Sociology of Georg Simmel* (New York: The Free Press, 1950), p. 402.

[10] For example, the Statute of Winchester of 1285.

[11] "The creators of the new police introduced a new concept in social control: the prevention of crime. Taking an argument of the Italian criminal law reformer, Beccaria, they claimed that regular patrolling, predicable detection of offenses, and rational punishment would deter *potential* offenders. They even extended Beccaria's argument, claiming that the sight of the police uniform itself would deter potential offenders....The notion of deterring potential offenses implied a new attitude toward social control, diverting attention from illegal behaviour to potential offenders, from act to actor. In so doing, the emphasis necessarily implied the forecasting ability of the police, especially to explain and predict criminal behaviour, thus rendering it amenable to control. Once the notion of preventing crimes had supplanted the notion of catching offenders, the focus of police actions on a 'dangerous class' became absurd. The nebulous idea of preventing criminal behaviour found perfect means of implementation in the concept of an identifiable, crime-producing 'dangerous class'; for only by focussing on crime producers could criminal behaviour be prevented, and the 'dangerous class,' by definition, produced the criminal behaviour." Monkkonen, pp. 40–41.

[12] Howard Saalman, *Haussmann: Paris Transformed* (New York: George Braziller, 1971), pp. 46–47.

[13] Karl von Clausewitz, *On War*, trans. Col. J. J. Graham (London: Routledge and Kegan Paul, 1966).

[14] "Times are past in which the mere enclosure of a place with walls, without any military preparations, could keep a place dry during an inundation of War sweeping over the whole country." Von Clausewitz, p. 195.

[15] Von Clausewitz establishes the conditions for these lines of communication: "Only those roads on which magazines, hospitals, stations, posts for dispatches and letters are organized under commandants with police and garrisons, can be looked upon as real lines of communication....An Army, even in its own country, has its prepared lines of communication, but it is not completely limited to them, and can in case of need change its line....An Army in an enemy's country on the contrary can as a rule only look upon those roads as lines of communication upon which it has advanced." Von Clausewitz, p. 115.

[16] After describing the new space of warfare, and the ideal means of controlling that space, von Clausewitz goes on to describe its character. He recommends a geometrical disposition of forces in order to establish virtually universal address of the field of battle — that is, an army prepared to advance or retreat on any of the cardinal points. The field of battle becomes a matrix of action.

[17] There are many paradigms of interpretation of the city: social, political, cultural and economic. The logistical interpretation sees the city's role in terms of the apparatus of war and the preparation for it, and the control of the inhabitants of the city on the part of the agents of the state. It is a rarer form of analysis, but unavoidable if a clear portrait of society is to be developed. In Canada today 60 per cent of government procurements are military, followed immediately by transport expenditures. In the United States the economy of violence — the war industry, crime, the drug industry — is greater than the rest of the Official Gross National Product. Add to that the cost of the more conventional agencies of control — federal, state and local police, inspectors, regulators and so on — and we might arrive at a national economy of the United States proportionately similar to those of the militaristic European nations prior to the great era of mercantilism, colonial imperialism, and the slave trade.

[18] This redundancy is reflected in the contemporary treatment awarded great cities by the conservative governments of capitalist nations. Giscard d'Estaing in France, Thatcher in Britain, Reagan in America — each have adopted programs for the dissolution of their great cities. Paris and London have both been threatened with programs to dismantle them into their constituent boroughs or *arrondissements*; New York remains menaced by the geographic devolution into its constituent economic classes. The city becomes expendable in the economy organized on military expansion, a condition observed in Jane Jacobs's study *Cities and the Wealth of Nations* (New York: Random House, 1984).

[19] Von Clausewitz, pp. 77–79.

[20] For instance, the prime task of education after the 1917 Bolshevik revolution was not political re-education, or building support for the revolutionary war on the Russian border, or even a campaign of literacy. The prime task for the propaganda arm of the party was to convince the newly created workers to accede to the schedules and practices of the contemporary city: to go to work on time, to work while there, to leave work at the appointed time, to sleep at night, to care for personal concerns only at particular times; in short, to participate in the structure of military discipline, to diminish friction.

[21] Edward Luttwak, *Strategy: The Logic of War and Peace* (Cambridge, Mass: Harvard University Press, 1987).

[22] We have only to see Israel's current plight to understand this concept: for twenty years Israel has maintained the occupied territories as a buffer against enemy states; now, in large part because of the effectiveness of the contemporary infrastructure of world communications, the occupied territories have **become** an enemy state, uncontainable by armed force.

[23] For instance, in Toronto the city's development often seems to proceed best when, at the political level, the Metropolitan and City governments are at their least co-operative. But even in times of apparently complete political acquiescence by the City in the face of Metropolitan ambitions, the mid-level "techno-structures" of the City and the Metropolis differentiate themselves. The Metropolitan engineering offices only operate in terms of "pure" systems, while the City engineers continue to think and work in compound systems with more sophisticated spatial consequences.

[24] Erich Jantsch, *The Self-Organizing Universe, Scientific and Human Implications of the Emerging Paradigm of Evolution* (Oxford: Pergamon Press, 1980).

[25] Ronald Wardhaugh, *An Introduction to Sociolinguistics* (New York: Basic Books, 1986), p. 57.

[26] D. DeCamp quoted in Wardhaugh, p. 60.

[27] Newton Frank Arthur Inc. & Agnew Communications Inc., "Toronto's Underground City," City of Toronto, 1988.

[28] City of Toronto Planning Department, "Toronto's Underground Pedestrian Network," 1987.

[29] Jan Morris, "Second Prize," originally published in *Saturday Night* (June 1984), pp. 44–49.

edited by Detlef Mertins

Audience, including Steven Fong, Nan Griffiths, Eric Haldenby, Brigitte Shim, Tom Emodi, Frank Palermo

The following is a partial record of the panel discussions that followed the presentation of the papers in the preceding section. The conference took place on June 9 and 10, 1988, at the auditorium of the Saint John High School in Saint John, New Brunswick.

Question I think that Peter Rose could have been a bit more optimistic about public spaces that are being created in Montreal. I refer to those little connections between St. Laurent and St. Denis that have recently been remade to accommodate traffic and pedestrians in a very friendly way. Would Peter like to comment on that perhaps?

Peter Rose It is just my manner. I seem to be a depressive person. But really, I am optimistic. It's my nature never to be too optimistic before the fact, because you can lose everything right up to the end. In terms of positive things that are going on, I agree with you about that whole area, the McGill ghetto and to the east. It's very lively, wonderful and healthy. But while the idea of making a pedestrian street connecting St. Denis and St. Laurent is an admirable one, there has been a strange ad hoc attitude to planning them. The manner in which they have been done is bizarre, different from block to block, generally impermanent, constructed of bad materials and wasteful of money.

My optimism is based on the fact that the right things are more or less being done. My pessimism is based on the fact that the quality of these things is still not high enough, and that these isolated pockets depend entirely on the intensity of the people for their success. It's a powerful phenomenon to see a street where three blocks are as lively as can be and then four don't exist at all and then somehow it pops up like a weed four blocks down the road. This defies urban design logic, but is a testament to the amount of blood in the veins of this city and the spirit of its citizens.

Question A question for Ken Greenberg. Is Beaux-Arts formality and symmetry an essential ingredient of the new urbanity?

Ken Greenberg It's very interesting to what extent one continually goes back into history and recycles urban ideas, but always with a difference. Certainly the critique of the modernist city has brought with it the utilization of formal devices in the layout of cities. But if one were to compare what is going on at the moment with the City Beautiful Movement of the turn of the century, I would say that the City Beautiful Movement was manipulating form in a very abstract way, while the current generation of dealing with form has actually tied that intimately into a consideration of uses and building types.

Question Going back to George Baird's talk, in which he put on the table the ideas of mobility, plurality and the historic city, I am wondering if the current reference to the history of the city isn't undermining our mobility in the city. If we just look at the work Ken Greenberg presented, isn't the real activity at the Consilium going to be 2,500 people moving up and down in an elevator from the parking garage, not people circumnavigating those new streets and colonnades in Scarborough on foot?

Ken Greenberg The important distinction to draw is between mobility and the automobile. In downtown North York, already 60 per cent of the people come there by transit. As these subcentres emerge in the suburbs there is a shift away from automobile use. To me the issue in suburban centres is to design them in such a way that they can work in the first instance with the automobile, but that they are capable of changing in time to increased movement by transit and on foot.

In respect of Trevor Boddy's point that the city is being suburbanized, I think that Mayor Art Eggleton has embarked on an extraordinarily misguided crusade in Toronto right now in the name of mobility. He is going to turn Bay Street and Yonge Street into one-way streets. If one looks at his proposal purely in terms of the number of people that are being moved, and one realizes that his proposal would do terrible damage to the transit system and to pedestrian movement in order to benefit a few more cars, it could be argued that the scheme would actually have a negative effect on the overall movement of people in the downtown.

Question This question comes out of a comparison of Gerald Forseth's and Peter Rose's presentations. Peter described some of the public spaces of Montreal as very clearly urban and very clearly public, but having lost their program of use, their reason to be. Then Gerald described the effect of the bonus system in Calgary, which promotes programmed amenities like the art gallery in the Nova Building, but also generates completely unpredictable form that blurs the distinction between private and public. What's going to happen when Calgary really goes bust and Nova Corporation goes down the toilet? By going on the cheap and trying to get public

256

elements that are clearly part of the public realm for nothing, are municipalities destroying the urban character of the city?

Gerald Forseth I agree that it is quite destructive. The first part of my paper was about the dismal effort that we have had on behalf of the public realm. There is a lack of public will, however, to recognize that these things do not come easily, that "you have to pay for the public life." But it's a part of the times and a part of the culture of a place like Calgary that people are more interested in natural environments like Banff Park than they are in the public spaces of the city. But as the city continues to grow these issues will have to be addressed.

Trevor Boddy I think that it could be strongly argued that it was never time for the sort of bonus system that Calgary came up with. The quality of those spaces that you showed — and you picked the best project, Nova — are more the result of a few people who really cared about the city and a good architect than the bonus system.

Detlef Mertins One of the things that has struck me about Calgary is that its bonus system was created in order to implement an urban vision, a progressive and obsessive positive vision for the future, and that it required a lot of public will to get off the ground. Since that time, there has obviously been a change of heart about that vision, especially by architects and planners. But I wonder whether that change of heart has been sufficiently shared by Calgarians to now warrant a major redirection of the planning effort, which suggests that there may have been something about that initial vision that made sense.

To the urban historicists, the Calgary case epitomizes all that was wrong about modernism, including its presumption that one could have a positive new vision for the future. And while I too am critical of the resultant urban mutation, I am charmed by what appears, in retrospect, as naive optimism in our collective ability to create a better world. To what extent do we allow ourselves to **project** for the future?

Peter Rose What is difficult in Calgary, and with the bonus system in general, is that it is not well planned or co-ordinated. The smaller pieces have to add up to something that is a public domain. One of the few recent examples that gives cause for optimism is Battery Park City in New York, where an elaborate system of public spaces has been created by the developers along with a number of enormous buildings. When the vision and the co-ordination are strong enough, it works. But it doesn't happen very often.

Trevor Boddy I agree that Battery Park City is working, but the key factor is the overwhelming pressure of development on that site and in that city. The bonus system only works in high-growth situations that even the healthiest city passes through but briefly. We have to find other ways to make viable public spaces that work in a non-boom or stable-state economy.

257

Ken Greenberg If we take Rockefeller Center, which was offered as an example of what Calgary might have been aspiring to, it is wonderful to have large private corporations that are philanthropic and make marvellous public amenities. However, no matter how wonderful they may be or how many of them there may be in the city, they are no substitute for public spaces. They are something different. Public spaces should last for centuries. Companies come and go. One can't depend on companies and the buildings that they build to substitute for the public life of the city. In the case of Battery Park City there is an absolute distinction to be drawn between the streets and the water's edge park, which now belong to the City of New York, and the other spaces of the buildings.

How do you move from the narrow interests of private companies to what really makes a city?
Phyllis Lambert

Question I want to ask a question about the responsibility of architects to force the public realm to do something about this. One of the problems that we face in Montreal now is this constant pressure of the private company in the making of public places and the city. How do you move from the narrow interests of private companies to what really makes a city, for a city is more than shopping and residential? I think it should be a requirement in those programs that you are setting up to create institutions. Or is it just a question of making the bones and waiting to see what happens?

Gerald Forseth When it comes to the creation of public spaces, there are partnerships of private and public interests being forged, tested and evolved. They probably complicate our lives more than simplify them, but it seems to be part of the economics, politics and social involvement of our cities now that things aren't as simple as they used to be. There seem to be large numbers of people willing to deal with larger numbers of people in the creation of public spaces. I think it does tend to suit the times.

Question After the presentations on suburbia today, I have to wonder why we should even bother with the suburbs. Who cares?

Tom Emodi There are a number of reasons. One is that the largest amount of our infrastructure is now in the suburbs and from a practical point of view we simply cannot throw it away. Another is that there is actually far more civic life there wanting to come out. It's trying to be there. If you go there and live there, you will see it and see that it isn't coming out easily. The physical urban form doesn't let it. A third is more abstract and ecological. There is no need for cities to spread at the moment. There are enough interstitial spaces in both the downtowns and the suburbs

258

that we can fill in for a long time. To treat the suburbs as a hazy fringe that we don't want to deal with is probably the most destructive thing that we could do to cities today.

Question I have a question for Kenneth. Historically, a suburb is a way of being quite distant from a community, despite the research that has proven that there is civic and community life out there. However, the idea that one has one's own land, which is private and often enclosed, is basic. How can we possibly imagine that these people who go directly to the suburbs to have a specific way of life, which allows them to withdraw from the company of others, will use all those public spaces that you want to offer?

Ken Greenberg A house in the City of Toronto costs roughly twice as much as a house in the suburbs. The market and cultural preferences are now such that most people who end up living in the suburbs, particularly the more recent suburbs that are being built on the outer periphery of the city, are not doing it because they are choosing a way of life. They cannot afford to live any place else. It's the place of last resort. To say that those people have opted for an alienated lifestyle is a little misleading.

Secondly, if you recall the slides, which Tom showed together, of the West Edmonton Mall and a suburban house, then you will recognize that there are potent images in the suburban situation for collective experience, which is a further complicating factor. And finally, it is important to recognize that there is far more development occurring outside of cities today than within cities. A place like downtown North York will soon have 20,000 to 30,000 people working there and as many living there. To say that one wouldn't provide public spaces for the common life of all of those people becomes slightly perverse. There is much evidence to suggest that where more urban forms are provided in such places, people use and enjoy them.

> **To treat the suburbs as a hazy fringe that we don't really want to deal with is probably the most destructive thing that we could do to cities today.**
> *Tom Emodi*

Tom Emodi I agree with the question more than know what the answer is. I don't believe that the majority of people in the suburbs are alienated and I don't believe that they are being forced out there by economic necessity. Maybe in Toronto. But many, many people are there by choice. They like it. The amount of public space that they require may actually be less than in the sort of walking cities of Europe. We may have to choose them and size them carefully and learn when enough is enough.

Question The phenomenon of the underground has been particularly strong over the past twenty years in Montreal, and I would like to ask Peter Rose whether that is still the direction we are going to follow to the year 2000.

Peter Rose I know it's there. I know that it turns a lot of people through the system and there is a lot of money invested in it. If I had my druthers, I would give it no bonuses, no breaks. I used to be more negative about it than I am even today. I used to refer to it as the worm in the stomach of a dog. Everything looks fine until suddenly the worm eats the dog and it falls over, and you realize something has gone wrong. And then you go to have it fixed.

   The underground is a commercial thing. It allows developers to put more commercial space on their particular piece of land. There is, as well, a matter of protection from the elements, but I think that it's not the principal part of it. I have a deep prejudice against it. I would rather see the streets healthy and strong and if there is enough energy and vitality left over, let the underground have some of it. But in so far as it has in the past sapped the life out of whole areas of the city, it strikes fear in

I would rather see the streets healthy and strong...the underground in Montreal strikes fear into my very soul.
Peter Rose

my very soul. St. Catherine Street is at great risk when you connect Simpsons through the Cadillac Fairview project through Eaton's through the new whatever it is to the Bay, and you put 500 stores in row without the necessity for coming out onto the street.

Trevor Boddy I think it so self-evidently obvious that cities are made of streets and streets alone, and that anything we do to promote streets is good, while anything that takes action or energy away from streets is wrong. I am reacting against the Team Ten orthodoxy that George Baird reminded us set the agenda of segregation even to this day.

Right now, the underground in Toronto is absolutely benign and harmless.
Ken Greenberg

Peter Rose The truth of the matter is that every city in the country, whether it is Vancouver or Calgary or Edmonton or Winnipeg, now has twenty-five or thirty years of this kind of development. Some of it is underground, some of it is in the air. We can't ignore it.

Trevor Boddy I would argue that the demolition of the Rideau Bus Mall in Ottawa is a signal event in Canadian urbanism. I would hope that it is followed by the demolition of the Calgary +15 bridges. I think that there will be a period of undoing the wrongs.

Peter Rose I would just like to make a comment on the Montreal underground. You can pack as much stuff underground as you want, just as you can build as much stuff above the ground as you want. The real issue is whether the underground should be a continuum under the public spaces of the streets, and thus be in competition with the streets. The city has to take a stronger stand about selling its own land.

George Baird

Question One simile for the continuous underground would be Chicago. Chicago was made by the fact that the railroad system from the west and the system from the east both stopped in Chicago. You had to get off one and go to the other. So people visited the town. In London there isn't a continuous underground. You go under and you come up again.

Ken Greenberg I never thought that I would say anything in favour of the underground, but I have been pushed so that I have to. Right now, the underground in Toronto, which is contained within a tight net of subway stations and is less dispersed than the one in Montreal, is absolutely benign and harmless. I would go so far as to say useful. Whereas it was initially a great threat to the life of the streets, now that the downtown has filled in and become fully active it wouldn't work if you were to suddenly empty all of those people from the underground onto the sidewalks. In some curious way that has to lead us back to a dialectical — pardon me Trevor — appreciation of the fact that the modernists tore the city apart to the extent that they did and made some holes. While we would never condone it at this point, some of the extraneous and odd elements that they introduced have contributed to the current vitality and workability of the city. One has to appreciate that, as circumstances change, these positions take on different meanings.

Peter Rose It's a layer you can add in Toronto and it's useful because you have a surplus of pressure on the street. But if you add it near a street that is just barely making it you kill the street.

Question I would like to address Frank Palermo's presentation; I feel that I have been provoked and in return I would like to challenge a few of your statements.

You spoke of streets from a general point of view, yet streets do not exist as an entity. We all know from ordinary experience that there are all sorts of streets. So when you say that streets are killed by automobiles, I think of all those dwellers of Manhattan walking like mad all over the place. And yet what city is more congested with cars than New York?

You said that in the past there was a sharp distinction between the private and the public. This was not so. It took centuries to empty the street. A very wide array of activities, which we consider today as being private, used to take place on the street,

Ken Greenberg

and many others, which we consider as public, used to take place inside or outside the home. The sharp division between inside and outside, private and public did not occur in Europe and even in the United States before the early 20th century.

I would also challenge your remarks about the **civic** quality of shopping centres. I would be the last to deny the importance of getting together, watching people, sitting in a safe environment, routine activities, and going to the same café every day. But I do not believe that these are civic activities. Civic activities took place in public spaces because they were legally collective territories where a group could signify something to the rest of the community. It is reductionist to consider that playful activities, consumerism or simply sitting around are civic activities.

The shopping mall would not have been possible without concentration of capital, which kills the activities around them. There is much statistical evidence from major American cities that those spaces siphon the life from the street. What I mean to say is that it is not because people go there that it is all right. It is just the opposite.

Frank Palermo I didn't imply that the street is dead or should be. I simply meant to make the point that there are elements of what I consider to be public life that take place in these indoor environments and that we might be able to learn something from those sorts of environments that would help us to make better streets, and that there are things that we might learn from streets that would help us make the indoor environments better. Really, it's that kind of thought that I've been pursuing.

Nan Griffiths I would just like to agree with you in principle. The phenomenon of popularity is really interesting, but your point that it's the lowest common denominator is what makes me anxious about the underground system and the overgrade. It's like Disneyworld and the replacement of what was once real.

Lance Berelowitz I want to pick up where the lady in the audience left off. I think it is an important challenge. What we are talking about is power and the extent to which power is exercised in the public domain. It seems very clear, and Don McKay's allusion to it was extremely provocative, that a public domain doesn't consist of programmed behaviour, but rather subversive behaviour. If you take away the venues for spontaneous subversive public behaviour, expressions of delight or hate, then these will surface elsewhere. Perhaps "surface" is not the right word to use in Don's case, because it will go underground. If you suppress vandalism, graffiti, defecation in public housing projects, etc., they go underground, they do not disappear. The problem with the tyranny of industrial capitalism as represented by the shopping mall, the underground system or the privatization of public space is that you simply block up the normal humanist channels of public expression for needs, desires and frustrations. Those things become more and more deviant and we end up living in a society which is more and more neurotic.

Phyllis Lambert

Donald McKay There is something very strange about a conference like this. If I take myself as an example, I am a young man. I have a secure job. I am white, Anglo-Saxon, male. I operate at the peak of what one generally calls the urban power structure in a sociological sense. I assume that, to a certain extent, everyone here shares most of the benefits of the privileged urban class, or expects to. That makes our conversation a remarkable conceit.

Now, I don't really think that we should run out and find some of those representative poor and drag them in. But the public space that we are talking about and the condition that we are talking about are enjoyed by only a few people, except subversively. In preparing for this paper, I spent several days dealing with crime analysts of various suburban police districts in Toronto. We would spend a day; they would drive me around and show me, literally, the domain of crime, mostly so called "victimless" crime — adolescent sex or serious drug trade — which is entirely private. The Jane/Finch district of Toronto is the biggest square mile of crime in Canada. It is the classic metropolitan suburban condition made up of a lot of public housing, in which the shopping malls are the only place of expression. That is to say, there is no active public realm and instead there is this private public realm that is being dis-

> **You are not going to fix the 300 square miles of Metropolitan Toronto that presently have no functioning urban domain overnight.**
> *Donald McKay*

cussed. In Ontario that realm is being reconsidered right now for the fact that it is such a pervasive realm within the city. I am not sure whether it should be there or not, whether it is an emerging public space or not. But for one-and-a-half million people it's their only public domain. And the province is busy reconsidering its laws on trespass in order to deal with minorities who do not even enjoy the fundamental privileges of those places.

You are not going to fix the 300 square miles of metropolitan Toronto that presently have no functioning urban domain overnight. So in the meantime, you are going to have to start thinking about how it is going to emerge, because it is going to find its way out one way or another. Or a larger and larger class of young men, and to a certain extent women, will be identified as dangerous, given police records and moved off the shopping mall.

The romanticization of the street in Toronto has already made many of the neighbourhoods uninhabitable for people with incomes under $100,000 a year. And so the edification of the public domain as we are discussing it here means that those people are relegated to that other domain and it seems perfectly reasonable for Palermo to begin to reconsider it because it's the one that most of those people have, and that deserves attention.

Question I'd like to deal with the question of ownership. The traditional city that Peter Rose talked about yesterday allowed for a great deal of variety and ownership; many people could own property on a street. The area that Don McKay talked about in Toronto, whether it's above ground or underground, is now owned in large blocks. Does it matter to the public space that all the things one sees around are under the ownership of a very small percentage of people?

...three positions within the conference: the mutants, who believe in the possibility of new forms...the modern squares, who are less activist and more conventional; and...the Camillo Sitte planners.
Trevor Boddy

Donald McKay It's a fundamental problem. In the 1930s legislation was written by the government of British Columbia to do with the implications of single ownership, primarily company towns. The legislation effectively made the streets and docks of companied logging towns part of the public domain, so that trade unions could legally organize workers.

I know that the world is owned by six hundred families, right? So are many of the great cities at great times in their development. It happens for a while. What is important, however, is that our concern should be public life in all of the exigencies of the expression of one individual and his personal experience in search of communication with another, or with more than one other. That means that we may have to continue to evolve not simply new space types, but new forms of administration, law and conditions of behaviour. I would propose that we develop multiple ones, and that we depend less upon governments to do that for us. Governments do these things in very single-minded ways, which inevitably suffer from the law of unexpected results. My paper is part of a larger cry for a certain amount of deregulation at the same time that the protection of the person might be enhanced.

Nan Griffiths It is difficult for us to imagine how we can influence the structure of these places or their changing. Most of us have, in some way or another, been involved in designing them, and we know that the fundamental question is not about design or architectures, but about ownership. It's the whole issue of public versus private.

Question Two things. First, out of simple curiosity: Frank, what's your advice about +15 at the end of the day in Calgary? And Don, what's your advice to the mayor on the one-way street?

Secondly, these are a remarkably disparate set of presentations and I have been trying to find some common way to look at them all. Obviously we're all looking at the same thing and seeing different aspects of it. Some of you are searching very hard

264

for the constants, those things that remain fairly continuous, and others of you seem to be very intent on identifying the things that come with rapid change. Both of those aspects of reality are present at any given time. I wonder if anyone on the panel would care to comment on what aspects of reality one should concentrate on in our capacity as shapers of public spaces?

Frank Palermo Hindsight is a terrific thing. If I were giving advice at the time that the system in Calgary was first being considered, I probably would have told them not to do it. The energy and financial commitment that went into making that system should have been put into making the existing public structure work better.

The position that I am taking now is that they obviously exist, that there is a very solid commitment to them and that there may be something that we could learn from them.

Donald McKay Mayor Eggleton of Toronto is clearly schizophrenic. My answer to him would be that he should decide whether he is the Mayor of the City of Toronto or the Chairman of Metropolitan Toronto. When he can actually come to terms with that schizophrenic condition, he would know whether Yonge Street was one-way or not. But if his ambition is really to become a sort of mayor/chairman of Toronto/Metropolitan Toronto, then my recommendation would be to draw a big red line around downtown-downtown and declare it an utterly free-fire zone, because dinking around with it at this stage is simply bejewelling a horse's ass. It is absurd. So

Michael Kirkland and Esmail
Baniassad at the opening

Mayor Eggleton of Toronto is clearly schizophrenic.
Donald McKay

he either takes responsibility for a condition where the core of the city is stable or if he is to establish growth in an apparently uncontrolled way, he literally pulls away from the controls. I suppose I am being slightly absurdist, but I think it would be reasonable at a certain point to quit trying to regulate growth and maybe something would emerge which would deal with the pressures.

Certainly there are building types in Manhattan emerging out of the incredible land development pressures there, which are engaging transformations of types that create a lot more public space than previous lower-density buildings simply because there are enormous spaces left at the ground level under them. Philip Johnson's building is one, but there are in fact at least half a dozen new buildings in mid-town where enormous spaces are left at ground level, if for no other reason than that during construction there is no other place to operate the site from. If Manhattan actually continues with this type, the public domain will actually grow in mid-town rather than shrink as it has been doing for some time.

Michael Kirkland There was a rather delicious insinuation in the question about

The city should in fact make itself inaccessible if that's what's necessary to preserve its integrity.
Michael Kirkland

the one-way streets in Toronto, which has to do with making the city more accessible to the metropolitan world as a shared asset. To compensate for the lack of urban places in the suburbs, one could argue that the metropolitan condition requires that you allow people to drive down there and enjoy the city as an alternative to the shopping mall. My interpretation of this situation goes along the lines of cruel love. The city should, in fact, make itself inaccessible if that's what's necessary to preserve its integrity, and thereby force the suburbs to see themselves in sharp contrast with it and to endure other painful conditions until they are able to reconstitute themselves, through the public system, and proffer the kinds of spaces they will learn to admire as inaccessible downtown.

Trevor Boddy The whole idea of metropolitan mutations is ontological; it only has meaning in relation to that form from which it was generated; it is a relational term. I assume that the gene pool from which our urban mutations were generated was the traditional city. One of the intentions of this conference was to look dispassionately at these new mutations. We have had a number of them put on the table. George Baird suggested that the conflation of theme park and shopping centre in the West Edmonton Mall may be one of these new forms. Don McKay and Frank Palermo made cases for the underground and +15 mutations. Pushing things a bit, I could identify three positions within the conference: the mutants, who believe in the possibility or advisability of these new forms; a middle camp — call them the modern squares — who are less activist and more conventional; and finally, perhaps led by Ken Greenberg, the Camillo Sitte planners.

It strikes me that these are gradations of positions and one can stand back now and look at attitudes toward the traditional city, new interventions, new types of urban space and see a variety of intentions. So I would like to come back to this idea of mutation, this ontological concept that relates back to something, and to talk about the various types of gene pools we have covered here. Obviously some of the mutants — the bus mall, the pedestrian Sparks Street Mall — have been rejected out of hand; no one has made a case for them. We have a fairly strong case today for underground cities, but a difficult argument. I would love Don to link the first part of his paper, the crypto-political part, with the actual activities in the underground city, because I find a great difficulty here. So I would first propose to you Detlef to come back and pursue the notion of mutations pro or con and then throw it back to the panel.

Detlef Mertins The proposition that urban forms are in the process of mutating

266

Christian Tiffault studying Halifax

serves several purposes. In the first instance, it's descriptive of what's actually been happening during the course of this century; Wall Street in New York or Bay Street in Toronto are characteristic "canyon" streets, which are traditional streets built up into the sky by the pressures of modern real estate; for me, these spaces are sublime, invigorating and — in terms of architectural theory — conceptually challenging, because they simply happened, they were not architecturally conceived. Of course, there are also mutations that are deliberate architectural conceptions; Mies' Toronto Dominion Centre, Revell's Nathan Phillips Square and Pei's Commerce Court are all examples of architects creating a distinctive and sophisticated 20th-century, metropolitan urbanity by reinterpreting traditional spatial types. Their work is more specific, but is akin to the creation of the "boulevard" in the late 19th century or even the "urban park," both of which were intentional formal responses to the intense concentration of population in the 19th-century industrial city. In terms of their origin, the underground and elevated pedestrian cities are neither purely developer-generated nor purely architect-generated; rather the idea has bounced back and forth between these realms and has engaged the political sphere as well. The impurity of these systems is intriguing; neither interior nor exterior, public nor private, controllable nor uncontrollable, these systems are the clearest reflections that we have of the murky, mixed-economy, I'll-scratch-your-back-if-you'll-scratch-mine world in which we operate. I really enjoy the irony in the fact that these realms implemented design controls inside and underground long before urban design controls became common outside, and yet these realms have virtually no credibility in terms of design.

The nature of architectural creativity should, to follow Trevor's observations about the term "mutation," become relational — not just in terms of site context, but in generational terms.
Detlef Mertins

But I have also chosen the term mutation because of its sinister and biological connotation. While I have no intention of reviving the very suspect proposition that architects can be doctors, that they can heal the disease of the city, the idea of the city as an organism has a significant history in the modern period precisely because the modern city is fundamentally uncontrollable and its growth and development cause disruption and pain. Indeed, architects have more often been hand-maidens of urban terrorism and torture than healers, even if they don't know it or won't admit it. Like Dr. Frankenstein, we are not in control of what we are creating. And, of course, that's exactly the reason why architects over the past two decades have withdrawn from experimentation into a conservative, let's-do-it-just-like-the-old-days practice. But while the new state of the art in urban design is relatively benign and popularly successful, it is nevertheless different from anything that has been done before; despite

267

its historicist polemic, the new urbanism is itself a mutation, which combines, to use a marketing slogan, "the best of the old with the best of the new." It's like new subdivision houses that are "traditional" on the outside and "modern" on the inside. Now, I'm not saying that this is bad, but rather that it's just not the final word; the process of change is continuing as new imperatives emerge.

The process of mutation, then, suggests ongoing change and successive generations of adaptations. If the development of the city or the metropolis can be seen, in a metaphorical way, to involve successive generations of mutations, each of which addresses new imperatives, then the very posture of architectural practice should be reformulated. The nature of architectural creativity should, to follow Trevor's observations about the term "mutation," become relational — not just in terms of site context, which is a different agenda — but in generational terms.

Michael Kirkland The word mutation is very loaded if one thinks of a world without any kind of control or possibility other than an occasional protest or the proffering of another mutation. Going back to Trevor's options, I would tend to err

We should have modesty...look at real values and determine which things have worked and which things haven't.
Phyllis Lambert

on the side of Camillo Sitte on the grounds that nothing at this conference or in my own experience suggests that the historical types that we have inherited are made obsolete by modern conditions, entirely. It is true that they require modification and refinement to address certain ephemeral modern peculiarities. But that doesn't in any way justify a renewal of that revolutionary zeal with which our forefathers abandoned the historical city as the point of departure.

It's certainly arguable to re-evaluate the modern city in the context of historical types and to ask in a very pointed way, "What's new?" I don't feel that we have succeeded in establishing anything new that would justify the search for mutations. I don't see what the alternative model is and, despite our modernist training in the pursuit of originality, it's time to admit that things haven't been going so well and all these inventions have had problems far worse that what they set out to address. Congestion, which has been the motive for the abandonment of the historical city, is a far less serious problem than +15s, transit malls, non-hierarchical open space, lack of address, overshadowing and all the other ills that have been visited upon us. It's time we had a certain humility.

Phyllis Lambert I'll just say what I have said on many occasions these last few days. If you ask what's new, I say Katowice. Katowice is a Polish socialist city just like Le Corbusier's "Plan Voisin" for central Paris (1925), which depicted an extraordinary situation in which you have a huge space consumed by cars, huge buildings, underpasses and the like. There was no consideration of what the consequences of those things would be. One of the consequences, of course, was that you have a centralized government that wipes out a whole sector of a city and brings in whole new populations; power is back into the hands of a very few people. It was highly fascistic and I think that it's one of the terrible scares in our cities today: the control of developers. The problems that we face in the city are the existence of buildings that go on for miles and miles, or whole blocks at a time with only one door. I agree with Michael that we should have modesty, look at real values and determine which things have worked and which things haven't.

Audience, including Joost Bakker, Lance Berelowitz and Catherine Alkenbreck

Lance Berelowitz While one might try to defend shopping malls by saying that they are just like the covered markets and arcades of Paris, Milan or Brussels, there are big differences. The traditional forms were integrated into a network of streets which structured and nourished these places. In the shopping mall, the opposite is true. Secondly, while the arcades and markets may have been private, they were small and limited. The shopping mall is a large concentration of capital with a private police. What's valuable about the street, in the final instance, is nothing romantic, or subversive. What the shopping mall deprives us of is the basic right of going in and out, not on the basis of an owner's rules, but on the basis of our own intentions and pleasure. When we are within a shopping mall we are not free.

Question I've been a mutant from day one. One of the weak parts of the conference has been to underestimate the force of mutant space. The +15s and undergrounds are probably the least effective of all the emerging public spaces that I've been looking at for a number of years. The major exclusion from the conference, in terms of emerging mutant spaces, are parking lots. The most significant public space in my neighbourhood in Toronto is the parking lot at the Summerhill liquor store. Parking lots are sadly missing here; they are important and optimistic centres of public activity that have been tremendously underestimated by architects.

As well, I would cite the whole collection of landscape open spaces inside cities, public districts that are on the verge of emerging. There is potential there that has not been discussed or documented at this conference. And the suburban arterials, which are beginning to change, are exciting and full of optimism. The emerging public spaces are the major public spaces in Canada. There is tremendous potential lying there; to turn back now to a Sitte-city is to ignore what is staring us in the face as a potential for this country.

Donald McKay Camillo Sitte is getting a bad rap. His argument was for those things which had been utterly unacknowledged as public spaces before he began to write about them. While his work has become codified and fixed, it was actually a very dialectical activity. Everyone is feeling around for a position. What's your answer? Mine is that the dialectical activity continued, that the work of one intelli-

Detlef Mertins

gent Viennese at the turn of the century doesn't become codified any more than the work of Venturi on Las Vegas. There is a kind of gliding evolution; there are a number of simultaneous phenomena, which is why I speak of the city in terms of multiple readings. We might begin to understand that there is not one thing or even one kind of thing or, in a very masculine way, one dominant thing, but rather a condition in which many things coexist. I am looking forward to the feminization of the practice of architecture; it's been in the boys' hands for four or five centuries too long.

Trevor Boddy Just a comment back to Don about Camillo Sitte, whom I respect. I presume that you are talking about Sitte's plea for organic structuring of cities based on his study of the medieval organism. But at no time did he engage in the dialectic of opposite scales. He was a participant in the dialectic but repudiated its existence and, in the end, his organicism was couched in the term "city planning according to artistic principles."

Lance Berelowitz I don't know whether I'm a modern square or an old-fashioned mutant. I was just leaning back a few minutes ago and happened to look at the roof of the fly tower behind my head. Sitting here on this stage, I seem to be on the dividing line of two realities. The graffiti on the roof of the fly tower is terrific, completely wild, like the slummiest alley in Toronto and very much opposed to the clean, crisp, manicured Victorian shed in front of me. If I were to make a single, simple motion it would be for a both/and condition, which is pluralistic, or to put it another way, to bring the graffiti to the front of house without bringing the house down.

Detlef Mertins I'd like to bring the discussion to a close with thanks to all the panelists and questioners, and a quotation from Camillo Sitte, whose ghost seems to have haunted the latter part of this session. I agree with Don McKay that Sitte is often misrepresented; while he certainly had harsh criticisms to make of his "modern" world, his own words reveal a complex position in which the relationship between tradition and modernity is dialectical, rather than the simplistic position often represented of choosing one or the other:

> Is it really possible to plan on paper the kind of effect that was produced by the passage of centuries? Could we actually derive any satisfaction from feigned naiveté and sheer artificiality? Certainly not. The vitality of the glorious old models should inspire us to something other than fruitless imitation. If we seek out the essential quality of this heritage and adapt it to modern conditions we shall be able to plant the seeds of new vitality in seemingly barren soil.

COMMENTARY: AN EMERGING DISCOURSE

Steven Fong

1. Post-card view of King Square,
Saint John, New Brunswick, c. 1900

King Square is a well formed and ordered space at the centre of Saint John, New Brunswick. In the surrounding grid of streets, there are various urban conditions, from sedate tree-lined streets with townhouses to an introverted hotel-cum-shopping mall and skybridges. In the evening, fast cars navigate the streets, participating in some sort of jerky, frenetic promenade. These are familiar ingredients of many cities besides Saint John. Fragments of traditional urbanism exist beside mute, acultural places, and both are in turn agitated by a restless, aimless mobility. Together, these phenomena constitute our current urban aspirations and predicaments. And so, it was in this appropriate context, both physically and intellectually, that a conference on Canadian urbanism was held.

This conference and its accompanying exhibition, a prodigious pan-Canadian sampler of urban spaces and discourses, were both curatorially aggressive in searching for new interpretations of the public realm and at the same time polemically oblique in positioning this effort in an international context. Implicit in the call for identifying "metropolitan mutations" is a critique of both European rationalism and American contextualism and their respective, corresponding preoccupations with the Traditional City and City Beautiful. However, most participants in this conference constructed more hermetic discourses.

The exhibition includes an inventory of Canadian public urban spaces. Of the nine examples cited, only three — Toronto, Mississauga and Vancouver — were conceived in light of any recent theory of urban design. The other six examples are historic and accretive (Ottawa, Quebec and Halifax), entrepreneurial (Edmonton), or the legacy of the 1960s fascination with multi-level, circulatory systems (Calgary's skyways and Montreal's tunnels).

George Baird's keynote address plotted a series of intergenerational adjustments to post-war discourse on urban design. However, Baird points out that these adjustments have not resulted in any definitive urban models. Instead, he sees a continuing crisis of representation of urbanism, where plausible urban models may be possible only through a kind of "hybridizing." However, by posing this possible trajectory based on accretive formulations, Baird implies a devaluation of the informative potential of utopias and ideal cities. Alongside Baird's sensibilities about hybrids one may also wish to include a fragmentary and potentially evocative urbanism whose physiognomy is based on theoretical paradigms. The results of this would be images and environments that may be no more or less appropriate than these other hybrid urban formulations.

Both Trevor Boddy and Peter Rose presented arguments for an understanding of traditional urban morphology, the former championing the street as the significant element of urbanity and the latter presenting both a morphological and behavioural assessment of Montreal's streets and spaces. Ken Greenberg transposed this argument to some new suburban "city centres," which in turn emulate the formal attributes of their denser forebears.

Boddy began his presentation by calling for recognition and support of the physical form of the traditional street. He went on to advocate the continuous street wall and sidewalk. Others have made a compelling case for this advocacy citing such

2. Contemporary post-card view of the Atrium at Market Square Redevelopment, Saint John, New Brunswick

20th-century streets as Fifth Avenue in New York. However, Boddy's case studies were often based on patterns of behaviour and physical characteristics that did not necessarily lend credence to his formal predilections.

Rose's observations about Montreal were more convincing, in part because of the subject matter itself. Montreal lends itself to comprehensive analysis of its patterns of form and use, because it has a unique and long-standing urban tradition. This uniqueness is problematic, for Montreal may have few attributes in common with other Canadian cities. This issue may have to be addressed as a sequel in this most urban of Canadian cities.

Other speakers rose to Baird's and curator Detlef Mertins's challenge to identify new versions of public life. These included Frank Palermo (Calgary +15s), Gerald Forseth (office lobbies), Tom Emodi (Halifax suburbs and parking lots), Donald McKay (the Toronto underground) and Michael Kirkland (urban expressways). Forseth presented the phenomenon of private corporations "doing good" in the ground-level lobbies of their urban headquarters. This somewhat fragile notion of public life begs the question of future recidivism. Emodi's discussion of suburban behaviour did not seem to coincide with any particular formal attributes; instead, he seemed to predict that these social customs might be a precursor to formal invention.

The McKay presentation identified three readings of urbanity. His urban paradigms — the Official City, the Shadow City, and the Metropolis — correspond to a similar segregation of urban scenes by Sebastiano Serlio in 1540. Serlio posited a series of parallel public domains, a composite city where citizenry with various motivations participate in various aspects of public life. In the Serlian world, prince, prostitute, merchant and thief have their respective places. McKay went on to conclude that new urban formulations exist in the overlap of the readings of the composite city.

Kirkland's presentation was the most ambiguous, an appropriate response to the dilemma of urban highways. Kirkland's ambivalence stemmed from a concern with definitional precision, a kind of text-book rigour about what constitutes street, square and park, and therefore a corresponding inability to "shoehorn" the exigencies of modern mobility into this taxonomy.

Another series of presentations were about a connection between public space and strong contextual anchors. For Lance Berelowitz, this was the relationship between Vancouver and its surrounding natural context. Nan Griffiths, in discussing urban conditions in Ottawa, saw this attachment to Nature as an internalized aspect of the Canadian psyche. Phyllis Lambert's presentation about the Park and Garden for the CCA in Montreal constituted an impacted assemblage of geographical, historical and cultural reference.

Discussions about Urbanism, like corresponding conversations about Culture, ride roughshod over traditional disciplinary fiefdoms as well as perceptions based on regional and class affiliations. Two days of this conference posed many questions. Given the example of the new Mississauga City Centre, can the physical simulation of a public domain nurture urbane behaviour? And with the West Edmonton Mall, are we now in the process of appropriating some ersatz, Disneyesque representation of a public domain without a "polis" (Arendt via Baird)?

In the final analysis, it was unclear as to whether or not the Trojan horse had indeed been pulled through the gates, or if hitherto unexplored discussions and objects of contemplation had been brought into the forum. A more precise vocabulary describing urban phenomena and the identification of a healthy Canadian urbanism were noteworthy achievements of this conference. However, it is doubtful if this conference prefigures, at this stage, anything more than certain linguistic adjustments in our understanding of the public realm. Saint John's sort of uneasy urbanism will continue, regardless of conferences like this. With this conference, architects and designers have been challenged to address these issues. At this point, convincing formal configurations corresponding to this discourse still seem to be only remote possibilities.

3. Post-card view of Prince William Street, Saint John, New Brunswick, c. 1900

4. Contemporary post-card view of King Street, Saint John, New Brunswick

COMMENTARY: RECONNECTING, RECLAIMING AND REINVENTING CITIES

Michael McMordie

Commentators on "Emerging Public Spaces" at the 1988 RAIC conference were divided between radical conservatives and conservative modernists. Yet, both sought the same experience of urbanity: richly varied encounters with people and places compressed within a dense, allusive habitation. The exchanges were about means, not ends.

The defence of the "old" against the "new" was a dominant conference theme. A need to explore the nature of the new — the modern — was evident. Mertins's quotation from Berman, "For the sake of modernism we must preserve the old and resist the new,"[1] epitomizes the rejection of 1920s modernism in favour of a deeper understanding of modernity. Modernity's roots reach back to the Renaissance, and its realization came in the 19th century. It has spawned different modernisms, of which the architectural and urban modernism of Le Corbusier and Gropius is one, "post"-modernism is another. Following Marx, Berman characterizes modern society as engaged in the continual reconstruction of its own foundations. Everything is in flux, nothing is stable and reliable, except the experience of change. The new metropolis of the 19th century gave this experience form and setting. As ideal and image, it was replaced, in turn, by a 20th-century city of towers and expressways. Speakers at the RAIC conference continued this dialectical encounter between the historic city and the modernisms of the 19th and 20th centuries.

Boddy and Rose led in the defence of the "old" against the "new," supported by Lambert and (implicitly) Berelowitz; Forseth, McKay and Palermo contemplated "new" alternatives with varying degrees of optimism. Griffiths and Kirkland explored enigmas created by 20th-century interventions in the historic fabric. Emodi and Greenberg looked to the accommodation and transformation of the "modern" exurban to the "historic" urban. These were the only speakers who discussed the

1. Medieval pedestrian passage, Chester, England

suburb as a problematic element that had, somehow, to be accommodated and transformed. All sought the sociological urbanity described by Mumford and Jacobs, a touchstone for the later 20th century apparently negated by the monuments to European modernism realized in North America in the 1950s and 1960s.[2]

The contributors persisted in preferring complexity, as experience and objective, in city building. The modernism of the mid-20th century had at first sought images of simplicity and clarity, in the effort to make modernity intelligible. Paradoxically this required complex manoeuvres of concealment of mechanical systems, servicing, historic change, and social interaction. Baird noted the issues that arose in the course of this evolution — plurality, mobility and the historic city — as central to the evolution of 20th-century urbanism. The public world, a "human artefact, the fabrication of human hands,"[3] is created pre-eminently in and through the city; its creation continues, whether the city is modern or historic. Its complexity arises from the human drive to find ways of living fully with whatever materials come to hand. Habitation, even of the newest cities, is bringing about their adaptation in just this way — a process of **bricolage** that designers are perverse not to recognize, accept and facilitate.[4]

This encounter between the ideal (simplicity) and the real (complexity) has led to a reconsideration of the most influential ideas of the prophets of clarity: Gropius, Le Corbusier and Mies van der Rohe. But only polemicists like Leon Krier have categorically rejected all their works. Their conceptions of modernism "destructured" the city, its structure "**methodically** threatened in order to be comprehended more clearly" and, as Derrida continues (discussing language), "to reveal not only its supports but also that secret place in which it is neither construction nor ruin but lability."[5]

That characteristic lability — instability, vulnerability — makes possible the continued remoulding of urban structure as a vessel for increasingly varied activities and experiences.[6]

The 20th-century pioneers took the city apart to see how it worked. (The approach was mechanical and Newtonian. In contrast the Scottish biologist Patrick Geddes understood the city ecologically.) When Le Corbusier and others assembled the parts they chose a simpler hierarchical order dominated by systems of communication, on the ground and in the air.[7] The conference's contributors who sought to change the city dealt, in one way or another, with the impact of transportation, especially the automobile, but also rapid transit. Those who, like Rose, simply praised the historic city of streets and squares and rejected underground and elevated layers of access and activity do not appear to have confronted those issues.

Those who recognized and accepted the 20th-century city sought to improve its connectedness. They accepted the changes in city form brought about by transport, which include sprawling suburbs fed by expressways and rapid transit below, above, or on the surface, and the other multi-level connections. Greenberg and Emodi pro-

2. The multi-level city: Waterloo Place, Edinburgh, Scotland

posed urban centres and public spaces for the suburbs. Griffiths explored the symbolic and historic issues raised by a disconnected monument and its setting. Palermo explored the implications of elevated walkways that weaken the dominance of the ground plane and reduce the priority given to the street.

Far from demonstrating the intractability of the modern city, these new devices and proposals show its plasticity. Despite the influences of the pure and simple theories of the 1920s, the cities we have built have been shaped even more by economic pragmatism and popular desires. These cities continue to change, as the exhibition shows, in ways that recapture aspects of the 19th-century urban experience, without reproducing 19th-century forms.

In arguments about the modern city, it is easy to romanticize the historic city. It condenses not only around street and market, but also against the walls of temple mound and citadel. These interrupted communications and segregated people by rank and activities, as did the city walls against which the first suburbs accumulated. These oldest cities were often dangerous and unhealthy, and visually attractive only to travellers with a passion for the picturesque. In the 19th century, urban squalor was attacked by expedients now often condemned. From Haussmann to Le Corbusier, reformers offered radical surgery for the Victorian ills of darkness, filth, congestion and crime. Unless we grasp the problems they confronted we can hardly understand their solutions. We also forget congenial precedents for 20th-century innovations now attacked. Chester's Rows, Milan's Galleria, Edinburgh's layers are a few that anticipated our pedestrian malls, walkways and bridges.

3. Victorian arcade, Norwich, England

The 19th-century city illustrates the problem of accommodating traditional ways of living to new technologies.[8] The cities' ills were already evident in London, overcrowded by the end of the 18th century. Their cure required the invention of new systems — for sanitation and water supply — but these lay in the future. For those who could afford it, suburban living, made possible by the new railways, became desirable for hygienic as well as social and aesthetic reasons. The rehabilitation of the historic centre was left for the later 19th and 20th centuries.

Two complementary processes are at work. Rehabilitation continues, amply documented by the exhibition and papers. There is also the process of adaptation and accommodation by which the hastily built settlements at the centre and the margins of the city become livable.[9] This includes both alterations by the inhabitants[10] and the creative accommodation by people to apparently uncongenial places as described, for instance, by Goffman.[11] Such transformations are too readily brought in evidence against architects. They may simply reveal divergent tastes in a pluralistic culture.

Ready acceptance of change is balanced by the current enthusiasm for urban conservation, which seeks to preserve or re-create points of historic reference. The process can be profound and subtle, dependent on creative scholarship, as Lambert's paper showed. On the other hand, the taste for restorations of dubious authenticity should be questioned; destruction of historic places occurs too often under the guise

4. The limit of disconnection from the city: the approach to West Edmonton Mall, Edmonton

of conservation. Such changes need to be resisted.

We arrive at the challenge of bringing together alternative visions of the city, from this century, the 19th century, and before. The process of habitation requires further mixing and blending of the crystalline categories by which the early modernists analyzed the city. Underground, elevated and street levels need to be merged and connected with greater subtlety and sensitivity.[12] Indoors and outdoors in climates that range between extremes require graded intermediates: awnings, arcades, pergolas. The ubiquitous atria need to be presented as a complement to the out-of-doors, not as an either/or alternative. Finally, the distinction between public and private spheres needs to be softened. Private use of public space is readily accepted in the case of hot-dog vendors and news agents on sidewalks and squares, but the public right to use such private spaces as shopping malls and commercial atria for political or social communication is not so well established.[13] All these adjustments increase the ways in which the city can serve its public, and so increase the varieties of life it will sustain.

Toronto's underground concourses, as interpreted by McKay, show the possibilities our changing cities offer. He finds in Toronto's underground network the rise of an alternative city, a Dionysian image of the city above ground. This gives further evidence of the city's capacity to accommodate alternative ways of living by creating new connections. Calgary's +15 system may have a similar potential, though not yet realized. The apparent absence of fringe and marginal uses in the Calgary system may reveal the city's relative immaturity, or simply an essential difference in character between an elevated and a subterranean environment. Both, however, add to the connectedness of their cities, and offer potential support for the marginal states and activities McKay describes.

As this suggests, the emphasis laid by Mertins on 19th-century dialectical modernity seems right. The contributors take alternative, sometimes opposing, positions that call for synthesis. All those who spoke clearly delight in the densely inhabited and interconnected city, which provides appropriately for private and public occasions with a variety of humane environments.

5. The arcade of the 20th-century Hudson's Bay Store, Calgary

Reflection on the analyses and proposals presented in these papers suggests some important conclusions. The connectedness, which supports Baird's mobility and plurality, depends on fineness of grain, a highly permeable fabric open to penetration in many places and many ways, and great variety: of density, texture and communications. Creation of these qualities is often defeated by current design and development practices.

Connections to the past are critical. Comparisons of older and newer states of the city make change visible. Just as the writing of history is a creative activity, based on the past but never fully congruent with it, so the reclamation and conservation of the historic city also requires invention.

Throughout history the work of invention has been stimulated and sheltered by

280

the city. Itself the greatest product of urban civilization, it has fostered creativity of all kinds. The conference papers have emphasized the work of architects and planners. Through their efforts they aid, or impede, the flow of experience that the city offers; they provide for meeting and mixing, withdrawal and reflection; they can make the city's own nature visible, and present images of urbanity. The city should speak of the possibilities it offers. Different varieties of modernism offer different versions of the city. The attempt to make the city seem clear and simple in this century was a response to the complexities and contradictions of the 19th century. We now realize that the city can never be simple; we once again can revel in its complexity.

6. The +15 level, Petro-Canada Building, Calgary

Notes

[1] Detlef Mertins, "The Challenge of Public Space," *RAIC UPDATE*, Vol. 11, No. 2, 1988.

[2] Especially Lewis Mumford, *The Culture of Cities*, and Jane Jacobs, *The Death and Life of Great American Cities*.

[3] Hannah Arendt, quoted by George Baird in "The Space of Appearance," this volume.

[4] "Every Starr perhaps a World of destined habitation," Milton, *The Shorter Oxford English Dictionary* (1959), p. 850.

[5] Jacques Derrida, *Writing and Difference*, trans. Alan Bass (Chicago: University of Chicago Press, 1978), p. 6.

[6] It is parallel to the adaptation and rehabilitation of individual buildings that now dominates architectural practice, and which has become thoroughly confused with historic conservation, to the detriment of both.

[7] When Christopher Alexander understood the problems with this approach he rejected his own earlier work. C. Alexander, "A City is Not a Tree," *Architectural Forum* (April-May 1965), pp. 58–62.

[8] The introduction of the factory system in the early 19th century is an example that has been extensively studied.

[9] It is worth remembering that "jerry-building" was coined in 18th-century England to describe the cheaply built and often unsound terraces with which speculators cashed in during boom periods.

[10] Like those to Le Corbusier's housing at Pessac described by Phillippe Boudon, *Lived-in Architecture: Le Corbusier's Pessac Revisited*, trans. Gerald Onn (Cambridge, Mass.: MIT Press, 1972).

[11] Erving Goffman, *Asylums: Essays on the Social Situation of Mental Patients and Other Inmates* (Chicago: Aldine, 1961).

[12] The exhibition shows, as a bad example, Calgary's +15 at an uninhabited Esso Plaza. However, this is one of the few places where the elevated pedestrian system provides easy and visible choices between inside and outside, elevated and ground level, particularly where the ground level has been made attractive. It is full of people at lunch on (frequent) warm and sunny days.

[13] "...Lawrence Tribe's argument that in the light of changed conditions — the decline of public streets and parks as meeting places, the rise of shopping centers, the high costs of access to electronic broadcasting, advertising, newspapers, and other means of communication — the First Amendment should be taken to protect the right to pass out leaflets in privately owned shopping centers in violation of the Owner's prohibitions." T. M. Scanlon, "Down from Liberalism," *New York Review* (April 28, 1988), p. 40, referring to Lawrence Tribe, *Constitutional Choices* (Cambridge, Mass.: Harvard University Press, 1985), p. 197f.

ACKNOWLEDGMENTS

The Publication

The RAIC ANNUAL is a publication of the Royal Architectural Institute of Canada, Chamberlain House, 328 Somerset West, Ottawa, Ontario, K2P 0J9, and is published by Little, Brown and Company (Canada) Limited, 146 Davenport Road, Toronto, Ontario, M5R 1J1

Editor	Detlef Mertins
Graphic Design	Adams & Associates Design Consultants Inc.
Production	Steve Eby
Copy Editing	Wayne Herrington
Typesetting	Rossignol & Associates
Printing	D. W. Friesen

Copyright © 1989 Royal Architectural Institute of Canada.
ISBN 0-316-56783-3   Printed and bound in Canada.

All original texts and photographs are printed with the permission of the authors.
Material included in this volume is, in part, from an exhibition and, in part, from a conference, both entitled "Metropolitan Mutations" and both sponsored by the Royal Architectural Institute of Canada and organized by the Research and Education Commission, under the Chairmanship of Prof. Esmail Baniassad. The conference was held on June 9 and 10, 1988, in Saint John, New Brunswick.

Sponsors

The Royal Architectural Institute of Canada gratefully acknowledges the financial contributions of the following sponsors for this publication, the exhibition and the conference:

The Canada Council
Alcan Aluminium Inc. (Canada and Italy)

Department of External Affairs
Canadian Embassy, Rome, Italy
Flos
University of Waterloo/Social Sciences & Humanities Research Council
Arriscraft Corporation

Concordia Estates Groups Inc.
Fiberglas Canada Inc.
GE Superabrasives Inc.
Olympia Floor and Wall Tile Co.
Shell Canada

Baird/Sampson, Architects
A. J. Diamond & Partner, Architects
Hotson & Bakker, Architects
Kuwabara Payne McKenna Blumberg, Architects
Mertins Architect

The Exhibition

Curation & Co-ordination	Detlef Mertins	
Research & Co-ordination Assistance	Brigitte Shim	
Graphic Design	Debbie Adams, Adams & Associates Design Consultants Inc.	
Installation Design	Detlef Mertins	
Triennale di Milano Photography	Robert Bean, Halifax Jack Buquet, Vancouver John Dean, Calgary and Edmonton Marc Fowler, Ottawa and Montreal Eugen Kedl, Quebec City Peter MacCallum, Toronto and Mississauga	
Typesetting	Canadian Composition Inc.	
Fabrication of Panels	Checkmate Photographic Centre Limited Jones & Morris Photo-Enlarging Limited	
Translation	Sogestran Inc.	
Drawings	**Calgary**	Bernard Jin, Francoise Lafontaine and Gerry Pilon under the direction of Brigitte Shim
	Edmonton	Peter Kurkjian, Ian MacLaren and Michael Szabo under the direction of Brigitte Shim
	Halifax	Brenda Webster, Stephen Blood, Paula Pittman, Mark Benoit, Donna Chong, Stephen Conger, Grant V. Dutnall, Sylvia Fong, Darryl Johnson, Andrew King, Brian Kucharski, Gordon Mackay, Brian Mombourquette, David Plant, Jennifer Richardson, Steve Rose, Peter Russell, Darren Spidell, Catherine Stevens, Sandi Tanaka under the direction of Frank Palermo and Tom Emodi, Technical University of Nova Scotia
	Mississauga & Vancouver	Douglas Dickinson, Michelle Gibson, Rob Lefebvre, Seth Matheson and Andrew Prus under the direction of Ryszard Sliwka, University of Waterloo
	Montreal	U2 Design Studio under the direction of Pieter Sijpkes with assistance of Howard Davies, McGill University
	Ottawa	Rudi Bortolamiol and Shawn Gardiner under the direction of Nan Griffiths, Carleton University
	Quebec City	Pascale Beaumont, Mathieu Gavazzi, Claude Laurin, Daniel Levasseur, Jordan Levine, Thanh-Tuyen Nguyen, Martine Savard, and Mary-Ann Schwering under the direction of Naomi S. Neumann, Université Laval
	Toronto	Andrew Jones and Robert Lange under the direction of Steven Fong and Brigitte Shim, University of Toronto

Co-ordination Assistance   David Weir, Gabrielle Crisante, Cathy Doherty, Andrew Dyke, Joan Hendricks, Mark Jaffar, Paul Noskewicz and Leon Phillips

The curator of the exhibition gratefully acknowledges the assistance of the following additional people and organizations:

Esmail Baniassad, Technical University of Nova Scotia
Larry Richards, University of Waterloo
James Bater, University of Waterloo
Bruce Anderson, McGill University
Gil Sutton, Carleton University
Robert Kirby, University of Calgary
Robert Sterling, University of Calgary
Joel Shack, University of British Columbia
Don Sinclair, City of Edmonton, Planning Department
James Low, City of Edmonton, Planning & Building Department
Alka Lukatela, City of Mississauga, Planning Department
City of Halifax, Planning Department
City of Quebec, Planning Department
City of Montreal, Planning Department
City of Ottawa, Planning Department
Hammerson Developments
Oxford Developments
Jones & Kirkland, Architects
Moriyama & Teshima, Architects
Joost Bakker, Hotson & Bakker, Architects
Maurice Sunderland, Architects
Webb Zerafa Menkes Housdon, Architects
Bregman & Hamann, Architects
Baird/Sampson, Architects
Harold Hanen & Associates
Thom Partnership, Architects
ARCOP Architects
Page & Steele, Architects
du Toit, Allsopp, Hillier
Moorehead, Corban, Fleming & McCarthy, Landscape Architects
Aldrich/Pears Associates
Panda Photography
Ron Vickers
Ken Brown Photography
Mildred Pulleyblank, Toronto Dominion Bank Archives
Michael McMordie
Brian McKay-Lyons
Howard Sutcliffe
Virginia Wright

Archival material courtesy Public Archives of Canada, City of Toronto Archives, Public Archives of Nova Scotia, Provincial Archives of Alberta, Vancouver Public Library, Hotson & Bakker, Architects, Mr. Charles Turpin, City of Toronto Planning & Development Department, City of Calgary Planning & Development Department, City of Mississauga Planning & Development Department, Toronto Dominion Bank Archives, Cadillac Fairview Corporation Archives, ARCOP Architects, City of Ottawa, Université Laval and the Department of Energy, Mines and Resources.

Conference

Curator *& Moderator*	Detlef Mertins
Co-ordinators	Tim Kehoe Bill Knorr Greg Murdock

Contributors

George Baird is a partner in the Toronto firm of Baird/Sampson, Architects and is Professor of Architecture at the University of Toronto. He has carried out important urban design studies for Toronto, Ottawa and Vancouver, and is the primary urban designer of the public space system for Toronto's Harbourfront development. His essays and commentaries have been widely published.

Lance Berelowitz is a designer who, until recently, lived and worked in Vancouver. A contributor to Canadian art and architecture magazines, his architectural career has taken him from Cape Town to London, Princeton, Paris and now Toronto. He was one of the organizers of the exhibition "Vancouver Revisions."

Trevor Boddy teaches history, theory and design at Carleton University's School of Architecture. He is currently researching and writing a cycle of essays on modernism, entitled *Canadian Architecture in the 20th Century*.

Tom Emodi is an architect in Halifax and teaches design and theory at the Faculty of Architecture at the Technical University of Nova Scotia, where he is Chairman of the Master's Program. Previously he was Head of the Diploma of Architecture Program at the Royal Melbourne (Australia) Institute of Technology.

Steven Fong is Chairman of the Program in Architecture at the University of Toronto. He is a graduate of Cornell University's architectural and urban design programs, and in practice has combined a wide range of architectural work with urban design projects. An architect in private practice in New York, his designs have received awards from Progressive Architecture and the ACSA, and have been published in international journals.

Gerald L. Forseth practices architecture in Calgary and has received numerous design awards for his work. He is a Director on Council of the RAIC, past-president of the Alberta Association of Architects, past-chairman of the internationally acclaimed Banff Sessions, Assistant Professor at the University of Calgary and an active member of many cultural organizations.

Kenneth Greenberg is a principal of Berridge Lewinberg Greenberg, a Toronto urban planning and urban design firm, and an Associate Professor of Environmental Studies at York University. He was previously Director of the Division of Architecture and Urban Design, Department of Planning and Development, City of Toronto.

Nan Griffiths is an Ottawa-based urban design consultant with Griffiths Rankin Cook/Griffiths, Architects and is Associate Professor of Architecture at Carleton University. In 1987, her study of, and recommendations to dismantle, the Rideau Street Transit Mall were accepted by Ottawa City Council.

J. Michael Kirkland is principal of Michael Kirkland, Architect in Toronto. Along with Edward Jones, he was architect of the Mississauga City Hall. His involvement in public space design includes the North York Civic Square, master plans for Harbourfront, Hamilton Waterfront and Etobicoke City Centre. As a consultant to the Harbourfront Corporation and the Domed Stadium he is currently designing a link through the Gardiner Corridor.

Phyllis Lambert is a Montreal architect, founder and Director of the Canadian Centre for Architecture, which will open in the spring of 1989. The CCA will be a unique and vital institution in Canada for the study of architecture. It has an extensive collection of books, prints, drawings, and photographs relating to architecture and an archives of the work of major Canadian architects. She is also a founder of Heritage Montreal.

Donald McKay is Associate Professor of Architecture at the University of Waterloo, and works as a planning consultant and designer in Toronto. A participant in numerous exhibitions and competitions, his work is increasingly being published. He is currently working on a book entitled *Interpretations of the Environment*.

Michael McMordie is Professor of Architecture at the Faculty of Environmental Design, University of Calgary. A graduate of the universities of Toronto and Edinburgh, he works principally in architectural theory and history. He is the author of articles on Canadian architects and architecture for the forthcoming *Cambridge Illustrated Dictionary of Twentieth Century Architecture*.

Detlef Mertins is an architect and critic based in Toronto, co-curator of the exhibition "Toronto Modern" (1987), curator/co-ordinator/editor of "Metropolitan Mutations" (1988), and now Professional Advisor for the Kitchener City Hall Competition.

Frank Palermo is an architect and planner in Halifax, Head of the Department of Urban and Rural Planning and Professor of Design at the Technical University of Nova Scotia. Previously he was Director of Downtown Planning for the City of Calgary.

Peter Rose is principal in the Montreal-based firm Peter Rose, Architects. He is designer and principal architect of the new headquarters for the Canadian Centre for Architecture in Montreal. Responsible for the 1983 Concept and Master Plan for the Old Port of Montreal, he is also founder and co-ordinator of Montreal's Alcan Lectures on Architecture.

Illustration Credits

Every effort has been made to trace the copyright ownership of the illustrations used in this volume. In some cases that has not proved possible and we would welcome the opportunity to include any omissions in future editions. We are grateful to the many organizations and individuals who have co-operated so readily in giving their permission to reproduce photographs, maps and diagrams. In the Exhibition section, sources are given with each illustration. The following list concerns the papers of the Conference section. The first item of the reference refers to the section or essay, while those figures after the oblique refer to the plate numbers within that particular section.

Baird/1: Les Éditions d'Architecture/2: Princeton University Press/3: Lund Humphries/4: Architectural Press/5,6,7: Studio Vista/8,17: Karl Dramer Verlag/9: Van Nostrand Reinhold/10: Faber and Faber/11,12: Yale University/13,16: Archives d'Architecture Moderne/14: James Stirling; Rose/1,13,16: McCord Museum/2,3,5,6,7,8,9,10,11,18: Peter Rose, Architect; Berelowitz/2: Éditions de Seuil/1: Vancouver Art Gallery/3 through 12: Lance Berelowitz; Boddy/1: Diamond & Myers, Architects/3: Glenbow Alberta Institute/5: Moshe Safdie, Architects/8,9: A. J. Diamond & Partner, Architects/10,11,12: Heritage Canada Foundation/ 2,4,6,7,13,14: Trevor Boddy; Griffiths/1,8: National Capital Commission/3: Musée du Louvre/5: McMichael Gallery/6,7: Public Archives of Canada/2,3,4,9,10,11,12: Nan Griffiths; Greenberg/1: City of New York/2,3: City of Toronto/4: City of Scarborough/5 through 11: Kenneth Greenberg; Kirkland/1,9: City of Toronto/2: Kryn Taconis/3: City of Toronto/4,5,6: Michael Kirkland/7: Henri Rossier/8: Istituto di Studi Romani/10: Paul Reuber, Architect/11: Ferguson & Ferguson, Architects/12,13: du Toit, Allsopp, Hillier; Lambert/1,10,11,12: Melvin Charney/2: Alan Stewart, Daniel Thibeault/3: McCord Museum/4: Atlas Publishing/5: Phyllis Lambert & Richard Paré/6,7: Peter Rose/8,9: Gerrard & Mackars; Palermo/1 through 9: Frank Palermo/10: Palermo & Cavanagh; Forseth/1: Rockefeller Center, Inc./2: City of Calgary/3,4,5: Gerald Forseth/6: Kohn, Pederson, Fox/7: Nova Corporation/8,9: J. H. Cook, Architects/ 10,11,12: D. Curran; McKay/4: Little Brown & Co./7: *Time* Magazine/13: King Publications/14: *Toronto Star*/15: McKay/16: Zeidler Architects/17: Ricoh; Emodi/2: *Life* Magazine/5: Victor Gruen & Larry Smith/6: MIT Press; McMordie/all illustrations by Michael McMordie.

The historic view of Halifax from the Citadel, today

Parade on Barrington Street, Halifax

Broken "history" on Granville Street, Halifax

PHOTOS BY ROBERT BEAN